INSIDERS' GUIDE® SERIES

IN:

PH   A

INSIDERS GUIDE

GUILFORD, CONNECTICUT
AN IMPRINT OF THE GLOBE PEQUOT PRESS

The prices and rates in this guidebook were confirmed at press time. We recommend, however, that you call establishments before traveling to obtain current information.

To buy books in quantity for corporate use or incentives, call **(800) 962–0973** or e-mail **premiums@GlobePequot.com**.

INSIDERS' GUIDE®

Copyright © 2007 Morris Book Publishing, LLC

Text design by LeAnna Weller Smith
Maps created by XNR Productions, Inc. © Morris Book Publishing, LLC

Library of Congress Cataloging-in-Publication Data
Mihaly, Mary E.
  Insiders' guide to Philadelphia / Mary Mihaly. — 1st ed.
        p. cm. — (Insiders' guide series)
  Includes index.
  ISBN-13: 978-0-7627-3840-3
  ISBN-10: 0-7627-3840-5
  1. Philadelphia (Pa.)—Guidebooks. I. Title.
  F158.18.M54 2007
  917.48'110444—dc22

                              2006033035

Manufactured in the United States of America
First Edition/First Printing

CONTENTS

CONTENTS

Directory of Maps

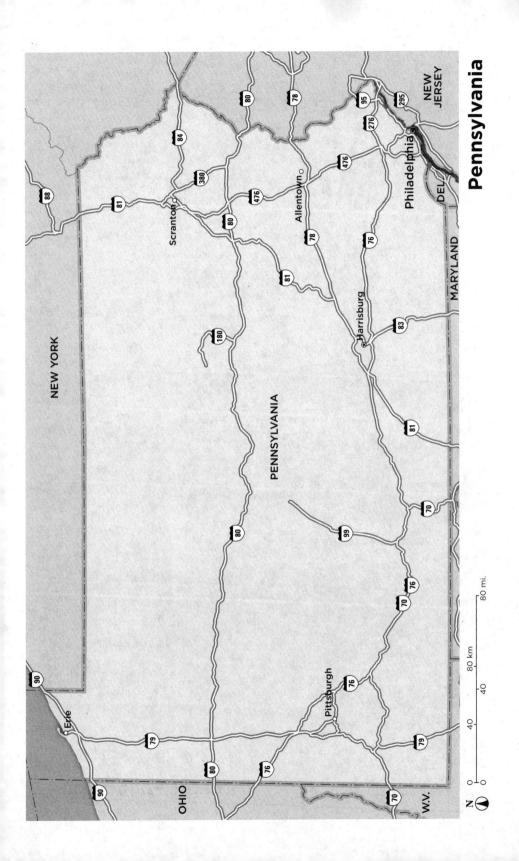

Pennsylvania

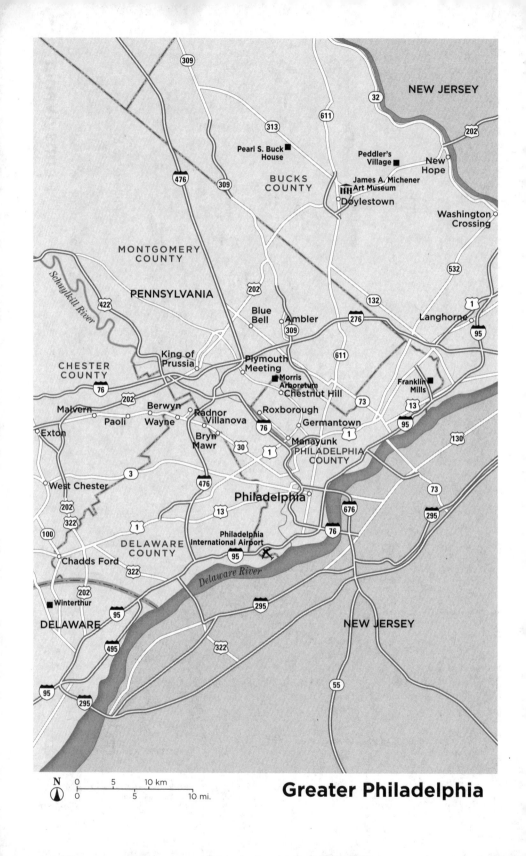

Greater Philadelphia

N

0 5 10 km
0 5 10 mi.

Center City

Delaware River

Schuylkill River

to Northern Liberties

95

30
676

Penn's Landing

Old City ELFRETH'S ALLEY
Painted Bride Art Center
Cultural District

German Society of Philadelphia
Edgar Allan Poe National Historic Site

Franklin Square
Chinatown
Friendship Gate
Chinese
Pennsylvania Convention Center

The Bourse
Independence National Historical Park

The Liberty Bell
Jewelers' Row
Washington Square

Independence Seaport Museum
Historic/Waterfront District

Reading Terminal Market
Masonic Temple
City Hall

Pennsylvania Hospital

Head House Square
South Street

to Mummers Museum
95

Mario Lanza Museum
Fabric Row

Park Hyatt Philadelphia at the Bellevue
Merriam Theater and Regional Performing Arts Center

Antique Row

Italian Market

Free Library of Philadelphia
Logan Square

Pennsylvania Academy of the Fine Arts

Academy of Music
University of the Arts

to Eastern State Penitentiary

The Shops at Liberty Place
AIA Bookstore and Design Center
Rittenhouse Square

Please Touch Museum for Children
Franklin Institute and Science Museum

College of Physicians/Mütter Museum

Philadelphia Museum of Art
Fairmount Waterworks

Eakins Oval

BENJAMIN FRANKLIN PKWY.

30th Street Station

Drexel University

University City

University of Pennsylvania
Wharton School

N

0   0.5   1 km
0   0.5   1 mi.

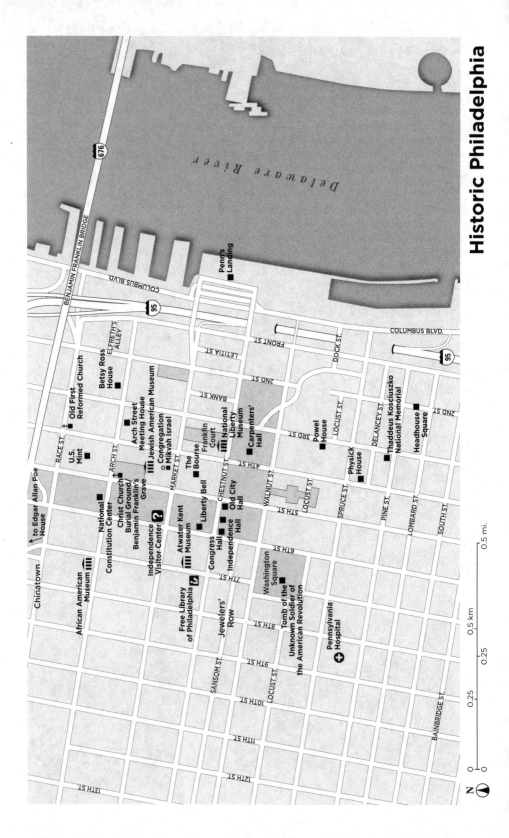

Historic Philadelphia

Delaware River

676

95

95

BENJAMIN FRANKLIN BRIDGE

COLUMBUS BLVD

COLUMBUS BLVD.

Penn's Landing

Chinatown

to Edgar Allan Poe House

African American Museum

Betsy Ross House

ELFRETH'S ALLEY

Old First Reformed Church

National Constitution Center

Christ Church Burial Ground/ Benjamin Franklin's Grave

U.S. Mint

RACE ST.

ARCH ST.

Arch Street Meeting House

Jewish American Museum

Congregation Mikvah Israel

The Bourse

Franklin Court

National Liberty Museum

Carpenters' Hall

LETITIA ST.

FRONT ST.

2ND ST.

BANK ST.

Independence Visitor Center

MARKET ST.

Liberty Bell

CHESTNUT ST.

Old City Hall

Atwater Kent Museum

Free Library of Philadelphia

Congress Hall

Independence Hall

WALNUT ST.

4TH ST.

3RD ST.

Powel House

Physick House

LOCUST ST.

DELANCEY ST.

Thaddeus Kosciuszko National Memorial

Headhouse Square

2ND ST.

DOCK ST.

5TH ST.

6TH ST.

7TH ST.

8TH ST.

9TH ST.

Jewelers' Row

SANSOM ST.

Washington Square

Tomb of the Unknown Soldier of the American Revolution

Pennsylvania Hospital

SPRUCE ST.

PINE ST.

LOMBARD ST.

SOUTH ST.

LOCUST ST.

10TH ST.

11TH ST.

12TH ST.

13TH ST.

BAINBRIDGE ST.

N

0   0.25   0.5 km

0   0.25   0.5 mi.

PREFACE

The first time I saw Philadelphia, I was in my early 20s on a business trip. I only remember the magnificent 30th Street Station and a memorable dinner at the Restaurant School (then located in a high-ceilinged row house just west of Rittenhouse Square).

The following year I drove from Ohio to Philly with two friends: It was 1976, the year of the nation's Bicentennial, and we had never been to such a party! None of us will forget lying on our backs with thousands of others in Independence Park, just a few feet from the Liberty Bell, watching the best darn fireworks show. . . . Nor will we forget our panic the first night, as the sun set and we realized we didn't have a place to stay. (We finally found a fleabag room somewhere outside the city for $11.)

How the city has changed since then! But one thing that hasn't changed is my devotion to Philadelphia. In the early '80s, my sisters and I were brainstorming about a getaway with our mother. We all had been to Philly separately and, though we didn't know the city well, we wanted to come back. We rode Amtrak for 11 hours until we reached that most-impressive 30th Street Station, and spent the next three days shopping, dining, and giggling non-stop.

That was the first of 20 consecutive annual trips to Philadelphia. We couldn't stay away; it was like coming home. (Actually, there was a two-year gap between our 19th and 20th trips. We're not sure why; I suppose life just intervened.) We were there during the Mayor Frank Rizzo years, and during the campaign to build something—*anything*—taller than William Penn's statue atop City Hall. We remember the trash strike and Project MOVE. For years we stayed at the Hershey Hotel at Broad and Locust Streets (now the Doubletree), where they gave you a big chocolate bar when you checked in. We had drinks at Apropos on Broad Street, scarfed down garlicky steaks at the Rusty Scupper in Headhouse Square, had roasted garlic appetizers at Mirabella on Locust, and became great friends with the Clevelanders who worked at Odeon on 12th Street—all of which have since gone to restaurant heaven.

After 20 years of exploring and enjoying Philadelphia, I figured I'd learned enough to write a book—and when the opportunity arose, that's what I did. What I didn't realize was how much more there was to learn and love about this city.

While history still shapes Philly's image, today there is so much more that distinguishes it. The medical, educational, and research community is unparalleled, from the nation's first and finest colleges and hospitals, to the weirdly irresistible Mütter Museum. Philadelphia is the country's premier restaurant town—a claim no one will dispute after one of Jim's messy cheesesteak sandwiches, or an exquisite dinner at the five-star Le Bec-Fin. And when you're in an artsy mood, nothing beats an afternoon at the famous Philadelphia Museum of Art, or a First Friday evening trolling the galleries in the happening Old City art district.

With the *Insiders' Guide to Philadelphia*, I set out to write a guidebook, but along the way it became almost a brag book. *Philadelphia* magazine once had a motto; it was "what every city magazine wants to be when it grows up." That's how I view Philly—it's what every city wants to be, and I can't help but brag about it.

HOW TO USE THIS BOOK

With dozens of information-packed chapters, from Antiques to History to Parks and Recreation, this book has been designed for everyone interested in learning about and exploring Philadelphia—visitors, new residents, even those who already live here. Whether you're seeing the city for the first time or have lived here for years, the *Insiders' Guide to Philadelphia* can help you get your bearings, get around, and enhance your understanding of the city in a straightforward, logical, and—we hope—fun way.

That doesn't mean you'll find every section organized identically. In the Restaurants chapter, for instance, listings are grouped first by geographic area, then by the type of cuisine within each area. It seemed likely that if readers were touring or living in one part of Greater Philadelphia, or interested in visiting a certain neighborhood, they would be interested in places to eat in the vicinity.

The Shopping chapter, too, is organized first by geographic area. Most people first consider a neighborhood or town in which they'll spend some shopping time, then learn about the mix of stores in that place.

For first-timers the History chapter will be a good introduction to Philadelphia because, unlike most tourism destinations, Philly's history really defines the scope and personality of your choices as a visitor. From the lush, shaded parks to its exclusive hotels, award-winning restaurants, and world-renowned arts organizations, history shaped the city dynamic, and it drives much of its economy today. As you tour Philadelphia, you will grow accustomed to looking beyond the obvi-ous historic icons, such as the Liberty Bell and Betsy Ross house. While those attractions are sure to inspire, there are lesser-known discoveries that are no less thrilling: The utopian backdrop of the White Dog Cafe, a heritage still influencing the cafe's social-minded activities. The 28,000-pipe organ in Macy's, formerly the cherished Wanamaker's department store. Or the colonial-era mansions dotting the landscape of Fairmount Park.

Perhaps your next stop in the book should be the Getting Here, Getting Around chapter. Once you have an idea of the city's history, that chapter will give you a perspective on where the landmark events took place, and how to find them.

From there, follow your interests. The Hotels and Bed-and-Breakfasts chapters will show you the wide range of lodging choices available, from historic inns on the National Register, to family-friendly hotels with swimming pools so the kids can splash around. The Kidstuff and Attractions chapters will help you plan your vacation days—but keep in mind that, in this city, most attractions are kid friendly, and most "kidstuff" sites are great fun for kids of any age. In some chapters—Arts, or even Parks and Recreation—you will find listings of places that easily could have appeared in Attractions, Kidstuff, or other chapters. That's the wonder of Philadelphia, that a wonderful restaurant like City Tavern, where the country's founding fathers debated the Declaration over mead and turkey legs, also is an attraction (and since most people go there to dine, we've included it in the Restaurants chapter).

In some sections we thought a pricing guide would be helpful. Prices for meals, admissions, and lodgings change every day, so we provided ranges in the form of dollar signs, with one ($) indicating the least expensive, and five ($$$$$) for the most pricey. Keys to the guides are given in the introductions to those chapters.

We also have provided four maps to aid you in planning your stay and getting around the city. The maps show (1) Pennsylvania, (2) Philadelphia and its suburbs, (3) Center City and surrounding neighborhoods, and (4) the Historic District. In addition, dozens of Insider's Tips (indicated by) are scattered throughout the book—tidbits of inside info not usually found in guidebooks.

After you peruse your *Insiders' Guide to Philadelphia,* we hope you will keep it on hand as a ready reference during your time in the city. And we hope you will forgive our biases, which surely emerge in the writing. For us, it was love at first sight with the City of Brotherly Love, and, we admit, we've tried to show you Philadelphia at its best.

AREA OVERVIEW

If you're lucky, you'll soon visit Philadelphia, where history is hip, where preservation is king, and where restaurants, jazz, culture, and kids rule.

It's a cleaner, higher-functioning city than it was 20 years ago. You'll find more art here now, more music, more dance and theatre companies, better food, and probably more glamour. The National Constitution Center, new stadiums for the city's pro football and baseball teams, and a long list of new eateries and nightclubs have added a tone of glitz and sophistication.

But it's still the history that brings some 30 million visitors to Philly each year—at least the first time. They come to walk in the steps of Ben Franklin and George Washington, to visit the rooms where the land of liberty was born. The Betsy Ross House, Elfreth's Alley, Franklin Court, Christ Church, and of course, the most famous icon of all, the Liberty Bell, all draw visitors.

Almost immediately, though, Philly's rich history overlaps with their modern-day experience: If they dine at Striped Bass, or Moshulu, or even grab a cheesesteak on the run, they're taking in a piece of history. Lodging at the posh Park Hyatt, once known simply as "the Bellevue," surrounds visitors with turn-of-the-20th-century elegance. Just pausing to people-watch from a bench in peaceful Rittenhouse Square puts one in the heart of William Penn's grand vision, more than three centuries old, of a borderless city with green, open squares.

A CITY OF DISTINCTIONS

Today, Philadelphia is as diverse as Penn had hoped—about 50 percent of the population is white, 40 percent African American, 6 percent Hispanic, and the remainder of residents are of Asian and other ethnic heritages. It's been nicknamed the "Quaker City" (for Penn's Quaker-inspired plans),

"Nation's Birthplace," "Cradle of the Revolution," "City of Neighborhoods," and the one we most often hear, the "City of Brotherly Love."

The list of contemporary accolades is long: Over the past few years, Philly has been among the top choices for "Best Walking Cities" (*Prevention* magazine), "Best Cities for Pets" (*Forbes* magazine), "Best Cities for Black Families" (*BET.com*), "America's Healthiest Cities" (*Natural Health* magazine), "Best Places for Business and Careers" (*Forbes*), "Top Cities for Business" (*Inc.* magazine), "Best Cities for Men" (*Men's Health*), and "America's Healthiest Cities for Women" (*Self* magazine). Philly was even awarded a "Five Dog Bone Award" from *Animal Fair* magazine, which named it the country's top city to visit with a pet.

Equally lengthy is the list of celebrities from Greater Philadelphia (many of whom still live here), including:

- actress Blythe Danner
- poker champion Annie Duke
- comedian Bill Cosby
- actor Billy Bob Thornton
- singer Patti LaBelle
- actor Will Smith
- actor Kevin Bacon
- actress Kelly Ripa
- author Buzz Bissinger

If you're over 55 and would enjoy seeing Philadelphia with an active, curious group of fellow travelers, consider enrolling with Elderhostel. The world's largest education and travel organization for mature individuals, Elderhostel stages hundreds of different theme-based trips around the world—including many to southeastern Pennsylvania. For more info, call (877) 426–8056 or check www.elderhostel.org.

CLOSE-UP

Philadelphia—A City of Firsts

It's known as the "Birthplace of Our Nation," but a free country isn't the only thing started in Philadelphia. It's said that no other city can claim as many "firsts." Some of our favorites:

- America's first public grammar school in 1689, now called the William Penn Charter School.
- The country's first public library, the Free Library of Philadelphia, founded in 1731 by Benjamin Franklin.
- The first public bank in America, the Pennsylvania Bank, opened in 1780. Later renamed the Bank of North America, it was the first incorporated bank chartered by the Continental Congress.
- The country's first stock exchange, organized in 1790.
- America's first botanical garden, Bartram's Gardens, in 1728.
- America's first hospital, the Pennsylvania Hospital, co-founded by Benjamin Franklin in 1751.
- America's first medical school, first nursing school, first dental school, first children's hospital, first cancer hospital, and first eye hospital.
- America's first volunteer fire department, the Union Fire Company, founded by Ben Franklin in 1736.
- The country's first mint, opened in 1792,

establishing the use of standardized coins for the country (instead of state currency, which had been used previously).
- In 1799, the country's first municipal water system, the Philadelphia Water Works.
- The country's first art school and art museum, the Pennsylvania Academy of the Fine Arts, in 1805.
- The oldest continually operating horticultural society in the United States, the Pennsylvania Horticultural Society.
- In 1829 the country's first large flower show (and still one of the most famous home-and-garden shows anywhere).
- America's first public zoo, the Philadelphia Zoo, in 1874.
- In 1876, the first World's Fair held in America, to mark the nation's centennial.
- In 1946, the world's first computer, ENIAC, at the University of Pennsylvania.
- The first American flag, sewn by Betsy Ross in 1777.
- The first written protest against slavery.
- The first German settlement in the New World.
- In 1744, the first novel published in America—*Pamela: or, Virtue Rewarded*, by Samuel Richardson.
- The country's first fire and life insurance companies.

Along with its history, Philadelphia's other major distinction is in its food traditions. Some, like cheesesteaks, are budget items—but every bit as tasty as a $200 meal at Le Bec-Fin, one of the city's most acclaimed eateries. Don't leave without trying a cheesesteak, made of thin slices of steak, fast-grilled with onions and served on a huge bun with an abundance of provolone and Cheez Wiz.

Hoagies are cold-cut feasts, sometimes called submarines or torpedoes. Also high on the Philly food list—and worth kicking back with, on that bench in Rittenhouse Square—are soft, warm pretzels, amply salted and with a good squeeze of mustard. Tastykakes, another Philly food icon, are packaged-treat decadence in the form of donuts, finger cakes, and cookie bars.

In any price range, Philadelphia is a food town, and competition between chefs always keeps the town buzzing about restaurants. Le Bec-Fin boasts five-star ratings, but don't overlook its classmates, the celebrated Susanna Foo, Lacroix, and Morimoto. Less expensive choices (but still top-rated) include Fork, Striped Bass, sexy Alma de Cuba, and our perennial favorite because it just has *so* much heart, the ever-progressive White Dog Cafe. BYOBs persist as the hot trend, a vehicle for talented newer chefs to step up as restaurateurs.

PROSPERING IN PHILLY

This city has come far since William Penn designed his five-square town: it's now the fifth-largest city in the United States, home to 1.5 million people, sometimes called the "buckle of the money belt" for its location halfway between New York City and Washington, D.C. Within a day's drive of Philadelphia are more than 100 million residents and six of the biggest U.S. markets.

Its transportation network, renowned educational and medical institutions, lively cultural landscape, and highly skilled workforce make Philadelphia ideal both for recruiting and for relocating. A report by *Business 2.0* magazine placed Philly among the country's "boom towns." With five medical schools and 120 hospitals, it's not surprising that more than 200 pharmaceutical and biotech research firms have located here. Technology giants such as Unisys, Meridian, Du Pont, and Safeguard are based here, along with

You can always read more about Philly by going to the Web sites of its daily and weekly newspapers, or by consulting Philadelphia *magazine (www.phillymag.com). But for the real skinny—or, at least, a different (and unedited) twist on it—check out some of the city's more popular blogs. Three that we like:* The Rittenhouse Review *(www.rittenhouse.blogspot.com),* Girlfriends' Locker Room *(www.pnionline.com/dnblog/fit/), and* Philebrity *(www.philebrity.com), where this morning we found a great photo of a Segway-riding cop in the 30th Street Station.*

pharmaceutical companies Pfizer, Aventis, Merck, Wyeth, and GlaxoSmithKline. In international trade, the facts are no less stunning: more than 2,000 foreign-owned companies in Philadelphia employ more than 60,000 workers, and the city hosts 33 foreign consuls—promoting more foreign trade all the time.

THE 'BURBS

Like every big city, Philadelphia sprawls—but from their colonial history to their hot new restaurants, Philly's suburbs are so Philly-like, they meld easily into city life.

In these parts, people identify their place of residence by county as often as by individual town. Bucks, Chester, Delaware, and Montgomery are the four counties which, along with Philadelphia County, comprise Greater Philadelphia. A brief look at each:

- Bucks County, an hour northeast of Philadelphia, has the personality of an actress—beguiling, vivacious, full of both vitality and mystique, not to mention physical beauty. This is where Washington crossed the Delaware on Christmas Eve, 1776—the spot is marked by Washington Crossing State Park on Route 32—and today is known for its hilly,

For instant access to the best Philadelphia info, go to www.gophila.com, the Web site of the Greater Philadelphia Tourism & Marketing Corporation (GPTMC). The "Culture Files" alone (www.gophila.com/culturefiles) bring up more than 300 Web pages on Greater Philly's arts and culture choices; other sections give you fast info on hotels, restaurants, attractions, and events. Two more great resources: the Independence Visitor Center (215-965-7676; www.independence visitorcenter.com) and the Philadelphia Convention & Visitors Bureau (215-636-3300; www.pcvb.org).

green landscape and eye-candy towns. New Hope, across the river from Lambertville, New Jersey, is an artists' colony, a bit commercial but great fun, full of boutiques and, like Lambertville, antiques shops. Mercer Museum in Doylestown, Peddler's Village, and Sesame Place are other popular stops.

- In Chester and Delaware Counties, which together form the Brandywine Valley, you'll find historic country homes for some of Philadelphia's most elite citizens. Just across the Delaware border at the Winterthur Museum, visitors can tour the fabulous DuPont country estate. Nearby are the famous Longwood Gardens, displaying 11,000 different kinds of plantings on its 1,050 acres of indoor and outdoor gardens, including the "Enchanted Woods" children's garden. Brandywine Battlefield Park and Tyler Arboretum round out the attractions, along with nine wineries (including award-winning Chadds Ford Winery) and, for home shoppers, the QVC Studio and store.

- From Valley Forge to Bryn Mawr, Montgomery County is a land of contrasts. The big tourist draw is Valley Forge Historical Park, the 3,600-acre outpost where George Washington and his troops spent the bitter winter of 1777-78, the months that shaped the Continental Army and its winning strategy. Today, restored buildings and miles of walking and horseback riding trails mark the terrain. The massive King of Prussia Mall is here, too. With Chester and Delaware Counties, Montgomery also is the locale for the burgeoning "Main Line" communities along Route 30, including Wayne, Bala Cynwyd, Bryn Mawr, Paoli, and Ardmore, which have grown with their own cultural, shopping, and dining opportunities.

Philadelphia Vital Statistics

Philadelphia mayor: John F. Street

Pennsylvania governor: Ed Rendell, former mayor of Philadelphia

Population: Center City, extended, 79,000 (includes Art Museum, Queen Village, South Waterfront, and Northern Liberties neighborhoods)
Philadelphia, 1,470,151
Greater Philadelphia 5-county area, 3,882,573

Area: Old City, 1 sq. mi.
City/County of Philadelphia, 136 sq. mi.
Pennsylvania, 44,888 sq. mi.

Nickname/Motto: "City of Brotherly Love," from William Penn's "Holy Experiment" to build a city without walls or neighborhood boundaries.

Climate: Hot summers and relatively mild winters, with an average of 200 days of sunshine annually.

Average high temperatures (F): fall, 67.2; winter, 38.3; spring, 61.6; summer, 84.4.

Average monthly precipitation (inches): fall, 3.91; winter, 4.14; spring, 3.48; summer, 4.45.

Important Dates in History:
1651 – William Penn's *Charter of Liberties* enacted.
1682 – Philadelphia founded by William Penn.
1774 – 1st Continental Congress meets in Philadelphia.
1776 – Patriots declare independence at Philadelphia's State House; Declaration of Independence is ratified July 4th.
1790 – Philadelphia begins 10-year term as U.S. Capital.
1846 – The Liberty Bell rings for the last time, commemorating George Washington's birthday.

Pennsylvania's major cities: Philadelphia (largest city), Harrisburg (capital), Pittsburgh, Erie, Scranton, Allentown.

Major colleges and universities: Temple University, Drexel University, branches of Penn State, University of Pennsylvania, Villanova University, Swarthmore College, Bryn Mawr College, LaSalle University, Lehigh University, Philadelphia University.

Major area employers: MBNA, DuPont, Merck & Co., Vanguard Group Inc., Lockheed Martin, Wyeth Pharmaceutical and Research, Boeing, GlaxoSmithKline.

Famous sons and daughters: Benjamin Franklin, Betsy Ross, Marian Anderson, Revolutionary War hero Thaddeus Kosciuszko, James A. Michener, Pearl S. Buck, Edgar Allan Poe (lived in Philly for two years).

Major airports/interstates: Philadelphia International Airport (PIA); I-95, I-76, I-276 (Pennsylvania Turnpike), I-676 (Vine Street Expressway), I-476 ("Blue Route").

Public transportation: SEPTA (Southeast Pennsylvania Transportation Authority) trolleys, buses, commuter trains, subways; PATCO (commuter rail to New Jersey); PHLASH (local shuttle bus).

Driving laws: Right on red is permitted; bus-only lanes strictly enforced; seatbelts must be worn at all times in moving vehicles; car must move to the far lane when passing a disabled vehicle or roadwork; speed limit on state highways is 55 mph.

Alcohol laws: The legal drinking age is 21; closing time for most bars is 2:00 A.M., 7 days a week. Wine and spirits are sold only in state stores; beer and wine coolers are available at many delis.

Daily newspaper: *The Philadelphia Inquirer;* daily circulation about 344,000, 761,000 Sunday.

Taxes: Lodging taxes 14 percent; restaurant meals and general sales taxes 7 percent; liquor 10 percent tax. No tax on clothing sales.

GETTING HERE, GETTING AROUND

Getting into most big cities, especially on the East or West Coast, is a migraine event, and getting around them is even worse.

Not so with Philadelphia! Freeways into the Center City keep traffic moving as smoothly as sleek ribbon, with easy-to-see signage that makes sense, and gorgeous greenery along the way. For those flying in, more than 25 airlines stage some 575 departures every day to 115 cities around the world. Just blocks from downtown, Amtrak's 30th Street Station's 11 train lines connect to every train destination in the nation.

Philadelphia is so ideally positioned—just a two-hour drive from New York City, 90 minutes from Baltimore, and three hours from Washington, D.C.—that getting here by plane, car, bus, or train is hassle-free. Once you're here, you're in a walking city, with dozens of historic sites inside the compact, 25-block Center City grid. Visitors too rushed for a stroll through history can easily hail one of the ubiquitous taxis constantly cruising the streets—and if you prefer to drive yourself, the grid is easy to negotiate, with plentiful parking in every section of town.

GETTING HERE BY CAR

If you're driving into Philadelphia, your route will be marvelously simple: Only a handful of major roadways lead into Philadelphia, and they connect with all surrounding regions.

From the north and northwest, the most common choice is the Pennsylvania Turnpike, or Interstate 80. Interstate 95, the primary north–south corridor running the length of the East Coast, brings travelers from New York and Washington, D.C.

From the west, the major route is Interstate 76 as it runs alongside the Schuylkill River approaching Philadelphia. Interstate 676, or the Vine Street Expressway, connects with I-76 and bisects Center City.

From southern New Jersey, Interstate 295 and the New Jersey Turnpike are primary routes to Philadelphia; alternatively, many visitors arrive via U.S. Routes 70, 73, and 55. The tranquil Atlantic City Expressway connects Philadelphia to the gambling mecca and beyond to the South "Jersey Shore" by the Garden State Parkway.

This efficient network has been in place for nearly two centuries: A number of roads into the city, 20 feet wide and built of crushed stone—complete with toll-gates—were completed by 1794 to facilitate the movement of goods. By 1821 paved toll highways connected Philadelphia to New York City, Baltimore, the state capital at Harrisburg, Reading, Lancaster, and into New Jersey. Fifty years later, some 300 miles of paved roads served Philadelphia, and in the early 1900s, the Pennsylvania Turnpike became the first statewide superhighway in the country.

One of the most popular routes into Philadelphia is by U.S. Route 30, known as the "Lincoln Highway"—into the city, that is, from every point west as far as California (though in other states the Lincoln Highway incorporates east–west routes in addition to US 30).

It is America's first transcontinental highway, conceived in 1913 by automobile

---

You'll never hear a Philadelphian refer to Interstate 76 as "I-76." That freeway is always called "the Schuylkill" ("skōō-kul"). Likewise, I-476 is known as the "Blue Route."

CLOSE-UP

Parking in Philadelphia

In every section of Center City, street parking is handy. You should never have to walk more than a block or two from your street-parked car to any restaurant, attraction, or historic site. Though it's technically illegal, many locals even park in the median, right in the middle of Broad Street heading toward South Philly!

If you feel more comfortable leaving your car in a lot, rates will be cheaper on the fringes of Center City—for instance, in the lot at 16th and Spring Streets, where you can park all day on the weekends for just $5.00.

Every hotel and inn in the city either has its own garage or valet parking, or the desk staff can guide you to safe parking nearby. If you want to plan your own parking before you visit, several parking companies have multiple locations:

• Central Parking System/Kinney System/ AllRight Parking, (215) 563-3650
• Parkway Corporation, (215) 569-8400
• Philadelphia Parking Authority, (215) 683-9600

---

icon Carl Fisher—the man who created the Indianapolis Speedway and Indy 500, and later transformed a southern swamp into Miami Beach. The Lincoln Highway was specifically planned for cars; at the time there were few good roads in the country. Fisher fantasized about a coast-to-coast highway made of gravel, and went to his fellow titans in the auto industry for financial backing.

He first approached Henry Ford, who turned him down. However, Frank A. Seiberling of Akron, Ohio—president of Goodyear Tire & Rubber Co.—and Henry Joy, president of Packard Motor Car Co., liked the idea. It was Joy, in fact, who proposed naming the highway after Abraham Lincoln. The road was built and triggered the nationwide "Good Roads movement," the foundation for today's national highway network.

If you're driving in the city, getting around is easy—once you're comfortable with the narrow, one-way streets and the

competition from aggressive taxi drivers. Just relax and plan to go around the block a few times when the one-ways trip you up.

The layout of Center City, where you'll find most hotels and historic attractions, is sensible and easy to learn; it follows the original grid format designed by William Penn nearly four centuries ago. The grid is compact, spanning just 25 blocks between the Schuylkill and Delaware Rivers. Between those boundaries, streets running north–south are numbered, while those running east–west are named for trees—Pine, Walnut, Spruce—with only a few exceptions, such as South Street (east–west) and Broad Street (north–south). Just watch for the "HOV lanes," reserved for bus and taxi traffic; city police take those lanes seriously, and if you're caught driving in one, your "souvenir" from the city could be a citation and a $100 fine.

After you park your car and start walking, curb cut-outs enhance accessibility, and Center City's five historic squares are great resting spots during a museum-hopping day.

GETTING HERE BY AIR

If you're flying to Philadelphia, chances are you'll fly into the Philadelphia International Airport (PHL), located about 7 miles from Center City and serving more than 20 air-lines with some 575 daily departures to 115 domestic and international destinations. Fifty percent of America's population is within a two-hour flight of Philly, and nearly 31.5 million travelers pass through PHL's 120 boarding gates each year.

PHL has come a long way since October 12, 1927—the day Charles A. Lindbergh flew onto the grassy runway to dedicate what was then known as Philadelphia Municipal Airport. The air-port has undergone major capital improvements in the past several years, including a $550-million International Terminal A-West, opened in 2003, which nearly doubled PHL's international gates. Because of capabilities created by adding the new terminal, Philadelphia now offers non-stop flights to Dublin, Cancun, Rome, Paris, London, Madrid, Glasgow, and Am-sterdam, among other faraway cities.

In 2004 Southwest Airlines and Fron-tier Airlines came to Philadelphia Interna-tional Airport, adding more than a dozen daily flights to cities west of the Rocky Mountains.

At this writing, PHL was served by the following passenger carriers:

- Air Canada, (888) 247-2262
- Air France, (800) 237-2747
- Air Jamaica, (800) 523-5585
- AirTran Airways, (800) AIRTRAN
- America West Airlines, (800) 235-9292
- American Airlines, (800) 433-7300
- American Eagle, (800) 433-7300
- British Airways, (800) AIRWAYS
- Continental Airlines, (800) 525-0280
- Continental Express, (800) 525-0280
- Delta Air Lines, (800) 221-1212
- Delta Connection, (800) 221-1212
- Frontier Airlines, (800) 432-IFLY
- Lufthansa German Airlines, (800) 645-3880
- Midwest Airlines, (800) 452-2022
- Northwest Airlines, (800) 452-2022
- Southwest Airlines, (800) 435-9792
- United Airlines, (800) 241-6522
- United Express, (800) 241-6522
- USAirways, (800) 428-4322
- USAirways Express, (800) 428-4322
- USA3000, (877) 872-3000

Getting to the airport from Center City is easy; I-76, I-95, and I-476 all offer direct access, and increased on-site parking has been added in recent years. Taxi service to the airport is affordable—just a $25 flat rate; call City Cab at (215) 492-6600, or Quaker City Cab, (215) 728-8000.

The SEPTA (Southeastern Pennsylva-nia Transportation Authority) R1 high-speed rail line connects to the airport for just $5.50 one way, with convenient stops at the 30th Street Station (Amtrak), Uni-versity City, and MarketEast/The Gallery on Market Street—the latter two being wheelchair-accessible rail stations. For more information on rail or bus service to the airport and around the city, contact SEPTA at (215) 580-7800, TDD (215) 580-7712, or go to www.septa.org.

Travelers with long layovers have hap-pily discovered that Philadelphia Interna-tional Airport is almost a destination in itself, with more food, drink, culture, and shopping choices than some small towns! Restaurants and shops include Cibo Bistro and Wine Bar, Caviar Assouline's gourmet foods, Fossil, Gap, Swatch, a PGA Tour Shop, and the Philadelphia Museum of Art gift shop.

At any given time, at least a dozen art, photography, and historic displays are shown in various terminals and con-courses. In the past they have included exhibits from the Museum of American Glass, photographs documenting Phillies Stadium history, examples from the Penn-sylvania Academy of the Fine Arts, arti-

CLOSE-UP

Taking a Limo

Limousines are another option for getting to the airport, and travelers have plenty of choices. Some of the larger limousine rental companies:

- A Executive Limousine, Inc., (215) 943-9464; www.aexecutivelimo.com
- BostonCoach, (610) 521-0500, or (800) 672-7676; www.bostoncoach.com; also offering wheelchair-accessible vehicles
- Callaway Transportation, (410) 795–8300; www.callawaytransportation.com
- Carey Worldwide Chauffered Services, (610) 595-2800; www.ecarey.com
- CAR ONE Sedan & Limousine, (215) 551-8400, or (800) 787-2271; www.car1limo.com
- Corporate Sedan Service, (888) 258-9555; www.sedanservice.com
- Crystal Limousine Inc., (610) 353-4324; e-mail crystal113@verizon.net
- Dav-El Limousine Service, (215) 334-7900, or (800) 727-1957; www.davel-phila.com

- David Tours and Travel, (215) 677-8300, or (877) 328-4349; www.davidtours.net
- Eagle Limousine & Motorcoach, (302) 325-4200; www.eaglelimo.com
- E.T.A. Worldwide, (856) 405-0054, (866) 382-5466; www.etalimousine.com
- Imperial Limousine Services, (215) 922-1133, (888) 245-6482; www.imperial limo.org; also offers wheelchair-accessible vehicles
- King Limousine & Transportation Service, Inc., (610) 265-3050, (800) 245-5460; www.kinglimoinc.com; also offers wheelchair-accessible vehicles
- Krapf's Coaches, Inc., (800) 548-9317; www.krapfbus.com; also offers wheelchair-accessible vehicles
- (800) BOOK-A-LIMO, (800) 266-5254; www.bookalimo.com
- Salem Limo, Inc., (215) 331-2468, (877) 875-1452; www.salem-limos.com
- Tropiano Transportation Services, Inc., (215) 643-5397, (800) 559-2040; www.tropianotransportation.com

facts from historic meeting houses of Greater Philadelphia, and showings from artists Nami Yamamoto, Warren Seelig, and Ava Blitz. Current exhibits can be checked at the airport's Web site, www.phl.org.

The airport Web site is a one-stop resource for all information relating to PHL, including parking (with lots ranging from $9.00 to $17.00 for 24 hours), directions to the airport, information on airlines, terminal maps, accessibility info, and current arrivals and departures. Travelers without Web access can phone the air-

port's general number, (215) 937-6937.

If you're renting a car at the airport, you will find information phones at all baggage claim areas. The following auto rental companies serve Philadelphia International; with the exception of Enterprise, travelers should proceed to Zone 2 outside the baggage claim area to pick up their cars. Autos equipped with hand controls are available from all agencies.

- Alamo, (800) 327-9633, TDD (800) 522-9292; www.goalamo.com

- Avis, (800) 331-1212, TDD (800) 331-2323; www.avis.com
- Budget, (800) 527-0700, TDD (800) 826-5510; www.drivebudget.com
- Dollar, (800) 800-4000, TDD (800) 826-5510; www.dollar.com
- Enterprise, (800) RENT-A-CAR, TDD (866) 534-9270; www.enterprise.com
- Hertz, (800) 654-3131, TDD (800) 328-6323; www.hertz.com
- National, (800) 227-7368, TDD (800) 328-6323; www.nationalcar.com

GETTING HERE BY TRAIN OR BUS

Amtrak brings more than 25,000 commuters daily into Center City, but it's also a relaxing and convenient method for traveling here from points north, south, and west. The 30th Street Station in Center City is Amtrak's main terminal, as well as the city's hub for the Acela Express, providing high-speed electric train service from Philadelphia to New York, New England, and Washington, D.C. For information, call Amtrak at (800) USA-RAIL or (215) 824-1600, or go to www.amtrak.com.

Those who opt to "leave the driving to us" can travel to Philly from thousands of towns across the country by Greyhound Bus Lines (800-231-2222 or www.greyhound.com). Other bus companies serving Greater Philadelphia include Martz Trailways (800-233-8604 or www.martztrailways.com), New Jersey Transit (215-569-3752, 800-582-5946, or www.njtransit.com), and Peter Pan Trailways (800-343-9999 or www.peterpan bus.com).

PUBLIC TRANSPORTATION

SEPTA operates the large network of rail, bus, subway, and streetcars throughout Philadelphia and its suburbs. Only two subway lines—Market-Frankford (east–west) and Broad Street (north–south) serve the city; buses and

Along with the array of shops and restaurants at Philadelphia International Airport comes another happy surprise: affordable prices. PHL pioneered the policy of anti-gouging at airports; all goods sold in airport stores carry the same price tag as in that store's Center City and shopping-mall counterparts. So, when you buy a sweater at the Gap at PHL, you will pay the same price as you'd pay at the Gap on Walnut Street— and if an item you purchase is not sold at "street price," your money is refunded. The airport's motto: "Same Store, Same Product, Same Price." For more info on airport shops, call (800) 937-3340, 24 hours.

streetcars are much more prolific. Cash fare is $2.00, with discounted tokens and passes sold at SEPTA sales offices. Seniors ride buses and streetcars free of charge during off-peak hours, and pay $1.00 for commuter trains.

For visitors, the easiest option is SEPTA's Day Pass, good for one full day of unlimited transportation on all City Transit, plus a one-way passage on the Airport Rail Line R1, connecting Center City with the airport and running every 30 minutes, for just $5.50. Day Passes can be purchased at the Independence Visitor Center at Market and Sixth Streets; for other locations call (215) 580-7800 from 6:00 A.M. to midnight, or get additional info at www.septa.org.

Wheelchair-accessible public transportation is likewise easy to find in Philadelphia, from SEPTA CCT (215-580-7700 or TDD 215-580-7853). More than 100 city and suburban bus routes are lift-equipped, and Market East and 30th Street Station regional rails, with routes to the airport, are fully accessible.

In addition, ADA Paratransit services are available (215-580-7145) for individuals registered in advance. Public transport from Center City to the South Jersey suburbs is offered by the Port Authority Transit Corporation (PATCO) Hi-Speedline rail service. Nearly 40,000 commuters from 13 stations use the service daily, arriving at four convenient Center City stops: on Locust at 9th/10th, Locust at 12th/13th, Locust at 15th/16th, or at 8th and Market Streets. Or, visitors can take a break from Center City touring and take PATCO for a scenic ride across the Ben Franklin Bridge to the Tweeter Center, Adventure Aquarium, and Camden Children's Garden in southern New Jersey. For information, visit PATCO's Web site at www.drpa.org/patco, or call (215) 922-4600.

For a quick connection to 19 Center City destinations between Penn's Landing and the Philadelphia Museum of Art—including most major downtown hotels—try the purple "Phlash" bus for a buck! An all-day ticket is just $4.00—seniors and kids under five ride free—and for a family of four, at $10.00 it's the least expensive all-day ticket in town. From March 1 through November 30, Phlash operates with direct connections to SEPTA, PATCO, Amtrak, and Airport rail lines, as well as the RiverLink Ferry and special events at museums and other hot spots such as Reading Terminal Market, The Bourse, and the Kimmel Center. Phlash runs every 12 minutes, 10:00 A.M. to 6:00 P.M., and offers a special Park & Ride parking discount at participating garages. For a map of "Phlash Point" stops in Center City, parking garages, and other info, visit www.phillyphlash.com.

The RiverLink Ferry takes commuters and visitors between the Philadelphia and Camden, New Jersey, waterfronts, Friday to Sunday, April 8 to 30, and seven days a week from May through September. In Philadelphia, catch the ferry at Penn's Landing; with a Phlash ticket, save $1.00 on the ferry. For information, call (215) 925-LINK or visit www.riverlinkferry.org.

CRUISING INTO PHILLY

It began in 2002 with just one sailing. By 2005 three cruise lines—Celebrity Cruises, Norwegian Cruise Lines, and Royal Caribbean Cruise Line (RCCL), the world's second-largest cruise line—were offering more than 30 sailings from the Philadelphia Cruise Terminal at Pier 1 in South Philadelphia, The Port of Philadelphia and Camden (PPC) (cleverly nicknamed "America's Berthplace"). More than 92,500 passengers came through the terminal that year, and port calls from additional lines, notably Seabourne and Silversea, were being planned at press time.

Philadelphia's new leisure cruising industry makes economic sense for travelers. The growing trend is called homeporting—the notion of starting a cruise as close to home as possible. With a quarter of the U.S. population living within a five-hour drive from Philly, cruising from a port close to home (as opposed to Florida or California, where just flying to the port adds significantly to a family's vacation cost) means big savings. They can even park at the cruise terminal for just $10 a day!

Another bonus of sailing from Philadelphia is the extra time that vacationers can spend at their cruise destinations, simply because Philly is closer to some of the more favored ports. Bermuda is the most popular destination, with New England/Canada cruises scoring a close second.

Since Pier 1's opening, the Delaware River Port Authority (DRPA) has invested $15 million in improving the facility. With the booming growth of cruising from Philadelphia, more expansions are planned. Already a system of remote-lot parking with trolley shuttles has been implemented and eased potential congestion in front of the terminal.

For cruisers, sailing from Philadelphia is a winning strategy, and they can enhance the experience with overnight stays in Philly. The "CruisePhilly First" program, available to all passengers sailing from the PPC, and Norwegian Cruise Line's "FreeStyle Philly," available to NCL's passengers, offer discounts on Philadelphia attractions, hotels, and restaurants, and the PPC itself promotes tours for cruise passengers visiting the city on port calls. Excursions to The Barnes Foundation, Valley Forge, Independence National Historical Park, the Amish Country, Brandywine Valley, and the Philadelphia Museum of Art are especially popular.

And, Philadelphia wins as well. Back in 2004, when only 60,000 cruise passengers sailed from PPC, CruisePhilly generated some $16 million in local business revenue—a figure that only grows with the number of cruise passengers.

For information on cruising from Philadelphia, or about special pre- and post-cruise packages, visit www.cruise philly.com or call (856) 968-2052.

HISTORY 🏛

By the time William Penn first stepped onto the land called Pennsylvania in 1682, it already had been explored—decades earlier—by Dutch and Swedish colonists.

Back in 1623, a Dutch stockade and trading post were the only structures in the busy city we know as Philadelphia. The region still was a place of dense, deep green forests. Bears, fox, and other wildlife were abundant, and the rivers were rich with fish. Most of the inhabitants were Lenni-Lenape Indians, a branch of the Delaware Tribe of the Algonquin Indians. Shawnee, too, were here, living in villages of 100 to 300 people along the Delaware River.

As treaties with Indians were signed mid-century, land was purchased and, beginning in 1643, Swedes, Dutch, Finns, and English settlers came and built cabins on the fertile farming land near the Delaware. The Indians were a presence—cordial neighbors, for the most part, trading with settlers for furs and tobacco.

William Penn, a Quaker, cleared the way for more organized settlement when he accepted the title to Pennsylvania in a land grant from King Charles II of England. Penn delegated the task of finding a site for Philadelphia, instructing his committee to find a spot with good river frontage, and Penn personally arrived to inaugurate and design the city in October 1682.

Using a rectangular grid pattern on just 1,200 acres, Penn planned the city streets between the Delaware and Schuylkill Rivers—a 22-by-8-block pattern, with a town square (now the location of City Hall) and four public squares. Penn had survived the terrible London fire of 1666 and knew well the perils of narrow streets lined with wooden buildings, so he laid out Philadelphia along broad boulevards. Wanting to treat European settlers and Native Americans equally, he specified that no city walls or neighborhood borders be used. Penn named east-west streets after trees and plants (though Sassafras was changed to Race Street for the horse-and-buggy races held there), with Front Street and subsequent numbered streets running parallel to the Delaware River. Penn's urban design was meant to facilitate future growth, and served as the basic format for dozens of future cities across America.

In March 1683, Philadelphia was named capital of the colony of Pennsylvania. Because of the region's fertile lands and riverside location, Philadelphia's population multiplied quickly to 7,000 residents by the early 1700s—mostly Quakers, or "Friends," from England, with growing numbers of Scottish, Irish, and German immigrants. Before the American Revolution began, Philadelphia had become a strategic port and a major city.

THE REVOLUTIONARY WAR BEGINS

No city was more vital to American independence than Philadelphia. After the French and Indian War in 1763, when Britain began tightening the reins on trade in the colonies, Philadelphia—the economic and political center—was the hub of discontent over the new policies. With unpopular taxes also being imposed, and no colonial representation in the British

---

One of the first major waves of immigrants into Philadelphia were European farmers, eager to work the affordable land. Most were English, Scottish, and Germans—or, in the German language, Deutsch—which is why the farm families in the surrounding countryside are known as the "Pennsylvania Dutch."

Parliament, the buzz in the 1770s was for
independence. Even Benjamin Franklin,
who was loyal to King George III until well
into the 1770s, became disenchanted and
talked of the "capricious English policy."

King George sent troops to the
colonies to help control unrest. In 1774
the First Continental Congress convened
at Carpenters' Hall in Philadelphia. Instead
of directly rejecting the British policies,
Congress decided on a commercial boy-
cott of British goods. But over the next
nine months, rebellion grew in Massachu-
setts and, in April 1775, the King's troops
attacked Concord and "the shot heard
'round the world" proclaimed that the
American Revolution had begun.

Still, the colonies sent delegates to
the Second Continental Congress in May
1775 to try to resolve the problems without going to war, meeting this time in
Independence Hall (then the Pennsylvania
State House). Though they were meeting
for peace, they established a Continental
army and named George Washington as
commander-in-chief.

Congress met a third time on July 4,
1776, no longer hoping for a peaceful resolution. John Adams, Benjamin Franklin,

Thomas Jefferson, Robert R. Livingston,
and Roger Sherman were appointed to
draft a Declaration of Independence. Jefferson wrote the first draft, presented to
Congress on June 28, and a vote was
called the afternoon of July 4. Nine of the
13 colonies voted to adopt the Declaration, and signatures were collected. (The
most flamboyant was that of John Han-
cock, who signed with a flourish so "King
George can read that without specta-
cles!")

Four days later, on July 8, 1776, the
Liberty Bell rang from the tower of Independence Hall, summoning some 8,000
patriots to hear the first reading of the
Declaration of Independence by Colonel
John Nixon. Aptly, the bell's inscription
read, "Proclaim LIBERTY throughout all
the Land unto all the inhabitants thereof."

By that day, we should note, the bell
already was cracked. It had been commis-
sioned by the Pennsylvania Assembly in
1751, to celebrate the 50th anniversary of
William Penn's state constitution. The
bell's inscription, a quote from Leviticus
25:10, was inspired by Penn's Quaker
philosophies and his liberal position on
Native American rights. It's believed that
the crack appeared the first time the bell
was rung, possibly because it was too
brittle.

That flaw didn't stop it from being
tolled frequently; the Liberty Bell was
rung to summon citizens for special
announcements as the war progressed;
when Benjamin Franklin traveled to England to debate colonial injustices; when
King George III was crowned in 1761; and
to call Philadelphians together to discuss
the Sugar Act in 1764 and the Stamp Act
in 1765.

Weeks before the British occupied
Philadelphia in October 1777, all bells
were removed from the city to keep them
from being melted down for cannon balls.
The Liberty Bell was hidden under the
floorboards of the Zion Reformed Church
in Allentown, Pennsylvania, until after the
war was over.

CLOSE-UP

The "Other" Liberty Bell

The Liberty Bell in Philadelphia may be the nation's most famous freedom-ringing bell, but it isn't the only one.

Just 30 minutes northeast of Philadelphia, in the second-floor lobby of the Bucks County Courthouse in Doylestown, sits the 400-pound Bucks County Bell, forged in 1813 by the same foundry that cast the Liberty Bell. This less-renowned symbol of freedom is half the size of its legendary counterpart—23 inches high, with a 72.2-inch circumference—and cost $211.20 to manufacture. Its first home was in the village of Newtown, but it was soon moved to Doylestown, the county seat, a more central location.

For years the Bucks County Bell tolled every 30 minutes and to announce convening court sessions. When a new court-house was built in 1877, the bell was moved there and continued tolling. When that courthouse was demolished in the 1970s, however, the bell was lost—for a while.

The bell was found in a Philadelphia junkyard and purchased for $15,000 by a William F. Berry, who kept it in his East Falls home. In 1989 philanthropist Horace Collins again purchased the bell for $15,000, and grade-school students from the Central Bucks School District collected 43,965 pennies to help pay for a frame for the bell. Bucks County Technical School students built a 1,000-pound ash frame for the bell. On March 15, 1995, the Bucks County Bell was returned to its home in the Courthouse, where it remains on display today.

WASHINGTON RESCUES INDEPENDENCE AND BEN FLIES A KITE

The Revolutionary War came to Philadelphia, and British troops occupied the homes of the city's elite. It was 25 miles northeast of the city, however, in pastoral Bucks County, that George Washington turned the tide of the war.

Bucks County had been settled, along with Philadelphia, in the 1600s. Some of the first European settlers paddled up the Delaware River, which forms the county's western boundaries, and stayed in what became the port town of Bristol in lower Bucks County. Others explored the river, establishing small settlements as they traveled north. With productive farmland and large agricultural stakes of those early families, Bucks County soon established itself as an enclave of the wealthy and genteel.

It also presented itself to George Washington as a strategic military outpost. His Long Island campaign of 1776 had been disastrous, he had been forced to retreat into Pennsylvania, and he desperately needed a victory. The Delaware River was the barrier. If he could get across, he and his soldiers could position themselves for a surprise attack on the British in New Jersey.

The plan was for the 2,400 ragged soldiers to cross during the night of December 25. The river was clogged with ice; soon after they entered the river, the weather suddenly changed and the men were fighting sleet and blinding snow. Two supporting divisions didn't make it, but Washington and his men got across.

That crossing was pivotal to our winning the Revolution. Washington went on to surprise the British troops at Trenton, New Jersey, the morning of December 26, 1776—a huge victory that revitalized his troops and renewed the faith of Americans that liberty would prevail.

It seems odd that the other legend of Revolutionary times, Benjamin Franklin, never served in the military. Instead, we honor Franklin for his wit and creative genius. A printing apprentice in his hometown of Boston, young Ben ran away to Philadelphia at 17 and, the next year, continued his printer's training in London. His publishing talents would serve him well, making him wealthy as a printer, publisher of the *Pennsylvania Gazette,* founder of the nation's first free library, publisher of the annual *Poor Richard: An Almanack,* author, legislator, international diplomat, scientist, inventor, economist, abolitionist, and signer of the Declaration of Independence. He documented the effects of electricity while flying a kite at the age of 44 and only stopped working and creating when he died at the age of 84.

Was it wit or philosophy that Ben Franklin employed when he wrote the following nugget of wisdom? Regardless, these are the words of a complex, curious, funny man:

"If you would not be forgotten,
As soon as you are dead & rotten,
Either write things worth reading,
Or do things worth the writing."

INTO THE 19TH CENTURY

When we think of "Philadelphia" and "history," the images are of Revolutionary War battles, Ben Franklin strolling past sedate brick buildings, and women dressed like Betsy Ross. So much of our quest for independence happened in Philadelphia, it's only natural that we dismiss the rest of the city's history.

The Revolution wasn't Philadelphia's only trauma: Before 1800 the city experienced two yellow fever epidemics, the first in 1762. The second, in 1793, killed 10 percent of the city's people, with lesser recurrences over the next five years and outbreaks of malaria to come.

Still, the city grew. It served as the nation's capital from 1777 to 1788 (except during nine months of British occupation), and again from 1790 to 1800. Residential areas spread west to Broad Street and along the river. Industry and culture made Philadelphia a thriving city; institutions such as the Walnut Street Theater, founded in 1809, and in 1805 the Pennsylvania Academy of the Fine Arts, along with private academies such as Friends Select and Germantown Friends School, are still popular today.

Immigrants swelled the city in waves: Industrialization, hastened by navigable rivers and the nearby eastern seaboard, created a huge need for laborers. By 1850 Philadelphia had become one of the world's largest producers of iron machinery and tools, glass, furniture, ships, textiles, and publishing. English commoners brought their skills in the 1820s, followed by Irish fleeing the 1840s potato famine. In the 1870s, Germans and central Europeans came seeking peace and refuge. Later, from the 1880s to the 1920s, Italians, Russians, and Jews from eastern Europe, and African Americans from the South came for work.

Philadelphia's responsibilities grew with its population. A Constitutional Convention met there in 1787 to fashion the U.S. Constitution that still stands as the backbone of our democracy today. The first mint in the country—in fact, the first building legis-lated by the U.S. government—was built in 1792. George and Martha Washington donated their personal household goods to use in making coins, just to see the mint succeed. David Rittenhouse, for whom the fashionable Rittenhouse Square neighborhood is named, was the mint's first director and greatest cham-pion. A second, larger mint was built in 1833, a third in 1901, and a fourth—the current mint, the largest in the world—opened in 1969.

Philadelphia again distinguished itself in the Civil War, becoming the first large city north of the Mason–Dixon line to become involved. Several regiments of Union infantry and cavalry were based here, and Philadelphia was a recruitment center for thousands of soldiers. Its indus-tries were primary suppliers of munitions, rifles, and uniforms for the army, and 11 warships were built in Philadelphia's Navy Yard. The city also was one of the first abolitionist centers.

Port activity soared after the Civil War, with cotton from the South support-ing Philadelphia's huge textile industry. Like most cities, urbanization welcomed the 20th century; as the manufacturing sector boomed, agriculture became less prominent.

A MODERN, COSMOPOLITAN CITY

With advances in every occupational cate-gory following the Industrial Revolution, the need for skilled and unskilled labor, as well as professionals, was relentless.

One of the major immigrant groups as the 20th century unfolded was Latinos, who actually had been in Philadelphia since the 18th century; in colonial times, the port traded regularly with Puerto Rico and Cuba. As Caribbean and Latin Ameri-can countries fought for their own inde-pendence in the 1800s, Philadelphia—the historic mecca for freedom fighters—was a destination for revolutionaries in exile.

Trade with Latin American countries focused on tobacco in the 1800s; as the 20th century loomed, Philadelphia's Spanish-speaking families clustered in new neighborhoods with other Latinos. The U.S. government hired Mexican labor-ers to work on Philadelphia's railroads during World War II, and post-war pros-perity brought a new Puerto Rican popu-lation for manufacturing and domestic service jobs.

Another major ethnic group are the Chinese, initially a "bachelor society" in America. Discriminatory laws prevented many from starting families or realizing their dreams and, as in other large cities, they worked in hand laundries and restau-rants, gradually settling in Chinatown. Those restrictions were lifted during World War II, and Chinese citizens joined their neighbors in starting families and pursuing careers. Once a "red-light dis-trict," Philadelphia's Chinatown today is a thriving village in the heart of the city.

African Americans, too, came to Philly from the South, drawn by jobs before and after World War II. As the migration to the suburbs began in the 1950s, those jobs began leaving as well, and the need for urban renewal became clear in the 1960s. Those initiatives brought the loss of some significant architecture in Central City, but the overall outcome was widespread sup-port of revitalization. Philadelphia would not be left to decay.

There have been more challenges in recent times: In the 1970s, Mayor Frank Rizzo was an icon among the city's work-ing class, but his management style was, in the view of some, old-school. No Philadelphians can forget the firebombing a few years later, ordered by Mayor Wilson Goode, of an entire city block occupied by the armed radicals of Project MOVE. And in 1990, the city teetered on the brink of bankruptcy.

Still, Philadelphia grows and thrives. Its urban region meshes with the sprawl that stretches from Boston to Washington, D.C.—a region that has been urbanized for

CLOSE-UP

Elfreth's Alley, the First Street

It seems out of place, this cobblestoned street of 33 homes in the heart of Old City, surrounded by trendy art galleries and artsy coffeehouses. But even in the early 1700s, Elfreth's Alley always welcomed those who walked to a different beat.

Its first resident was Jeremiah Elfreth, a young blacksmith who built the Alley's first homes here in 1713. By mid-century, he owned more than half the street and was renting homes to ship builders, sea captains, and artisans, many of whose occupations no longer exist today: curriers, glass bevellers, soap pressers, saddlers, sail makers, and tinsmiths. Thousands of individuals and families have lived on the tiny street over the last three centuries: From the 1790 census we see an entry for "Elizabeth Chandler, Spinster." In 1810 Magt. Fry lists his occupation as "Huckster", and the 1900 census lists a Jacob Doran, "Hustler."

During the Industrial Age in the early 1900s, the Alley filled with immigrants and other laborers; some homes became rooming houses and one dwelling was a stove factory. The last house built was in 1836, the only four-story dwelling on the street. Two were torn down in the 1940s—numbers 136 and 138—but the remaining homes were saved from demolition by a national preservation effort in the 1950s, and in 1958, Elfreth's Alley, the country's oldest residential street, became a National Historic Landmark.

The Alley today looks much the same as it did in the late 1700s. Each year thousands of visitors stroll the cobblestones, past the Georgian and Federal-style homes so typical of Philadelphia residences during that period. Two of the homes are museums, open to the public; the others are occupied by families—making Elfreth's Alley a true neighborhood, just as it was 300 years ago.

300 years. At the same time, its open green spaces, from the immense Fairmount Park to bucolic Bucks County, rival any city's natural attractions.

In Philadelphia, the more things change, the more they stay the same: every Fourth of July, children who are descendants of the men who signed the Declaration of Independence gather at the new Liberty Bell Center, across from Independence Hall. There, at 2:00 P.M., the children tap the Liberty Bell 13 times, honoring their ancestors and patriots from the original 13 states. In Philadelphia, we still let freedom ring.

HOTELS

From cobblestone streets to the Liberty Bell, Philadelphia is one of the country's biggest family travel destinations. Every year some 16.2 million leisure visitors, plus 6.6 million business travelers, pour into the city. What's more, they stay twice as long as in the past: In 1990, visitors only spent an average of 1.8 days here; just 12 years later, in 2002, they stayed an average of 3.6 days—and all of those folks need a place to stay.

Some of that increase in tourism and business travel is due to a boost in tourism promotion through the Greater Philadelphia Tourism Marketing Corporation, who do an outstanding job of pitching Philadelphia through the media and through GPTMC's Web site, www.gophila .com. Another factor is the city's new Convention Center, opened in 2000, which brought tens of thousands more people into the city for meetings and conferences.

Anyone coming to Philadelphia has thousands of choices in lodging; the four-county suburban area, not counting the city itself, offers an astounding 16,400 hotels. They range from roadside motels along the interstates to posh establishments like the Ritz Carlton and Four Seasons, to hunting lodges in outlying villages. In 2003 about 11.6 million rooms were available to visitors.

Not surprisingly, the choices include every hotel chain, opening the city to travelers on any budget, or those who prefer any combination of amenities. In fact, since Philadelphia's is such a tourism-based economy, the vast majority of hotels in the city and environs are chains; many more individualized, entrepreneurial establishments appear in the Bed-and-Breakfasts and Historic Inns chapter. Our hotel selections, though extensive, are a relatively small sampling of what is available in Greater Philadelphia. For more information on national chain hotels in the city and its suburbs, you can visit the hotels' Web sites (e.g., www.hilton.com, www.marriott.com, www.knightsinn.com, etc.), or go to www.gophila.com.

Unless otherwise stated, the hotels herein have at least a few wheelchair-accessible rooms. They also have some smoking and some pet-friendly rooms, unless we've included information to the contrary, and all of the hotels listed welcome children.

PRICE CODE

Because Philadelphia is a popular East Coast city, expect higher room prices overall than in many regions of the country. Our prices represent the average room rate for a one-night stay, for two adults, in high season. They do not include taxes: 6 percent for Pennsylvania sales tax, 1 percent for Philadelphia sales tax, and 6 percent for Philadelphia's hotel occupancy tax. In other municipalities outside the city limits, the rate may vary slightly.

$	Less than $99
$$	$100 to $150
$$$	$151 to $200
$$$$	$201 to $250
$$$$$	More than $250

AIRPORT AREA

Embassy Suites Philadelphia $$$$
9000 Bartram Avenue
(215) 365-4500, (800) 362-2779
www.philadelphiaairport.embsuites.com
This hotel is a step up from airport hotels you've stayed in elsewhere. Located 1 mile from Philadelphia International Airport, Embassy Suites, like most airport hotels, caters largely to business travelers, so the luxury level is competitive. All 263 two-room suites include a private master

bedroom, refrigerator, microwave, coffee-maker, and dataport, while the property itself features an indoor pool, sauna, fitness center, and tropical atrium lobby. In the evening guests are invited to a manager's wine reception, and breakfast is full and cooked to order. You might miss your plane for a second order of hash browns; if you can tear yourself away, shuttle service to the airport is complimentary.

Hampton Inn
Philadelphia Airport $$$
8600 Bartram Avenue
(215) 966-1300, (800) 426-7866
www.hamptoninn.com/hi/philadelphia-airport

You'll know this Hampton Inn is a popular airport hotel by the crowded parking lot at Ruby Tuesday's restaurant next door. Renovated in 2005, Hampton Inn has 152 guest rooms, including five junior suites. All rooms include coffeemaker, dataport, high-speed Internet access, cable TV, and air conditioning, and breakfast is complimentary. Guests also find a fitness center, ATM, outdoor pool, and free on-site parking. A coin laundry is available for extended-stay guests, and business services include meeting rooms, audio-visual equipment rental, and fax and express mail services.

Hilton Philadelphia Airport $$
4509 Island Avenue
(215) 365-4150, (800) 445-8667
www.hilton.com

With 331 rooms and two restaurants, this Hilton is large even for an airport hotel. Renovated in 2005, the hotel has a gift shop, clothing store, and coin laundry, and offers a full range of business services, including notary public, audio-visual equipment rental, and secretarial service. Public areas feature a pool table, workout room, large indoor swimming pool, heated whirlpool, and video arcade, while all rooms have a desk, sitting area, two phone lines, and high-speed Internet

access. Three suites also have refrigerators and dining areas, and some rooms offer roll-in showers for wheelchair access.

Philadelphia Airport Marriott $$$
One Arrivals Road
(215) 492-9000, (800) 682-4087
www.marriott.com

You can't get much closer to the airport than connecting to it via a sky bridge. The Marriott connects to Terminal B, a tremendous convenience for both business and leisure travelers. At 414 rooms, it's even larger than the Hilton and includes three concierge levels and five suites. Along with ready access to all hotel eateries and shops, the Marriott has its own lounge and restaurant, and travel-weary guests can get pampered at the Spa at Paul & Kay's with body scrubs, wraps, and facials. In the Concierge Lounge, they'll receive continental breakfast, lunch, and evening hors d'oeuvres; the hotel also offers a fitness center, indoor pool, ballroom, and meeting spaces. High-speed Internet access is available for a fee; all rooms have two phone lines, voice mail, coffeemaker, turndown service, and complimentary newspaper delivery. No pets are permitted except service animals.

Ramada Inn
Philadelphia International Airport $
76 Industrial Highway (Route 291), Essington
(610) 521-9600, (800) 277-3900
www.phillyramadainn.com

This 292-room Ramada Inn is the bargain of the airport hotels. Located 3 miles south of the airport, the Ramada offers free 24-hour shuttle service and features a heated, outdoor Olympic-size pool, restaurant and lounge, weight room, free parking, coin-operated laundry, and for groups a ballroom, three banquet rooms, and three boardrooms. Guest rooms have private balconies, coffeemaker, dataport and, in some rooms, wheelchair access.

AVENUE OF THE ARTS AND CONVENTION CENTER

Courtyard Philadelphia Downtown $$$$
21 Juniper Street
(215) 496-3200
http://marriott.com

The only building closer to City Hall, at the heart of Center City, is City Hall itself. Just across the street, Courtyard Philadelphia, built in 1926, was formerly City Hall Annex; today it's a 498-room hotel (including 21 suites) with oversize desks, two phone lines and dataports in all guest rooms. Amenities include choice of down/feather or foam pillows, washer/dryer, in-room coffeemaker, newspaper delivered to room, voice mail and desk-level electrical outlet; features of the property include indoor pool, fitness center with cardio equipment and free weights, and whirlpool. Guest rooms are wired for Internet access; meeting rooms and public areas are wireless-accessible.

Crowne Plaza Hotel Philadelphia—Center City $$$
1800 Market Street
(215) 561-7500, (888) 303-1746
www.ichotelsgroup.com

In such a busy city, it's not always easy to relax and rejuvenate. The Crowne Plaza aims to help guests unwind with such comfort-aids as pillowtop mattress, sleep CD, relaxation tips, and their choice of seven different pillows. They can also relax in the outdoor rooftop pool with great cityscape views, or by working out in the 24-hour fitness center with rowing machine, stairmasters, universal station, and other exercise equipment. All 445 guest rooms have high-speed Internet access, coffeemaker, two-line phone with voice mail, work desk, and morning newspaper delivered to the room. Guests traveling on business will find a computer, copying machine, fax, and printer in the business center. Staff is multilingual; no pets are allowed.

In many cities people dine in hotels as a last resort—but in Philadelphia, some of the hottest nightlife, restaurants, and spas are based in hotels, so don't overlook them when you're looking for a great meal or nightclub! As one Washington Post reporter wrote, "Much of the city's activity is [at] the hotels, which gives visitors the chance to spend a weekend or longer in places with history whispering from the walls."

Doubletree Hotel Philadelphia $$
237 South Broad Street
(215) 893-1600
http://doubletree.hilton.com/en/dt/hotels

Some will remember this hotel as the Hershey (and being handed a Hershey's chocolate bar when they checked in; now you get a warm chocolate chip cookie). Located just across from the Kimmel Center and Academy of Music, no hotel could be handier for concertgoers. Features include tour services, indoor pool and whirlpool, sauna, fitness center, sundeck (with terrific views of Broad Street and Center City), racquetball courts, and a rooftop garden and jogging track. Business support services and banquet space are available for groups and business travelers; room amenities include coffeemaker, high-speed Internet access, complimentary weekday newspaper, two phone lines with voice mail, cable TV, and desk.

Hampton Inn Philadelphia Center City $$
1301 Race Street
(215) 665-9100
www.hamptoninn.hilton.com

Adjacent to the Pennsylvania Convention Center, this 250-room hotel has all the amenities expected of a convention-center hotel: valet parking, meeting and banquet facilities, audio-visual equipment, ATM, secretarial services and business center, as well as video-conferencing capabilities. Guests aren't charged for using a calling card from their rooms, which are equipped with coffeemaker, dataport, desk, two phone lines with voice mail, and speaker phone. A newspaper and hot breakfast are complimentary; guests who want to stretch their legs can walk to the Reading Terminal, just around the corner, for one of the best hearty breakfasts in the city. Some rooms also have a Jacuzzi and microwave.

Hilton Garden Inn
Philadelphia Center City $$$
1100 Arch Street
(215) 923-0100
www.hiltongardenphilly.com

Location isn't the only thing the Hilton Garden Inn has going for it—although, parked adjacent from the Pennsylvania Convention Center, its location couldn't be more convenient for business travelers. All 279 rooms and suites have high-speed Internet access, complimentary remote printing with the hotel's business center, two phone lines with speaker phone, voice mail, dataports, and a large desk with desk-level outlets and ergonomic chair. Weekdays, newspapers are complimentary; guests also are invited to use the heated indoor pool and Jacuzzi, and renovated fitness center. Rooms also have refrigerators, microwave ovens, and coffeemakers.

Holiday Inn
Philadelphia—Historic District $$$
400 Arch Street
(215) 923-8660
http://hiphiladelphia-historicdistrict
.felcor.com

A colonial flair marks the decor in this Holiday Inn, with the country's most historic square mile as its setting, but guests still live with modern amenities. Use of the rooftop pool and fitness center are complimentary, as are morning newspapers delivered to all 364 guest rooms and seven suites. High-speed Internet access, phone with voice mail, and work desk are standard, while suites have a dining table and larger sitting area. For extended-stay guests, on-site self-laundry facilities are

available, and business services include photocopying, fax, and printer. Cable TV features three family-friendly channels; pets are not permitted.

Loews Philadelphia Hotel $$$$
1200 Market Street
(215) 627-1200
www.loewshotels.com/hotels/philadelphia

When it opened in 1932, the PSFS bank building, now a National Historic Landmark, was an art deco wonder of exotic woods, tall ceilings, and carved glass. After a multimillion-dollar renovation, this sleek hotel has 583 guest rooms, including 37 suites, all with a writing desk and in-room coffeemaker; suites also have fax, printer, modem, and three phones. The Family Concierge counsels guests on kids' amenities, including games, special menus, tours, and welcome gifts. Those with trouble sleeping can borrow non-snore or hypoallergenic pillows; additional extras-on-loan include chenille throws, air purifier, putting green game, workout clothes, rain poncho, and reading glasses. Pets are welcome.

Park Hyatt Philadelphia
at the Bellevue $$$$
Broad and Walnut Streets
(215) 893-1234
www.hyatt.com

Formerly the Bellevue-Stratford—and still thought of as "The Bellevue"—this is a true Philadelphia icon. Guests have included Jacob Astor, John Wayne, Jimmy Durante, Katharine Hepburn, and the Vanderbilt family, and every U.S. president since Theodore Roosevelt has visited. Furnishings are classic and elegant; standard amenities include turndown service, in-room safes sized to fit a laptop, wireless Internet service, desk with dataport, robes, voice mail, three phones, and daily newspaper. Guests are welcome to use the 93,000-square-foot Sporting Club with state-of-the-art fitness equipment, racquetball, indoor track, and whirlpool. They also have 24-hour access to the business center with photocopying, fax, and secretarial services, as well as a computer work station. Bliss, the new restaurant, joins the Bellevue's other eateries (The Palm, Zanzibar Blue, among others) and lower-level shops, including Tiffany & Co., Nicole Miller, Origins, Polo Ralph Lauren, and other high-end boutiques.

Ritz-Carlton Philadelphia $$$$$
Ten Avenue of the Arts
(Broad Street)
(215) 523-8000
www.ritzcarlton.com/hotels/philadelphia
Puttin' on the Ritz means personal service, from the Technology Butler's assistance in hooking up your laptop, to the Bath Butler's drawing your hot bath after a long afternoon at Tiffany's. Attention to detail is the norm, including complimentary overnight shoe shine, evening turndown, pillow menu, complimentary morning newspaper, overnight laundry service, and twice-daily housekeeping. A massage therapist will visit guest rooms on request, or guests can visit the Richel D'Ambra Spa for their pampering. Contemporary American cuisine is served in The Grill; light dining and afternoon tea happen in The Rotunda; after dinner, many repair to The Vault, an intimate tobacco lounge. Of 303 guest rooms, 36 are suites, 47 are club-level rooms and suites, and the entire 31st floor is The Penthouse.

Rodeway Inn $$
1208 Walnut Street
(215) 546-7000
www.choicehotels.com
Located in a Victorian-style row building, Rodeway is smack in the middle of the action—within a 500-foot radius of more than 200 restaurants, bars, and clubs! It's a deal, with free continental breakfast, a 60,000-square-foot gym with sauna, Jacuzzi, and pool nearby (for a $10 fee) and 24-hour concierge services. Rooms are equipped with dataport, air conditioning, and cable TV, and pets are welcome for a $25 fee. Discounted parking is available.

In preparing to host the 2000 Republican National Convention, Philadelphia nearly doubled its Center City hotel rooms from 6,000 to 11,000, and boosted airport rooms to 4,500, in order to accommodate the 55,000 delegates and press who would be attending.

Travelodge Philadelphia $
1227 Race Street
(215) 564-2888
www.travelodge.com
Travelodge is another great deal, positioned across the street from the convention center for budget-conscious business travelers. Newspaper, high-speed Internet access, local calls and continental breakfast all are complimentary, and rooms are equipped with cable TV (30 channels including Showtime and two HBO channels) and coffeemaker. The staff is multilingual, and wheelchair-accessible rooms are available. Parking is available nearby.

OLD CITY

Best Western
Independence Park Hotel $$$$
235 Chestnut Street
(215) 922-4443, (800) 624-2988
www.independenceparkinn.com
Billing themselves as a "civilized alternative," this Best Western is listed on the National Register of Historic Places and is decidedly more posh than the popular roadside motel image. Guest rooms are distinctive with high ceilings, furnished with classic pieces, and have two phone lines, modem, coffeemaker, and cable TV. Two courtyard-level boardrooms feature Chippendale-style furnishings, while the business center offers photocopying, fax, a personal computer, and secretarial services. Guests enjoy a complimentary European breakfast (including make-your-own Belgian waffles) in the glass-enclosed courtyard and afternoon tea in the Grand Parlor, complete with fireplace and leather settees.

Comfort Inn
Downtown/Historic Area $$
100 North Columbus Boulevard
(215) 627-7900
www.choicehotels.com

Located on the waterfront, this Comfort Inn offers wonderful river and skyline views and close proximity to Penn's Landing, South Street, and other destination neighborhoods. Guest rooms offer all the conveniences: coffeemakers, cable/satellite TV, and high-speed Internet; weekday newspaper and continental breakfast are complimentary. Some rooms have microwave and refrigerator (which can also be rented for rooms if not provided), and wheelchair-accessible rooms are available, as are an exercise room, meeting rooms, and fax machine. Parking is available. No pets are allowed.

Hyatt Regency Philadelphia $$$$
200 South Columbus Boulevard
(215) 928-1234
http://pennslanding.hyatt.com

Presiding over Philadelphia's revitalized waterfront is the Hyatt Regency, the city's newest hotel with a commanding 22-story tower and views of the downtown skyline and the Delaware River. The 350-room hotel was built to convey elegance, with a lobby of beveled woods and marbled floors with jade green accents. Guest rooms, too, spell luxury with two phone lines, high-speed Internet access, laptop safes, work area, granite countertops and French doors in the bath, and coffeemaker. Public areas offer wired and wireless Internet access. Use of the health club is complimentary, along with the skylit indoor pool, sun deck, sauna, and lockers—though many guests opt simply to walk or jog along the Delaware. The business center is open 24 hours.

Omni Hotel at
Independence Park $$$$
401 Chestnut Street
(215) 925-0000
www.omnihotels.com

Overlooking Independence National Historic Park, the 150-room Omni has larger-than-usual guest rooms (350 square feet), all outfitted with two-line phone, executive desk with modem outlet, marble bath, plush robes, and coffeemaker. Just because the hotel is on the elegant side, however, doesn't mean families aren't welcome, and the Omni offers a Kids Program. Business guests can receive packages around the clock. Wheelchair access, Braille signage, audible/strobe-light alarm systems, and multilingual concierge services are available, as are complimentary shoe shine, business support services, and horse-drawn carriage rides. A complimentary *USAToday* is delivered to guests' doors.

Penn's View Hotel $$$
Front and Market Streets
(215) 922-7600, (800) 331-7634
www.pennsviewhotel.com

As a family-owned boutique hotel, the 51-room Penn's View can offer personalized attention to guests, including tastings in the world-class wine bar at the hotel's Ristorante Panorama, where the wine list changes weekly. Its wine preservation and dispensing system, or "cruvinet," is the world's largest, custom-built for the Penn's View, allowing them to preserve the vitality of up to 120 open bottles of wine for an extended period. Guest rooms are decorated with Chippendale-style furniture and include terry robes, morning newspaper, cable TV, and a complimentary continental breakfast, while some deluxe rooms have a whirlpool and fireplace. Wireless Internet access throughout the hotel is free to all guests, as is use of the fitness room.

Probably the city's most infamous "hotel" was the Eastern State Penitentiary. Opened in 1829, it was ultra-modern for its time; the Pen could boast that it had central heating, running water, and flush toilets before the White House! Famous "guests" included gangster Al Capone and bank robber Willie Sutton.

Sheraton Society Hill $$$

One Dock Street (Second and Walnut Streets)
(215) 238-6000
www.starwoodhotels.com

One of the Sheraton Society Hill's claims to fame is its soaring atrium lounge, one of Philadelphia's first. A closer look at the public areas gives guests a unique thrill: Artifacts from the past 200 years, unearthed during an archaeological dig prior to the hotel's construction, are displayed throughout the hotel—a fascinating exhibit, given that the nation's founders lived, communed, and strategized in this very neighborhood. Guest rooms feature oversize work desk and ergonomic desk chair, voice mail, dataport, and coffeemaker, while the hotel offers complimentary fitness room, indoor heated pool, and computer rental. A plus for business travelers: complimentary morning shuttle to any Center City business.

RITTENHOUSE ROW

Hotel Windsor $$

1700 Benjamin Franklin Parkway
(877) 784-8379
www.windsorhotel.com

Another small property is the Hotel Windsor, with 110 spacious studios and one-bedroom suites, many with private balconies. This hotel is popular with extended-stay business travelers as all rooms have fully equipped kitchens, oversize desks, two-line phones with dataports, voice mail, large walk-in closets, and complimentary high-speed Internet access. Some rooms offer separate living areas; guests also are invited to use the rooftop pool and sundeck in season. The fitness center is open 24 hours, and both same-day laundry service and self-laundry facilities are available. The Windsor also has a gift shop and two restaurants on site, Asia on the Parkway and Peacock on the Parkway.

Latham Hotel $$

135 South 17th Street
(215) 563-7474, (877) LATHAM1
www.lathamhotel.com

A true Rittenhouse Row jewel, the Latham, built in 1907, is listed on the National Register of Historic Places and belongs to the Historic Hotels of America. Built in 1907 on the site of philanthropist William Bucknell's home, the marble-lobbied Latham opened in 1915 as an upscale apartment house, and re-opened in 1970 as a 139-room, European-style boutique hotel for business travelers. All rooms feature voice mail, coffeemakers, robes and free high-speed Internet access, along with complimentary weekday newspapers and turndown service on request. Fax and copy services are available, as well as a fitness room and business center with computer.

Radisson Plaza-Warwick Hotel Philadelphia $$$

1701 Locust Street
(215) 735-6000, (800) 333-3333
www.radisson.com

Listed on the National Register of Historic Places, the Warwick is a Rittenhouse Row icon. Built in 1926 in the English Renaissance style, it has 545 rooms, yet exudes the ambience of a boutique hotel. Rooms are spacious, each with a large desk, two phone lines, voice mail, speaker phone, coffeemaker and high-speed Internet access. A business center, complimentary newspaper (choice of USAToday or Wall Street Journal), 24-hour fitness room, multilingual staff, ATM, and meeting rooms accommodating up to 400 people round out the business amenities. For Plaza Club Level guests, extras include complimentary continental breakfast, bottled water, evening hors d'oeuvres and beverages, and use of the Club Lounge with large-screen television.

The Rittenhouse Hotel $$$$$
210 West Rittenhouse Square
(215) 546-9000, (800) 635-1042
www.rittenhousehotel.com
This hotel might be the classiest address
in the city. Its logo depicts a sketch of Rittenhouse Park, one of the small common
areas designed by William Penn as quiet,
green oases. The hotel's 98 guest rooms
include 11 suites; guests are pampered
with pillowtop mattress, 310-count linen
sheets, marble baths, Aveda bath amenities, robe and slippers, and TV in the bathroom. High-speed Internet access is
complimentary; guests can work while
they look out oversize windows at Rittenhouse Square or the cityscape; they also
have voice mail, dual-line speaker phones,
laptop-size in-room safe, and complimentary use of guest computer. Selected
suites also include washer, dryer, and
whirlpool. A world-class spa is located on
the premises; shoe shine and morning
newspaper delivery are complimentary,
and town-car transportation is available.

Sofitel Philadelphia $$$
120 South 17th Street
(215) 569-8300
www.sofitel.com
At 17th and Sansom, the Sofitel places
guests ideally, both for doing business in
the financial district, and for up-market
shopping along Rittenhouse Row. It's
located on the site of the former Philadel-
phia Stock Exchange and makes business
travel easy, with a currency exchange
office, dry cleaning, fitness center, updated
security management, cable/satellite TV,
dataport, and bathroom telephone. Of 306
rooms, eight are wheelchair accessible and
68 are suites. The on-site restaurant, Chez
Colette, has a four-diamond rating; the
lobby lounge, La Bourse, features nightly
entertainment.

Westin Philadelphia $$$$$
99 South 17th Street at Liberty Place
(215) 563-1600
www.starwoodhotels.com/westin
Traveling spouses will appreciate the
Westin's prime location—connected to
Liberty Place shops—where they can
indulge in Coach bags and Godiva choco-
lates. Working at the Westin, though, is
convenient with high-speed Internet
access in all rooms, dual-line telephones,
and in-room fax, copier, and printer. Thick
terry robes, Starbucks coffee and cof-
feemaker, complimentary weekday news-
paper, video check-out, WestinWORKOUT
Powered by Reebok Gym, sauna, Westin
Kids Club, and 3- and 5-mile walking and
jogging maps designed and certified by
Runner's World Magazine, enhance every-
one's experience. Even Pooch can travel in
luxury here, with Westin's "Heavenly Dog
Bed" available on request.

UNIVERSITY CITY

The Hilton Inn at Penn $$$
3600 Sansom Street
(215) 222-0200, (800) HILTONS
www.theinnatpenn.com
Newly renovated, the 238 guest rooms at
the Inn at Penn are equipped with two
dual-line phones, voice mail, dataports,
high-speed and wireless Internet access,
and laptop-size safe. For a touch of luxury,
rooms also offer WEBTV, terry cloth
robes, and refreshment center. The 24-
hour fitness center has cardio and weight-
training gear, and for business travelers,
the multilingual staff include a notary
public. Audio-visual equipment rental,
photocopying and video conferencing
also are available.

Sheraton University City Hotel $$$
36th and Chestnut Streets
(215) 387-8000
www.starwoodhotels.com/sheraton
Both business and leisure travelers find a
good home here, with amenities ranging
from high-speed Internet access, dataport,
dual-line telephones, complimentary
newspaper, and executive desks, to cribs,
coffeemakers, and the "Sheraton Sweet
Sleeper dog bed." Both the fitness center
and outdoor pool are open to all guests,

and babysitting services are available. There may be a deposit for pets.

WEST SUBURBS

Chestnut Hill Hotel **$$**
8229 Germantown Avenue, Chestnut Hill
(215) 242-5905, (800) 628-9744
www.chestnuthillhotel.com
Even during the Civil War, Chestnut Hill was known for its "Summer Hausen"—at 9 miles northwest of the city, it served as a remote getaway destination for colonial Philadelphians. Built in 1864, the 36-room Chestnut Hill Hotel has always been among those guest homes welcoming business-weary travelers. Today, however, the hotel offers guests modular phone hook-ups with dataport, cable TV with HBO, and voice mail. Standard rooms have double beds, while deluxe are furnished with either one queen or two full beds. The four suites also offer an adjoining sitting room with sleeper sofa. Fax and photocopying are available, parking is free, and all guests receive a complimentary continental breakfast.

MainStay Suites **$$$**
440 American Avenue, King of Prussia
(484) 690-3000
www.choicehotels.com
For families and long-term visits, MainStay has thought of everything, down to the pancake flippers. Every room is a suite, and each has a full kitchen with utensils, dishes, and cooking gear. Suites also have their own private, direct phone numbers with two-line speaker phones, voice mail, high-speed Internet access, and, if you don't want to cook your own breakfast, guests are offered complimentary continental breakfast. An indoor heated pool and hot tub, fitness center, laundry facility, weekday newspaper, and sun deck are among the other amenities; to avoid waiting in line during busy times, a kiosk machine is available for quick check-in.

BUCKS COUNTY

New Hope Motel in the Woods **$$**
400 West Bridge Street, New Hope
(215) 862-2800
www.newhopemotelinthewoods.com
This is a place for people who don't just want a hotel, they want an experience. It begins with a few minutes watching the resident family of ducks in the pond. Then, after a hike in the nearby Washington Crossing Historic State Park, a popcorn break while you watch some big-screen TV in the "covered bridge lounge." This is a five-acre sanctuary, eight buildings with 28 guest rooms. Some have fireplaces, or guests can warm themselves with a swim in the heated outdoor pool. Rooms have dataports and voice mail, and coffee is available all day.

The Warrington **$**
701 Easton Road, Warrington
(215) 343-0373
Don't look for a cookie-cutter business hotel here. The Warrington is a country lodge, built in the comfy old motel style—all at ground level, set on 12 acres of greenery. Though it's without pretense, it still offers the expected amenities—meeting and banquet facilities, satellite TV, dataports in rooms, fitness center, and complimentary continental breakfast. After a day of antiquing, guests can relax in the outdoor heated pool, and kids can romp in the playground.

BED-AND-BREAKFASTS
AND HISTORIC INNS

Visitors from other regions of the country often are surprised at how old the buildings are along the eastern seaboard. It's true; history began there a full century before the Midwest was settled, and it was even later that towns started appearing west of the Mississippi River.

Spending the night in an 18th-century farmhouse gives a special thrill. The floorboards creak (or even slant), stairways might be steeper and more narrow, and features such as inlaid parquet, 12-foot ceilings, pocket doors, and transoms suggest a slower, more peaceful, more sociable lifestyle from the past.

Perhaps because historic buildings have been so carefully preserved in Philadelphia, the region boasts an unusual number of bed-and-breakfasts and historic inns—though no one can say for sure how many are in operation. More than 500 B&Bs belong to the Pennsylvania Bed & Breakfast Association; many B&Bs do not join their state or regional associations, so we can assume there are several hundred more, but at least 250 operate in Greater Philadelphia. At least 40 B&Bs belong to the Bucks County association alone, and many historic inns are not bed-and-breakfasts.

In general terms, a bed-and-breakfast or inn is a small property, with 25 or less rooms. Unlike most hotels and motels, the inn's owners or hosts usually are on-site around the clock, and the decor is distinctive. Rooms in most inns are individually decorated; often the innkeepers even name the rooms. In recent years, the B&B industry has burgeoned and become much more competitive, forcing inns to upgrade and become more luxurious. It's much more common now to find whirlpools, in-room refrigerators, bedroom fireplaces, and other posh amenities that most B&B owners would have scoffed at a decade or two ago.

Their clientele has changed as well: Many more small inns are family friendly these days, and "theme" B&Bs have emerged. Christian B&Bs and gay B&Bs compete with business hotels and sports lodges for consumers' dollars; many attract guests by offering classes as varied as fly-fishing, tole painting, and baking.

Before booking a stay at a B&B or inn, it's wise to learn as much as possible about the property. Are there elevators, or will you be lugging your bags to a third-floor room? Will you have a private bath? Is there Internet access? Wheelchair access? (Few historic homes are wheelchair accessible, though some have incorporated ramps, wider doors, and other aids.) Do the owners have cats? Are children allowed? If so, is there an age limit? Many B&Bs require a two-night stay, especially if they're located in popular tourist regions.

Historic buildings often will have neither elevators nor wheelchair access, especially if the B&B is in a home. You should also ask about the breakfast; we have stayed at B&Bs where breakfast consists of a bagel you toast yourself; others serve a lavish meal. If there's something you cannot tolerate, either because of allergies or personal preference, let the innkeeper know before you book a room.

You also should ask about the smoking policy. If you smoke in a room where smoking is taboo, many B&B owners will have the room cleaned and apply the cost to your charge card—and if they decide their draperies and carpets smell like your smoke, that cleaning fee could be hundreds of dollars. Likewise, some B&B owners object to alcohol on the premises, even in the privacy of your room, so if you like to relax with a glass of wine in your room, be sure to ask about the alcohol policy before you book.

A few words about prices at B&Bs and inns: In recent years, B&B prices have risen to become competitive with hotels. Philadelphia is a major tourist city in the East, and prices will reflect the fact that this city is hot.

When booking a room in Philadelphia, be sure to add 13 percent to the room rate for taxes: 6 percent for Pennsylvania sales tax, 1 percent for Philadelphia sales tax, and 6 percent for the hotel occupancy tax. Tax rates may vary slightly, once you leave the Philadelphia city limits.

PRICE CODE

Staying at an elegant inn may not always be the most economical choice, especially in Greater Philadelphia, but it will be a memorable one. Rates are subject to change, so we use the price code below to indicate the price range of our listed properties' average rates per night for two adults in high season, before taxes.

$	Less than $100
$$	$100 to $150
$$$	$151 to $200
$$$$	$201 to $250
$$$$$	More than $250

CENTER CITY AND UNIVERSITY CITY

Antique Row Bed & Breakfast $
341 South 12th Street
(215) 592-7802
www.antiquerowbnb.com

Antiques lovers will be in their element here, surrounded by some of the finest vintage and antiques shops in the East. This early-1800s home is a typical Philadelphia row house with rooms and suites available. Guests share baths, though extended-stay apartment suites have private baths, and all accommodations have individually controlled air conditioning and cable TV. The decor features primitive and folk art, with antiques and Early American–style furnishings juxtaposed with contemporary pieces. A full breakfast is served in the dining room, or you can prepare it yourself at your convenience. This B&B is less posh than many, but it's a great value.

La Reserve Center City Bed and Breakfast $$
1804 Pine Street
(215) 735-0582, (800) 354-8401
www.lareservebandb.com

This is a luxurious B&B at affordable rates. Located a few blocks from high-end Rittenhouse Square, La Reserve is an 1853 town house with four guest rooms and two suites. Guests are welcome to play the vintage Steinway grand piano in the parlor, or relax in the salon under soaring 15-foot ceilings, or in the cozy TV lounge. Complimentary wireless high-speed Internet access is available throughout the house, and copier and fax are available. All rooms have a desk, robes, satellite TV, complimentary bottled water, and air conditioning, and a full breakfast is served every morning. No minimum stay is required.

Morris House Hotel $$$
225 South Eighth Street
(215) 922-2446
www.morrishousehotel.com

This 1787 Society Hill hotel is listed on the National Register of Historic Places and is the only Center City lodging with its own private garden, making it ideal for small weddings or other parties. The Morris family—whose ancestor, Anthony Morris, was Philadelphia's mayor in the late 1600s—occupied this home for 120 years. Its 15 guest rooms have been restored down to the smallest detail, while introducing modern amenities such as private baths, air conditioning, wireless high-speed Internet access, and phones in every room. Most have hardwood floors,

If you don't want to research all of Greater Philadelphia's B&B options, help is available from A Bed and Breakfast Connection of Philadelphia. This reservation service can answer your questions by phone or e-mail, help you choose the perfect B&B for you, or you can use their online order form to make your own reservations. Staff periodically visit all inns listed at the site to be sure they meet high standards. Visit www.bnbphiladelphia.com, e-mail bnb@bnbphiladelphia.com, or phone (610) 687-3565 or (800) 448-3610 with questions.

and two suites also offer private sitting rooms. Continental breakfast is served in two dining rooms (with original fireplaces). Parking is available at a garage across the street. Credit cards are preferred; if paying by cash, a $200 deposit is required at check-in.

New Market B&B $
New Market and
Head House Square
(610) 687-3565, (800) 448-3619
www.bedandbreakfast.com/
pennsylvania/new-market-bb.html
Staying at this small (two guest rooms, both with private baths), 1811 brick town house puts guests in the heart of historic Philadelphia. This is the neighborhood where homes have coal bins and boot scrapers at the door. The interior has been remodeled but is faithful to the period, with the original wooden floor planks, old spiral stairs with buttery-yellow pine supports, and a working fireplace in the third-floor bedroom. Brick walls are exposed, giving the home an older feel. One reviewer reported seeing cats on the premises. Breakfast is "continental-plus." South Street shopping and clubs are a short walk away.

Penn's View Inn $$
14 North Front Street
(215) 922-7600, (800) 331-7634
www.pennsviewhotel.com
Beautiful views of the Delaware River

await at this historic inn that dates back to 1828. Six of the 38 individually decorated rooms have river views; others have working fireplaces, whirlpool tubs, and marble baths. Dataports, cable TV, telephones, and air conditioning are in every room, and an elevator takes you to upper floors. Unlike most Philadelphia inns, Penn's View does not require a minimum two-night stay, and children are permitted. The inn has a liquor license, and dinner is available. Breakfast, included in room rate, is "continental-plus," and a daily newspaper is complimentary.

Rittenhouse Square
Bed & Breakfast $$$$$
1715 Rittenhouse Square
(215) 546-6500, (877) 791-6500
www.rittenhousebb.com
In the center of one of the city's most fashionable neighborhoods, Rittenhouse Square B&B is a refuge of refined elegance. This early 1900s carriage house pampers its guests with plush robes, nightly turndown service, cable TV, computer work stations with Internet access, and 24-hour concierge service. A complimentary wine and snack reception is offered each evening in the lobby. Furnishings are luxurious; the effect is one of quiet, artful sophistication. All 10 guest rooms have private baths, an amenities basket, whirlpool tub, coffeepot, and telephone. The reception desk is open 24 hours, and breakfast is continental. No minimum stay is required.

In Philadelphia, there's historic, and there's historic. Especially when strolling past row houses and other buildings in Old City, scan the façade for a small plaque, hung high on the first-floor level. (No, it won't say, "George Washington slept here," though in this neighborhood it's a distinct possibility!) Those plaques identify certain structures as being listed on the National Register of Historic Places—a difficult-to-achieve designation that ensures that the building is not only old, but that any renovation to it adheres to strict federal guidelines, preserving it for future generations.

Society Hill Hotel $$
301 Chestnut Street
(215) 925-1919
www.societyhillhotel.com

Once a rooming house for longshoremen who sailed into Philadelphia from ports worldwide, Society Hill Hotel prides itself on having been the city's first "bed and breakfast hotel." Now an "urban inn," it sits in Independence National Historical Park in Old City. While the location is convenient, guests should know that the 12 guest rooms are placed in four floors—and there is no elevator or bellman on the premises. The climb is rewarded, however, with breakfast served in your room, along with a complimentary newspaper. Six of the rooms are two-room suites and all have private baths. Downstairs, a full-service restaurant and bar is open seven days a week, with great views of Independence Park.

Spruce Hill Manor $$
331 South 46th Street
(215) 472-2213, (866) 521-2975
www.sprucehillmanor.com

This stately Edwardian mansion is located in University City, in walking distance of the University of Pennsylvania—though if you don't feel like walking anywhere, Spruce Hill offers a chauffeur service. All of the four guest accommodations are suites, with bedroom, private bath, sitting room, and kitchenette. The interior features original oak and mahogany woodwork, stained glass windows, and antique furnishings, and all suites are equipped with dish TV, VCR, telephone, air conditioning, and free parking—a rarity in the city. A two-night stay is required, and children over 10 are welcome.

1011 Clinton Bed & Breakfast $$$
(or Ten-Eleven Clinton
Bed & Breakfast)
1011 Clinton Street
(215) 923-8144

This Federal-style town house is quintessential colonial Philadelphia in appearance—red brick façade, black shutters, and a courtyard abloom with flowers. It's a lovely urban retreat, sitting on a Registered Historic Street; all structures were built in 1836. All five accommodations are suites (one with two bedrooms), with individual phone lines, spacious work spaces, reclining chairs and sofas, computer access, and full kitchens, complete with refrigerators stocked with breakfast foods and beverages. Well-behaved dogs are welcome as well.

The Thomas Bond House $$
129 South Second Street
(215) 923-8523
www.winston-salem-inn.com/philadelphia

Located in Old City across the street from the historic City Tavern, this restored 1769 town house is listed on the National Register of Historic Places. The most luxurious of the 12 rooms are on the second floor; those have whirlpool tubs with showers, oriental rugs, and Chippendale period furniture. Other rooms have queen or double poster, iron, or cannonball beds, and all have private baths. On weekends, breakfast is sumptuous (weekday breakfast is "continental-plus") and complimentary wine and cheese is offered in the evenings. Children over 10 are welcome, but pets are not.

NORTH AND SOUTH PHILLY

The Columns on Clinton   **$$**
922 Clinton Street
(215) 627-7598

On the edge of South Philly, this 1854 Federal town house sports some impressive features, including a grand staircase topped by a stained glass skylight. Each of the six guest rooms is designed around a theme from Philadelphia's history. Two rooms have private baths; the others are shared, and some rooms are furnished with all-cotton and natural fabrics. Breakfast is continental. No minimum stay is required; children are welcome, and accommodations for guest pets are limited.

Cornerstone Bed & Breakfast   **$$$**
3300 Baring Street
(215) 387-6065
www.cornerstonebandb.com

Once you leave Center City and get into the outer neighborhoods, the properties often become more spacious and imposing. This church-stone mansion, built around 1870, has red oak and black walnut floors, 12-foot ceilings, and a staircase of Honduran mahogany. Seven stained-glass windows grace the home. All guest rooms have a desk, and wireless or phone-wire Internet access. A full gourmet breakfast is offered daily, and you can invite a guest for $15 extra. Smoking is permitted on the wrap-around porch and on the grounds; anyone smoking inside the house will find a $500 cleaning fee charged to their credit card. Children over 13 are welcome, pets are not.

Germantown B&B   **$**
5925 Wayne Avenue
(215) 848-1375
www.bedandbreakfast.com/
pennsylvania/germantown-bb.html

This northwestern corner of Philadelphia has its own history and charm, and this many-gabled Victorian, built in 1888, is a looker. It's surrounded by homes in a mix of architectural styles, dating from pre-

For a list of gay-owned lodging and other gay-owned businesses in Philadelphia, go to www.gophila.com/gay/index.htm. The page lists gay-focused shopping, restaurants and cafes, cultural attractions, and events, as well as the ongoing "Philadelphia Freedom" package.

Revolutionary days through the late 1800s. Just several blocks from Fairmount Park, the B&B is a 15-minute commuter train ride from Center City. There's only one guest room in this inn; it has a private bath, and a minimum stay is required—or a $5.00 surcharge for staying only one night. Smoking is allowed on the front porch only. Pets are taboo, but children can be accommodated by prior arrangement.

Trade Winds Bed and Breakfast   **$**
943 Lombard Street
(215) 592-8644
www.tradewindsbedandbreakfast.com

This Queen's Village inn is set in a town house more than two centuries old, furnished with art and antiques from the owner's worldwide travels. Of the three guest rooms, one has a private bath; the others share a bath. The master suite is appointed with a queen canopy and working fireplace, while the double-bed room, with an antique brass bed, displays a finely executed *trompe l'oeil*. All rooms have coffeemakers, small refrigerators, cable TV, and phone; breakfast is supplied in the room. Children are welcome, as are well-behaved small pets.

WESTERN SUBURBS

Anam Cara Bed & Breakfast   **$$**
52 Wooddale Avenue,
Chestnut Hill
(215) 242-4327
www.anamcarabandb.com

The owner, a native of Ireland, creates the tone at this B&B. All three guest rooms have private baths, and for extra

They're not exactly B&Bs, but travelers on a budget might consider Philadelphia's five youth hostels. Call ahead to ask about rates, possible age restrictions (most hostels now rent to guests of any age), and security—where to stow your bags while you tour around:

- Bank Street Hostel (Old City), 32 South Bank Street, (800) 392-4678
- Old Reformed Church's Youth Hostel (Old City), Fourth and Race Streets, (215) 922-6366
- Chamounix Mansion Youth Hostel (Fairmount Park near Zoo and Art Museum), Chamounix Drive, West Fairmount, (215) 878-3676
- Divine Tracy Hotel (University City), 20 South 36th Street, (215) 382-4310
- International House of Philadelphia (University City), 3701 Chestnut Street, (215) 387-5125; guests must show a student or academic I.D.

relaxation, many guests opt to hire co-owner Jack Gann, a licensed massage therapist whose range of therapies includes massage, reflexology, and other relaxation modalities. Complimentary sherry is offered. A minimum two-night stay is required on weekends; extended-stay suites are also available, featuring dining room, kitchen, desk/chair, cable TV and VCR, washer/dryer, and private phone line. Children are welcome; small pets may be permitted in extended-stay suites.

Bed & Breakfast at Walnut Hill $$
541 Chandler's Mill Road,
Kennett Square
(610) 444-3703
www.bbonline.com/pa/walnuthill/
Located midway between Philadelphia and Lancaster County—Pennsylvania's Amish country—Walnut Hill sits on land that William Penn originally granted to his daughter, Letitia, in 1701. The B&B itself is a former mill house; during the Revolutionary War a Loyalist brigade, called the Queen's American Rangers, camped on the hillside facing the B&B site on their way to the Battle of Brandywine. The home's history is apparent in its details,

down to the wide-plank floors and German box lots. Guests are served a full gourmet country breakfast in the common room, complete with homemade breads and spreads, as well as afternoon refreshments. Three guest rooms are available, and most weekends a two-night minimum is required.

1800 Tory Inne $$$$
734 North Chester Road,
West Chester
(610) 431-2788
www.toryinne.com
Built in 1800, the stone-built Tory Inne was the former Jesse Reece house, the first general store and Post Office in the hamlet of Goshenville, and is listed on the National Register of Historic Places. This is an upscale inn; the three spacious rooms are furnished with king mahogany four-poster beds, fitted with Egyptian cotton linens. All rooms have large private balconies, cable TV, high-speed Internet access, and air conditioning. A full English breakfast is served by candlelight in the dining room; guests also receive turndown service and truffles on their pillows. Children over 16 are welcome, pets are not allowed, and there is no minimum stay requirement.

Fairville Inn Bed and Breakfast $$$
506 Kennett Pike, Route 52,
Chadds Ford
(610) 388-5900, (877) 285-7772
www.fairvilleinn.com

Listed on the National Register of Historic Places, Fairville Inn was built in 1857; today its three buildings host guests in a total of 13 guest rooms and two suites. All rooms feature a private bath, satellite TV, phone, and individually controlled air conditioning; the suites also have private decks and fireplaces. Fresh flowers throughout the inn add to the elegant-country ambience. Guests are served a full breakfast with hot entree, and afternoon tea with cheeses, crackers, and home-baked treats. Kids over 15 are welcome. No pets are allowed, and guests caught smoking will be charged a $250 cleaning fee.

Faunbrook Bed and Breakfast $$$
699 Rosedale Avenue,
West Chester
(800) 505-3233
www.faunbrook.com

In its heyday, Faunbrook was a carefully landscaped estate; swans graced its two ponds ringed with stately oaks and chestnut trees, statuary, and gazebos. The home, built in 1860, at that time was topped by a weathervane with a "faun" pointing to the wind. The gazebo and a pond remain, along with a winter porch, library, and ice house. Of the six guest rooms, two have working fireplaces. Guests are given a full breakfast; they can book a single night's stay for a $15 surcharge. No pets are allowed; ask about children.

General Lafayette Inn & Brewery $$
646 Germantown Pike,
Lafayette Hill
(610) 941-0600, (800) 251-0181
www.generallafayetteinn.com

Located at the westernmost tip of Lafayette Park just outside Chestnut Hill, the General Lafayette has five guest rooms, three with private baths. All rooms are located in the secluded guest house and include cable TV, phones, and air conditioning; breakfast is self-serve continental. Guests have access to the kitchen 24 hours; each morning it's stocked with fresh breakfast foods and juices. The restaurant and tavern are connected to the guest house by a brick path; they're a handy spot for relaxing with an artisanal brew and listening to local musicians. Pets are not allowed; ask about limitations on children.

General Warren Inne $$
Old Lancaster Highway, Malvern
(610) 296-3637
www.generalwarren.com

As histories go, the General Warren's is provocative: Owned by John Penn (Philadelphia founder William Penn's grandson) during the Revolutionary War, this 18th-century inn became a Tory stronghold; John Penn was a Loyalist. His cohorts met here to strategize and plot against the Revolution, and the famous Paoli Massacre was planned and launched here in 1777 as General "Mad Anthony" Wayne camped 1 mile south of the inn. Today, eight suites are furnished with mine antiques, including cannonball and cherry four-poster beds, and all include private baths, cable TV with VCR, telephones, and high-speed dataports. Six of the suites have fireplaces; one has a whirlpool tub.

Hamanassett Bed & Breakfast $$$
115 Indian Springs Drive,
Chester Heights
(610) 459-3000, (877) 836-8212
www.hamanassett.com

Casual elegance is the mode at Hamanassett, where a quick tour of the grounds reveals terraces and topiaries, and rooms are appointed with fine antiques and heirlooms in English country style. No detail is overlooked: bed sheets are pressed, in-room coffeemakers are abundantly stocked, and soft drinks and bottled water are available 24 hours. Guests will be relieved to find the innkeepers even thought to install good reading lights—an amenity all too rare in B&Bs. Wireless high-speed Internet access is available throughout the home, and a gourmet breakfast is served by candlelight with antique china and silver. There are seven guest rooms and a child- and pet-friendly carriage house with air conditioning, phone, and a front porch with rockers.

Inn at Whitewing Farm $$$$
P.O. Box 98,
Kennett Square, PA 19348-0098
(610) 388-2664
www.whitewingfarm.com

The 10 rooms and suites at this elegant 1700s farmhouse are almost apartment-like, they're that warm and welcoming. Some have working fireplaces, private decks and terraces, and are furnished with antiques, while the inviting public areas include the gathering room, game room, library, tennis court, chip-and-putt golf course, pond, pool, and six-person whirlpool. The real draw, however, might be the grounds; they showcase the seasons, from bursting with thousands of daffodils in spring, to the croaking of the resident frog family in the fall. Full breakfast is served daily, as are afternoon and evening cordials. A two-night minimum is required on weekends, and weekend and holiday rates are boosted slightly.

Kennett House Bed & Breakfast $$$
503 West State Street,
Kennett Square
(610) 444-9592, (800) 820-9592
www.kennetthouse.com

This granite, foursquare-style mansion was built in 1910 and is an impressive example of Arts and Crafts design. The interior features chestnut and rosewood woodwork, oriental rugs and antiques, and the three guest accommodations (two rooms, one suite) offer cable TV, four-poster queen beds, air conditioning, private baths, and spacious armoires. The guest refrigerator is always stocked with snacks, and the full breakfast each morning is made with fresh, local ingredients. The historic village is a short drive from the Brandywine Valley's most famous attractions, Winterthur Museum and Longwood Gardens.

Silverstone Bed & Breakfast $
8840 Stenton Avenue,
Chestnut Hill
(215) 242-1471

Small shops on cobblestone streets are Silverstone's neighbors, making it a great close-by getaway destination. All three rooms have private baths and a private kitchen and laundry room are offered for guests' convenience, so it's an ideal lodging for families. One of the innkeepers is a registered nutritionist and is happy to consult on any dietary needs. Between them they speak five languages, so they can accommodate almost any culture. A full breakfast is served on a flexible schedule. Children are welcome, pets can be admitted at owners' discretion, and no minimum stay is required.

Sweetwater Farm $$$
50 Sweetwater Road,
Glen Mills
(610) 459-4711, (800) 793-3892
www.sweetwaterfarmbb.com

Set on 50 acres in the Brandywine Valley, this farm began as part of an original land grant from William Penn to the Hemphill family. Today, miles of hiking trails wind through the acreage, and guests can relax in the outdoor pool and hot tub, or on the pillared porch. Sweetwater Farm has seven guest rooms: three in the 1734 Quaker farm house, and four in the more formal Georgian wing. In addition, families can choose between five pet- and child-friendly cottages on the grounds. All accommodations have phones, private baths, air conditioning, and cable TV, and the three-course gourmet breakfast is served on the patio or in the Manor House. The price code refers to the average weekday rate; weekend rates are higher, and cottages are priced from $125 to $275.

Tudor House
Bed and Breakfast $$
207 Bryn Mawr Avenue,
Bala Cynwyd
(610) 617-9247
www.tudorhousebandb.com

This is neither the largest nor the most historic B&B on the menu, but it's a good value. There are only two guest accommodations: the loft, in the main building, and the carriage house. The loft offers a full-size bed and sofa bed, sleeping four adults for less than $100. The carriage house is newer, built in 2003, with a private entrance, full bath, queen bed, sofa and loveseat, cable TV, and a wet bar. Neither children nor pets are permitted, and a two-day minimum stay is required on weekends. Breakfast is "continental-plus."

BUCKS COUNTY AND LAMBERTVILLE AREA

Brick Hotel   **$$**
1 East Washington Avenue, Newtown
(215) 860-8313
www.brickhotel.com
It's pretty as a picture, with its white picket fence, tidy gardens, and broad front porch. The Brick Hotel has 15 guest rooms, some with Jacuzzi and fireplace, TV/VCR, desk, or living area. All have air conditioning, private baths, and garden or town views. A full country breakfast is served. Weekend prices are higher, and no pets are allowed. Dinner is available at the inn's Garden Grille restaurant, along with live music, events such as wine tastings, and dining al fresco in summer.

Bridgestreet House   **$$**
75 Bridge Street,
Lambertville
(609) 397-2503
Furnished with Victorian-era antiques, the Federal-style Bridgestreet House was built in 1850 and restored in 2000, and is listed on the National Register of Historic Places. The five guest rooms all have private baths, robes, cable TV, and air conditioning, and fresh fruit, homemade cookies, and chocolates are always available. The expanded continental breakfast features homemade breads and muffins, and wine and cheese is served in the early evening. Children and pets are not permitted, and a

two-night minimum stay is required on weekends.

Chimney Hill Estate Inn   **$$$**
207 Goat Hill Road,
Lambertville
(609) 397-1516, (800) 211-4667
www.chimneyhillinn.com
High on a hill overlooking the riverside town sits Cherry Hill Estate—an 1820 fieldstone Greek Revival house and restored dairy barn. It's an interesting complex—a working llama and alpaca farm, with eight acres of fields and gardens, minutes away from the biggest antiques mecca in the region. All 12 guest rooms are equipped with private baths, robes, coffeepot, cable TV, VCR phones, compact kitchens with microwave and refrigerator, dataport, fireplaces, and two-person whirlpool tubs. No pets; children over 12 are welcome.

Doylestown Inn   **$$$**
18 West State Street, Doylestown
(215) 345-6610
www.doylestowninn.com
Anchoring the center of one of Bucks County's most endearing small towns is the Doylestown Inn, a haven for travelers since 1902. In 2001 it was restored, including the skylighted, four-story atrium and all 11 guest rooms. Private baths, jetted tubs, dataport, cable TV, phone, desk, refrigerator, minibar, and individual heating and air conditioning controls are standard, and premium rooms have sitting areas and fireplaces. Complimentary coffee, "continental-plus" breakfast, and newspaper are served up each morning. Children are welcome, no pets.

Evermay-on-the-Delaware   **$$$**
889 River Road, Erwinna
(610) 294-9100
www.evermay.com
With the floral wallpaper, ruffled curtains, and Victorian antiques, Evermay might be a little over-the-top for some tastes—but we'll get over that, because it's a beautiful inn. Built in 1780, the inn is listed on the National Register of Historic Places. It sits on 25

acres of pasture and woodland—a bit of which houses Evermay's sheep—and guests who aren't in the mood to cozy up to the fireplace can stroll along the canal towpath, enjoying the scenery from another era. Breakfast is "continental-plus," and turn-down service includes sherry and fruit in the 18 guest rooms and suites, all of which have private baths. No children or pets.

Golden Pheasant Inn $$
763 River Road (Route 32),
Erwinna
(610) 294-9595, (800) 830-4474
www.goldenpheasant.com

In 1699, when William Penn sold the 7,500 acres surrounding the Golden Pheasant site to the London Company, early settlers couldn't have imagined the development that would happen there along the Delaware River, especially once the Delaware Canal opened. "Delaware House," precursor to the Golden Pheasant, was built in 1857, one of many that served men working on the canal. Constructed of local fieldstone, the inn has wood-burning fireplaces, exposed stone walls, recessed windows, beamed ceilings, and the original tap room—thanks to its current owners, who restored the inn in its original period style before opening in 1986. The six rooms and cottage suite all have river and canal views, and are furnished with French, English, and American antiques. The suite has a Jacuzzi tub and patio. A two-night stay is required on weekends.

Inn at Bowman's Hill $$$$$
518 Lurgan Road, New Hope
(215) 862-8090
www.theinnatbowmanshill.com

If you need your getaway to be defined by sheer luxury, this is your place. Located next to a wildflower preserve, this inn has five rooms, all fitted with king feath-erbeds, Italian tile and travertine baths, luxurious linens, fireplaces, high-speed Internet access, TV, DVD player, heated whirlpools, Egyptian cotton towels, and fresh flowers. In addition, the Tower Suite is a 500-square-foot space with cathedral ceilings, sitting room, and private entrance. The signature English or gour-met breakfast is served al fresco on the terrace or in your room, and newspaper, bottled water, soft drinks, and afternoon tea sandwiches also are offered. Visit the orchid room-conservatory; the pool and hot tub open Memorial Day. Not surpris-ingly, no kids or pets are allowed.

Lambertville House $$$$$
32 Bridge Street,
Lambertville
(609) 397-0200, (888) 867-8859
www.lambertvillehouse.com

Back in Captain John Lambert's day, his stagecoach stop was known simply as Lambert's Inn—but it was a class operation even then. It was the lodging of choice for traveling dignitaries, including President Andrew Johnson and Ulysses S. Grant, and today it's listed on the National Regis-ter of Historic Places. The 26 rooms and two suites feature fireplaces, jetted tubs and, for a lucky few, private courtyard bal-conies. All rooms are equipped with robes, cable TV, cordless phones, complimentary high-speed Internet access, and coffee service outside the room. Breakfast is "continental-plus," and pets are not allowed.

Main Street Manor
Bed and Breakfast $$
194 Main Street, Flemington
(908) 782-4928
www.mainstreetmanor.com

Main Street Manor, built in 1901, is the only B&B in this small town—site of the Lindbergh-Hauptmann trial—and, of course, one of the five guest rooms is aptly named the "Lindbergh Room." It's the largest accommodation, with a spa-cious private balcony and, in the bath, a sink with lion's-paw legs. Other rooms fea-ture claw-foot tub, sleigh bed, or stained glass windows. Guests can lounge in the two parlors furnished with period antiques, or on the broad veranda over-looking the front garden. The dining room is paneled in an Arts and Crafts style and is lit by a cranberry-glass chandelier. Guests eat a full breakfast; the menu changes with seasonal, local products, and specialties include an herb, potato, and mushroom frittata, or pumpkin pancakes. No pets or children are allowed.

Martin Coryell House   **$$$**
111 North Union Street,
Lambertville
(609) 397-8981, (866) 397-8981
www.martincoryellhouse.com
The original owners of this 1864, Federal-style brick mansion, a designated Historic Place, were descendants of Emmanuel Coryell, founder of Lambertville. The home was restored in 2003 and modern conveniences were blended with the historical features. The Italianate front porch, wainscoted dining room and elegant parlor are faithful to the original; the six guest rooms offer cable TV, desk, high-speed Internet access, phone, air conditioning, coffeepot, fireplace, and whirlpool tub. Fax machine and copier are available on-site as well. A minimum two-night stay may be required on weekends, and children and pets are not allowed.

Woolverton Inn   **$$$$**
6 Woolverton Road, Stockton
(609) 397-0802, (888) 264-6648
www.woolvertoninn.com
Guests can pick their own version of luxury at this 1792 manor house, set on 300 acres pretty enough to inspire poetry. For extreme elegance, try the Sojourn Loft, a two-level private cottage where, at $425 in high season, you get a fireplace, refrigerator/freezer, and great views. All five cottages feature fireplaces, as do some of the eight rooms in the main house. Fresh flowers, robes, complimentary newspaper and bottled water, and Egyptian towels and bed linens are standard fare. Some rooms feature original oils by American Impressionists, while others have two-person whirlpools and showers, or private gardens or screened-in porches. A full country breakfast is served at this true luxury destination.

GAY-OWNED OR GAY-FRIENDLY INNS

Alexander Inn   **$$**
301 South 12th Street,
Philadelphia
(215) 923-3535, (877) ALE-XINN
www.alexanderinn.com
Just around the corner from Center City's Antique Row, the Alexander began as an upscale apartment building. Today the 48-room inn provides guests with a 24-hour fitness room, 24-hour fresh fruit and snack table, and 24-hour "e-mail access computers." All rooms have DirecTV, including eight movie channels, and a continental breakfast is served. The lobby welcomes guests (but not their pets) with fresh flowers, stained glass windows, oak moldings, marble tile floors, and great artwork. At $99 for single rooms and an elevator to get you to them, the Alexander Inn is a Center City deal—but guests who like to sleep in a cool room might put off their stay until the off-season; the inn is not air conditioned.

The Gables   **$$**
4520 Chester Avenue,
Philadelphia
(215) 662-1918
www.gablesbb.com
Victorian buffs will love this University City mansion that won the Historical Society's "Best Preservation Award" and was named "Best Urban Getaway" by *Philadelphia* magazine. The stunning wraparound porch invites guests to linger; inside they'll find parlors trimmed in natural chestnut and cherry wood, oak floors with inlays of mahogany, ash and cherry, and period wallpaper. Rooms are furnished in 19th-century antiques and include cable TV, high-speed wireless Internet access, robes, CD player, fireplace, VCR and telephone, and most have private baths. Five of the 10 rooms are on the third floor. A full breakfast is served, including the innkeeper's signature apple walnut muffins, and children over 10 are welcome.

RESTAURANTS

If your image of Philadelphia food stops at soft pretzels and cheesesteak, think again: No less than nine four-star restaurants, and one five-star, have heightened culinary awareness throughout Philly's neighborhoods. Bistros, wine bars, gelaterias, and sports bars happily thrive alongside steakhouses, romantic dining escapes, and the city's latest hot trend, the newly prolific BYOB.

Philly's restaurant scene has been building for several decades now. It's moved past being a "renaissance"; great dining is in the city's fabric, an essential part of the Philadelphia lifestyle. Much of the credit for this development goes to Georges Perrier, who came here with fellow cooking student Peter von Starck and opened La Panetière in 1967. Several years later, Perrier struck out on his own with the acclaimed five-star Le Bec-Fin. He moved his exclusive eatery to Walnut Street in 1983, thus establishing Philly's "Restaurant Row," where today Le Bec-Fin is joined by Striped Bass, Susanna Foo, and other fine dining choices. Perrier, one of the city's most colorful characters, is a true local celebrity, often appearing on "Late Night With David Letterman" and other network TV shows.

Of course there were restaurants in Philadelphia before Perrier and his fine-dining contemporaries redefined the eating-out scene. Old Original Bookbinders began serving up thick chowder in 1865. Close behind it came Reading Terminal Market in 1892, and vendors at the Italian Market began peddling artisanal cheeses, baked goods, fish, meats, and produce soon after the turn of the last century.

After the success of restaurants along Restaurant Row, the 1980s and '90s brought a fast infusion of great places to eat. Perrier found formidable competition in Jean-Marie "Papa" Lacroix, chef at The Fountain in the Four Seasons Hotel; their rivalry and constant pursuit of excellence brought international recognition to both chefs. They mentored a long list of chefs who have gone on to open their own successful restaurants.

All the while, restaurants of diverse ethnic flavors appeared. Joseph Poon, known as the ambassador of Chinatown, opened his Asian Fusion Restaurant in 1997; the neighborhood now boasts more than 35 restaurants, plus bakeries, groceries, and a Chinese cookie factory, as well as Thai, Japanese, Vietnamese, Malaysian, Burmese, and Hong Kong–style restaurants.

Italian restaurants made names for themselves in South Philly, from white-tablecloth dining to cheesesteaks at famous Pat's, and his equally famous foe, Geno's. Around University City, diners choose from Ethiopian, Mexican, Indian, Senegalese, Japanese, and French restaurants, as well as the progressive-social activism served with meals at the White Dog Cafe.

In the last decade, more celebrities have emerged. The Nuevo-Latino flavors at ¡Pasión! (1998) inspired the opening three years later of Alma de Cuba, with perhaps the sexiest ambience of any restaurant we've seen, and more Cuban cuisine followed. As Old City reemerged, the popular bistro Fork and restaurants by culinary star Stephen Starr (Buddakan, Tangerine, Bluezette, and Cafe Spice, among others) brought new energy to the dining scene.

Speaking of food celebrities, none hears more applause than the Iron Chef himself, especially when his dazzling restaurant, Morimoto—another Stephen Starr creation—is being reviewed.

This is a city of great restaurants, and we've organized them here by community and, in Philadelphia proper, by neighborhood, because we believe that's the format people use in deciding where to dine in Philly. Every section of town offers an abundance of choices. Because BYOB restaurants are so popular, we've clustered them in their own section; you don't want to visit Philadelphia without sampling this new breed. Sunday brunch, too, is a Philly tradition, so we've provided a brunch category as well.

All restaurants listed have non-smoking policies, so you needn't be bothered by cigarette and cigar smoke, and unless we've indicated otherwise, all restaurants honor major credit cards. Do keep in mind, though, that Philadelphia is an old city, and many restaurants are located in row houses and other old structures—and, consequently, may not be wheelchair accessible. If that's an issue with your party, it's best to call ahead.

Remember, too, that Philadelphia is an East Coast city, and restaurant prices may be higher than in other parts of the country. We've included a price code, below, to ward off "sticker shock"; dollar signs indicate the price range for two dinners without tax, tip, or beverage. But not to worry: in Philly, there are plenty of good eats for every budget.

PRICE CODE

$	Less than $30
$$	$30 to $50
$$$	$51 to $80
$$$$	More than $80

PHILADELPHIA

Center City

Alma de Cuba $$$$
1623 Walnut Street
(215) 988-1799
www.almadecubarestaurant.com
The music and ambience are so Latino-hot sexy in this place, it wouldn't have surprised me a bit if Antonio Banderas had tangoed over and sat down beside me. The black-and-white photo treatment is

pure Old Havana. Come even if you're on a budget and indulge in appetizers, like royal palm dates, stuffed with almonds and wrapped in bacon with cabrales blue cheese, or the ham croquettes—smoked pork and Serrano ham cream-filled croquettes with Dijon aioli.

Astral Plane $$$
1708 Lombard Street
(215) 546-6230
www.theastralplane.com
When we discovered this place 20 years ago, we thought we had entered a Bohemian paradise. With draping parachute fabric covering the ceiling, an exotic solid-black bathroom, and plush/mismatched furnishings, it took a while before we noticed the movie memorabilia clustered throughout the small dining room. Top celebrities who've given their seal of approval include George Clooney, Mick Jagger, and Bette Midler. Astral Plane's old standbys, such as the spinach salad with blue cheese, apples, walnuts, red onion, golden raisins, and Dijon vinaigrette, never disappoint. You'll be tempted to fill up on the bread, which appears in a huge basket every few moments, it seems. But save some room for the real food; we recommend the pork chop stuffed with bacon, apples, and pecans.

Capogiro Gelato $
119 South 13th Street
(215) 351-0900
www.capogirogelato.com
We knew about artisanal cheese makers, but artisanal gelato? Stephanie Reitano, owner of this new gelateria at 13th and Sansom Streets, explains how it happens, for five hours every morning before the shop opens. She has experimented (and succeeded) with such offbeat flavors as Caribbean breadfruit, avocado, and spicy cajun peanut, but our favorite is pistachio. In the fall Reitano shops local farms for produce and churns out seasonal flavors such as pumpkin, acorn squash, and fig. The creamy gelato is made fresh every

CLOSE-UP

Taking Tea

Everyone should "take tea" from time to time. The next time you feel like dressing in your Sunday best and joining the ladies for High Tea, consider one of these—but be sure to call for reservations first:

- The Park Hyatt at the Bellevue. When it comes to pure elegance, the Ethel Barrymore Room at the Bellevue has no rival. Three courses are served, including seasonal sandwiches. Tea is served Tuesday, Thursday, Saturday, and Sunday; ask about the kids' menu and prices (200 South Broad Street, 215–893–1776; http://park.hyatt.com).
- Chestnut Hill Community Centre Women's Exchange. Set in the Centre garden, this tea easily conveys the spirit of 19th-century formal teas on the lawn. The most affordable of the three choices (under $10 at this writing)—homemade scones, petits fours, cheese crackers, and sandwiches—are served, Tuesday through Saturday, with proceeds going to charity (8419 Germantown Avenue, 215–247–5911).
- Ritz-Carlton. You'll see some strutting at this tea, held in the Ritz's Rotunda just off the main entrance, Wednesday through Sunday. Nibble on the chef's pastry selection—or, for an extra fee, champagne and strawberries (10 South Broad Street, 215–523–8000; www .ritzcarlton.com/hotels/philadelphia).

morning; at lunchtime try a gelato con brioche—a thick slab of sugar-sprinkled egg bread topped with two gelatos. Well, it's *almost* a sandwich.

Fork $$
306 Market Street
(215) 625-9425
www.forkrestaurant.com

The most fun menu selections at Fork are the veggie sides, such as sautéed spinach, yucca frites, and carrot or ginger mashed potatoes; regulars often order two or three instead of an entree. Catering to the Old City nightclub crowd, Fork also offers an interesting late-night menu (after 10:30 P.M. weeknights, 11:30 P.M. weekends); we stopped in then and had sesame flat bread with lobster, tomato, basil, mozzarella, and caramelized leeks. Don't worry if you get late-night munchies and can't rustle up a date—grab a stool at the bar. You won't be alone.

Fountain Restaurant at Four Seasons $$$$
Four Seasons Hotel
1 Logan Square
(215) 963-1500
www.fourseasons.com

We have never visited the Fountain without seeing a celebrity. The design of the room is quite formal, with lavish fabrics and warm woods creating a sense of opulence. The food is consistently honored by such publications as *Bon Appétit;* we had the simple house salad with shallot dressing, then Maine lobster with a mushroom galette, and understood why. After dinner, repair to the Swann Lounge for a cocktail and delicious people-watching.

Franklin Fountain $
116 Market Street
(215) 627-1899
www.franklinfountain.com

When was the last time you tried a lime rickey? Uh-huh, we thought so. How about a Parisian Flip, laced with Angostura bitters and an egg? Then you're due for a stop at Franklin Fountain, a replica 1900 soda fountain, serving beverages whose recipes were devised more than a century ago. At least 25 nonalcoholic drinks are served, including Thirst-Ades in lemon, lime, and orange, squeezed from whole fruits. Honoring one of Philly's favorite inventions—the ice-cream soda, created here in 1874—root-beer floats, cherry bombs, and other treats are a wonderful respite on a hot shopping day.

Friday Saturday Sunday $$$
261 South 21st Street
(215) 546-4232
www.frisatsun.com

This space is so cramped, and the tables so tiny, that I often feel as if I'm crashing someone's private celebration when I eat at this always-crowded restaurant—but all discomfort is forgotten with the first taste of their signature mushroom soup. Who wouldn't be comforted by this concoction that uses far more cream, butter, half-and-half, and brandy than chicken stock? Bottles of wine are only $10 over retail, a great deal for this class of restaurant.

Joseph Poon Asian Fusion Restaurant $$
1002 Arch Street
(215) 928-9333
www.josephpoon.com

Mr. Poon is the self-appointed ambassador of Philadelphia's Chinatown; you might see him in the kitchen or conducting his "Wok 'n Walk" tours of the neighborhood—but wherever you find him, he's talking up Chinatown. He pioneered pan-Asian fusion cuisine in these parts; we recommend the scallop cake starter and king salmon with spinach chips. On his Web

site, click on "Calligraphy" and learn to read, write, and speak a bit of Chinese.

Lacroix $$$$
210 West Rittenhouse Square
(215) 790-2533
www.rittenhousehotel.com

True to its prestigious address, Lacroix at the Rittenhouse bespeaks excellence. Named the country's best new restaurant by *Esquire* magazine when it opened in 2003, Lacroix has since received a James Beard Award and Mondavi Award, among many others, for excellence in dining. The decor is minimalist—no distractions from the view overlooking Rittenhouse Square—and chef Jean-Marie Lacroix's famous dishes include skate "T-bone" and sweet onion soup with sweetbreads.

Le Bar Lyonnais $$$$
1523 Walnut Street
(215) 567-1000
www.lebecfin.com

This little bistro is downstairs from its big brother, the renowned Le Bec-Fin—and, in fact, is overseen by Bernard Perrier, whose big (well, older) brother, the renowned Georges Perrier, owns both restaurants. As much as we love Le Bec-Fin, we almost like Le Bar Lyonnais better; you need no reservations (so get there early in the evening), and at about $60 per person before wine, it's more affordable than the $135-plus prix fixe upstairs. It's more casual, too, but don't dress down; senators, sports stars, and TV celebrities stop in every night. If you enjoy an Irish coffee nightcap, Le Bar Lyonnais serves one of the best in the city.

Le Bec-Fin $$$$
1523 Walnut Street
(215) 567-1000
www.lebecfin.com

One of the few true destination restaurants, Le Bec-Fin is the anchor and *grande dame* of Rittenhouse Row. Chef Georges Perrier is notorious for demanding perfection from his servers, his chefs, and his suppliers; he has been known to return an entire restaurant-size floral shipment because of one wilted flower. So you can imagine the exquisite food and service here. All meals are prix fixe; if $135 for dinner is too steep for your budget, come for a very special $45 lunch—but for either meal, save room for dessert. The famous towering dessert cart features up to 20 offerings, and patrons are expected to sample at least four or five. Make reservations as far in advance as possible.

Meritage $$$$
500 South 20th Street
(215) 985-1922
www.meritagephiladelphia.com
Only 12 tables grace this exclusive little bar serving classic regional foods (French, Italian, American). Shortly after opening in 2004, Meritage made a name by offering four-course tasting menus, pairing wines with the dishes. The restaurant is just far enough from Walnut Street to keep the sophistication but lose the pretension. If you don't go for the tasting menu, try Spanish tapas or monkfish piccata—and if wine isn't your thing, never fear; Meritage offers more than 50 single-malt scotches and 10 specialty bourbons.

Monk's $$
264 South 16th Street
(215) 545-7005
www.monkscafe.com
"If you are a Bordeaux drinker, then we have beer for you," say the owners of Monk's, claiming to be able to persuade anyone to like beer. We dunno about that, but we definitely enjoyed the food, starting with mussels (each variety cooked in a different beer). We chose Ghent mussels with fumé, garlic, caramelized leeks, bacon, parsley, and blue cheese, then moved on to New Zealand lamb with fries and their signature bourbon mayonnaise on the side.

BYOB restaurants are hatching like rabbits across Greater Philadelphia, and they're some of the city's most popular spots. Although inviting patrons to bring their own vino is unusual in most cities, the reason for their success here is no mystery: A liquor license in this region can cost from $300,000 to $600,000. (Yes, there are five zeros in those numbers!) Compounding the problem is the small number of licenses available in each neighborhood. Not to be deterred, the new generation of chefs decided to open BYOBs instead, and the concept is a huge hit!

Morimoto $$$$
723 Chestnut Street
(215) 413-9070
www.morimotorestaurant.com
If you've ever wondered whether the famous TV chefs really knew what they were doing, here's your evidence: "Iron Chef" Masaharu Morimoto presents the finest *omakase*—the daily chef's selection, a multi-course tasting menu, literally translated to, "leave yourself in my hands"—in these parts. A smaller-but-filling version is offered at lunch. The interior of the place is stunning, with softly backlit furnishings that gradually change color every few minutes. Chef Morimoto himself often cooks, so look for him behind the sushi bar, and if you're ordering dessert, try the wasabi tiramisu.

Moshulu $$
Penn's Landing
401 South Columbus Boulevard
(215) 923-2500
www.moshulu.com
The menu isn't the real story with this restaurant. It's straightforward, affordable, tasty, and not too adventurous. The attraction here is the setting: Moshulu is the biggest, oldest four-masted sailing ship still in the water. More than a century

If you're not into Italian food, head for the Italian Market anyway, because alongside the Italian bakers, cheese importers, produce vendors, and butchers, you'll find Mexican food at Taqueria La Veracruzana, home of the best tamales and chile relleno tacos in the city. And if Vietnamese fare is your craving, stop at Nam Phoung for a salad or hot pot (Taqueria Veracruzana, 908 Washington Avenue, 215-465-1440; Nam Phoung, 1100 Washington Avenue, 215-468-0410).

old, the ship has circled the globe 54 times, served in World Wars I and II, and was first launched as a restaurant in 1975. After a fire and pier collapse, Moshulu reopened in 2003. The interior is elegant, and we found the crab-crusted tilapia and Thai filet mignon excellent—but if you'd rather have a drink and a burger, and a great view of the Delaware River, take a seat on deck.

¡Pasión!   **$$$**
211 South 15th Street
(215) 875-9895
www.pasionrestaurant.com
You can almost taste the passion that goes into the cooking at this aptly named restaurant. It must be true love—why else would a chef claim to have created more than 100 versions of ceviche, the citrusy seafood? The food here is spicy and interesting; churrasco is served impaled on a stick of sugar cane, and the braised baby goat is so tender you can almost hear it say, "Baaah!"

Phoebe's   **$**
2214 South Street
(215) 546-4811
The menu here is basic barbecue: chicken, pork, ribs, with huge portions and a sweet-as-honey Oklahoma-style sauce. The coleslaw is fresh and the collard greens are peppery. Phoebe's is comfort-food heaven, which explains why so many

Philadelphians stop for takeout on their way home after work.

Planet Hoagie   **$**
1211 Walnut Street
(215) 928-8883
www.planethoagie.com
You walk into this place and wonder why you didn't come up with this idea first: more than 60 varieties of hoagies every day, including the Chicken Corleone (grilled chicken, roasted red peppers, honey mustard, fresh grated cheese) and a long list of vegetarian options. We tried the Verdura (roasted eggplant, broccoli rabe, roasted red peppers, sharp provolone) and a caesar salad. Since we first discovered them a year ago, five more Planet Hoagies have opened in the area, so they're doing something right.

Sansom Street Oyster House   **$$**
1516 Sansom Street
(215) 567-7683
www.sansomoysters.com
You can find more upscale seafood houses in the Rittenhouse Row neighborhood, but none more friendly than the Sansom Street. "Serve It Fresh!" is the motto in this dining room, which has been filled with slurping oyster-lovers since 1901. The raw bar is extensive; check your pretenses at the door.

Striped Bass   **$$$$**
1500 Walnut Street
(215) 732-4444
www.stripedbassrestaurant.com
After a five-month renovation, we noticed the changes: cylindrical chandeliers of 5,600 hand-placed crystals, hanging from the 28-foot ceiling; hundreds of yards of theatrical-gray fabric draping the huge windows—and, we were shocked to see, steak and foie gras on the formerly all-seafood menu. But no matter; Striped Bass still dazzles, from our English pea soup with morel custard starter, through the peanut-crusted Hawaiian ono in Thai curry-broth entree, into the carrot tart dessert with cream-cheese ice cream. To

Pet-Friendly Dining

Not everyone wants to dine with Pooch slurping at the next table, but many pet owners love having their animals with them at dinner. These restaurants are happy to accommodate:

- American Bar & Grill has outdoor dining in the warmer months. Pets are welcome (499 East Uwchlan Avenue, Chester Springs, 610-280-0800).
- Devon Seafood Grill in Rittenhouse Square offers pets a bowl of water in its outdoor cafe (225 South 18th Street, 215-546-5940).
- Fork is one of the Old City eateries that allows pets as soon as the sidewalk cafe opens in the spring (306 Market Street, 215-625-9425; www.forkrestaurant.com).
- Labrador Coffee in beautiful Chestnut Hill is full of dog lovers; they're shown to the small outdoor garden, where they have light dining and dessert while the dogs enjoy water and a treat (8139 Germantown Avenue, 215-247-8487).
- For pets with an appetite, Le Bus in Manayunk offers "casual cuisine" and water for dogs (4266 Main Street, 215-487-2663).
- Peacock on the Parkway is both pet-friendly and family-friendly. Pups get a treat while the family dines outdoors (1700 Benjamin Franklin Parkway, 215-569-8888).
- Philadelphia Fish & Co. welcomes owners with leashed pets at its outdoor seating (207 Chestnut Street, 215-625-8605; www.philadelphia fish.com).
- Rita's Water Ice helps both pets and their owners cool down—pets with water, owners with their own treats (430 Lancaster Avenue, Malvern, 610-644-2920; www.ritasice.com).

be honest, we liked the old decor better; this one sets a chillier tone to the cavernous space. But this is the power-dinner restaurant of Rittenhouse Row, and the focus is on the food.

Susanna Foo Chinese Cuisine $$$
1512 Walnut Street
(215) 545-2666
www.susannafoo.com
When Susanna Foo opened more than 15 years ago, it was applauded as an innovator in classic Chinese cuisine. This may be the finest Chinese food you will ever eat; it consistently earns Mobil four-star and AAA four-diamond awards; famous restaurant critic John Mariani named Susanna Foo one of the 15 best restaurants in the Northeast. You cannot go wrong with any choice on the menu—but we have particularly fond memories of the lemon mascarpone cheesecake with pistachio crust, drizzled with cherry wine sauce. You cannot imagine a more sublime taste in your mouth.

Tria $
123 South 18th Street
(215) 972-8742
www.triacafe.com
When you want to go out but don't need a big sit-down meal, Tria is the place. Light dining and drinks—grazing, in other words—are the focus here, where it's easy to snack on one of several bruschetta choices, some mixed greens with a bold

gorgonzola dressing, and a cheese selection. The beer list is fairly sophisticated with plenty of Belgian and German brews, and a few from Canada and Japan.

Manayunk and Kelly Drive

Bourbon Blue $$
2 Rector Street, Manayunk
(215) 508-3360
www.bourbonblue.com

Awarded a "Best of Philly" in its first year of operation, Bourbon Blue does New Orleans right, from the blackened catfish and jambalaya, right through to the beignets we ordered for dessert. Even the decor evokes the French Quarter, with high ceilings, exposed brick, and a wrought-iron balcony. The restaurant is located just off Manayunk's busy Main Street, so it's handy for a post-shopping bite.

Jake's $$$
4365 Main Street, Manayunk
(215) 483-0444
www.jakesrestaurant.com

We first discovered Jake's in the late 1980s, soon after it opened, and we're still drawn by the great service, funky-sophisticated decor and convenience for lunch during a Main Street shopping binge—not to mention its memorable dishes like sweet potato soup with goat cheese dumpling. On our last visit we tried grilled calf's liver over apple, potato, and bacon hash—an ideal fall entree—and for hearty appetites, the lump crab cakes with a mountain of yam fries. Jake's earns its status as a Manayunk icon.

Verge $$$$
4101 Kelly Drive
(215) 689-0050

You've never heard of some of the concoctions on this menu, which changes every six weeks—but a bit of adventurous spirit will pay off here, with dishes like achiote-rubbed salmon with lime jam; a buckwheat crepe filled with ham, chèvre, and fresh figs; and the surprisingly light sweet-corn flan. The wine list is affordable and unusual, focusing on small wineries. We settled in easily to the friendly, neighborhood-restaurant feel of the place.

South Philly

Paradiso Restaurant & Wine Bar $$$$
1627 East Passyunk Avenue
(215) 271-2066
www.paradisophilly.com

In this neighborhood, it's almost required that the wine list include a respectable selection of Italian regionals, and Paradiso doesn't disappoint—but you'll also find a few other interesting bottles, such as those from Argentina, New Zealand, and the Finger Lakes. We started with the butternut squash and ricotta crespelle (on the sweet side, but delicious anyway) and moved on to grilled tuna (rare) atop shaved fennel and blood oranges. We also enjoyed the octopus braised in white wine and olive oil with Yukon Gold potatoes. The food at this small restaurant is magnifico but half the tables were empty; we hope more diners take notice and business picks up.

University City and West Philadelphia

Cereality $
3631 Walnut Street
(215) 222-1162

We're pretty much staying away from chain restaurants in this guide, but there are only three Cereality Cafes in the country—and readers need to know about this place. More fun than a sushi bar, salad bar, and sundae bar combined, Cereality attracts customers with slogans like, "95 percent of Americans like cereal. 57 percent like sex. We've got cereal." And boy, do they—more than 30 different kinds for breakfast, served

White Dog Cafe

You might think you're in a parallel universe at first, when you first notice the dogs. They're everywhere: dog lamps, dog coffee mugs, dog salt and pepper shakers, dog paintings on the walls.

It's part of the restaurant's legacy from one-time resident Madame Helena P. Blavatsky, scholar, eccentric, and founder of the Theosophical Society. According to the legend, Madame Blavatsky in 1875 had a severe infection in her leg, but when doctors wanted to amputate, she sent them away, exclaiming, "Fancy my leg going to the spirit land before me!" A white dog sauntered into the room, climbed on the bed and slept across Madame Blavatsky's leg for several nights—and soon her diseased leg was cured.

While the white dog gave owner Judy Wicks her restaurant's name, it is her own commitment to serving not only her customers, but her community and the earth—and a bit of inspiration from Madame Blavatsky—that prompts Wicks to sponsor programs such as "Table for Six Billion, Please!" In this "sister restaurant project," the White Dog targets areas of the world that need more dialogue with other nations. Using their mutual interest in food as a starting point, restaurants in Nicaragua, Lithuania, Vietnam, Cuba, Thailand, Mexico, and The Netherlands work with the White Dog toward a common goal: ensuring that every nation "has a place at the global table."

That's only the beginning of the White Dog's social activism. Staff and customers come together several times a year to rehab homes, build community gardens, and organize other quality-of-life improvement projects. Every Saturday customers who bring an elderly person to "Take a Senior to Lunch" get a 50 percent discount on the tab. On select Monday nights, storytellings give a voice to disenfranchised Philadelphians, including the homeless and ex-offenders. Eco-tours, "parties for peace," events to promote sustainable farming, and annual multicultural nights to celebrate diversity—including a Rum & Reggae party, Noche Latina, and Native American Thanksgiving Dinner, keep the calendar full.

And if all of those activities weren't progressive and service-oriented enough, the White Dog donates 20 percent of its pre-tax profits, every day of the year, to non-profit projects and organizations, including its own White Dog Cafe Foundation.

The restaurant's food has developed along with its social agenda, with a menu mixing the familiar and the new introduced each week. Sweet potato and lemon grass soup might appear alongside grilled yellowfin tuna, and for brunch you can enjoy roasted red pepper grits with rock shrimp and Amish cheddar—made, like all White Dog dishes, with as many locally produced ingredients as possible.

After you dine, step next door to the White Dog's gift shop, offering local crafts and Whole World Products, thus promoting an inclusive, sustainable global economy. The shop's name? What else could it be but, The Black Cat. (White Dog Cafe, 3420 Sansom Street, 215-386-9224; www.whitedog.com; The Black Cat, 3426 Sansom Street, 215-386-6664; www.blackcatshop.com.)

by wait help in pajamas. You get two scoops of cereal, one topping (selected from over 30 choices), and milk for one price, or you can choose one of Cereality's custom mixes, as well as cereal smoothies or breakfast bars. If you like your custom-mix, box a few servings and take it home.

Marigold Kitchen $$$
501 South 45th Street
(215) 222-3699
Tucked deep in the West Philly pocket known as Spruce Hill, Marigold Kitchen has served generations of students, professors, and young families. Its new owner has replaced the box of toys in the corner with contemporary art; instead of meatloaf and fried chicken, the menu now offers such dishes as coffee-braised lamb shoulder on chestnut puree, goat cheese mousse, and ginger-pomegranate sorbet. The restaurant still has a "homey" feel, but it feels more like a home where grown-ups live.

BUCKS COUNTY

Golden Pheasant Inn $$$
763 River Road, Erwinna
(610) 294-9595
http://goldenpheasant.com
In the mid-1850s, this fieldstone inn, sitting between the Delaware River and the Canal, was a barge stop where canal workers could get salt cakes, beer, a change of mules, and a bed. Today it's on the National Register of Historic Places, still doing double-duty as an inn and restaurant. The cozy dining room over-looks the canal and features French cuisine, variations of lamb, duck, scallops, and filet mignon dishes.

Lambertville Station
Restaurant $$$
11 Bridge Street,
Lambertville, New Jersey
(609) 397-8300
www.lambertvillestation.com
Just across the river from New Hope, this beautifully restored 1867 railway station serves a straightforward steak-and-seafood menu. Signature dishes include dijon-rosemary encrusted rack of lamb, rare ahi tuna with wasabi puree, and Chesapeake lump crab cakes. The restaurant is open 365 days a year; the pub downstairs serves more casual fare and features entertainment nightly.

Landing Restaurant $$$
22 North Main Street, New Hope
(215) 862-5711
www.landingrestaurant.com
Not only is The Landing handy in the heart of New Hope, it also serves from all of its menus, all day. You can have prime rib at 3:00 P.M. or a burger at 8:00 P.M. We did try the prime rib, as well as a fried calamari

What's a cheesesteak? Aside from Ben Franklin, cheesesteaks might be the most famous thing ever produced in Philadelphia. Invented in 1932 by the "King of Steaks" Pat Olivieri, a cheesesteak is a soft Italian roll filled with greasy, thinly sliced beef, provolone (or Cheez Whiz), and a small mountain of grilled onions. Finding a great cheesesteak is easy, just ask anyone for directions to Pat's, Geno's, or Jim's, and they'll direct you to the nearest cheesesteak fix. The three restaurants are rivals and the acknowledged champs at building these gastronomical wonders.

- Pat's King of Steaks (1237 East Passuyunk Avenue, 215-468-1546; www.patskingofsteaks.com)
- Geno's (1219 South Ninth Street, 215-389-0659; www.genossteaks.com)
- Jim's Steaks (400 South Street, 215-928-1911; www.jimssteaks.com)

with cilantro-lime sauce appetizer, and enjoyed them both. Perched on the river-bank, the setting couldn't be prettier.

Marsha Brown $$$
15 South Main Street,
New Hope
(215) 862-7044
www.marshabrownrestaurant.com
Set in a 125-year-old stone church, Marsha Brown bills itself as a "refined Creole kitchen and lounge," and we wouldn't disagree. The menu relies largely on seafood and meats with a Creole prepa-ration, along with Marsha's own southern family favorites, including eggplant Ophelia—layered, like lasagna, but with eggplant instead of noodles, and crab-meat and shrimp instead of meat, all drenched in a creamy bisque—and spicy coconut shrimp. All entrees are served with a generous "Church Salad." On the far wall Marsha proclaims her approach to food, and to life: "God is in the Details."

Odette's Restaurant $$$
274 South River Road,
New Hope
(215) 862-2432
www.odettes.com
Odette's life journey took her from the live stage to the Delaware River. Once a star of the Ziegfeld Follies, Odette appeared in 27 movies and a long list of Broadway shows before she settled in this 200-year-old inn just south of New Hope. She brought her love of entertaining to her new fine-dining restaurant, incorporating a piano bar. The cuisine is continental, fea-turing predictable but delicious beef, fowl, seafood, and pasta dishes.

CHESTER COUNTY

Teikoku $$$
5492 West Chester Pike,
Newtown Square
(610) 644-8270
www.teikokurestaurant.com
Simplicity is the key at Teikoku, with its

Those who sip regularly at Great Tea International probably won't be happy that we're disclosing the location of their favorite tea sanctuary. From the tinkly music to the origami garlands, soothing waterfalls, and paper lanterns, this Zen hideaway is a city worker's dream escape. The menu of green, oolong, black, white, and herbal teas is lengthy, and the staff are happy to help you negotiate through the many choices (1724 Sansom Street, 215-568-7827).

great feng shui and tone of serenity. The dining room resembles an outdoor court-yard, lined with bamboo wall coverings and exotic greenery, and accented with a stone garden. Both Japanese and Thai cooking are featured. The sushi is some of the best we've tried, but Teikoku's real claim to fame is its expansive sake list. Learn about the rice wine while you sip a Saketini, a cold drink of sake and vodka, garnished with a cucumber.

MONTGOMERY COUNTY

Arpeggio $$
Spring House Village Center
Bethlehem Pike at
Norristown Road
(215) 646-5055
One of the proliferation of BYOBs that have sprung up across Greater Philadel-phia in the past few years, Arpeggio is a casual shopping-plaza neighborhood restaurant, focusing on Mediterranean cui-sine. We liked their pizzas best, baked in a wood-burning oven, though their typical Mediterranean foods—hummus, baba ghannoush, pita—are made on the prem-ises and also were quite good.

Bianca $$$$
24 North Merion Avenue,
Bryn Mawr
(610) 519-0999
www.biancarestaurant.com

You would be hard put to find more elegant comfort food than the decadent fare at Bianca. We started our evening with cappuccino-style exotic mushroom soup, and moved on to smoked duck breast with barley-apple pilaf. Another in our party was most happy with his roast chicken stuffed with chestnuts and melted foie gras. The sides alone are worth the drive out to the Main Line; we tried truffle-whipped potatoes and parmesan bread soufflé. We skipped the handmade pastas, although they looked divine, and saved just enough room for the rosemary ice cream and gooey-centered chocolate cake.

**Blue Horse
Restaurant and Tavern $$
602 Skippack Pike,
Blue Bell
(215) 641-9100
www.thebluehorse.net**
We arrived just in time for complimentary hors d'oeuvres and tapas, and lingered to enjoy the works by local artists, displayed around the circa-1700 inn; all pieces are for sale. We liked the menu's range, too; you can order spaghetti marinara for $8.00 or a three-course prix fixe dinner for $28. Blue Horse also hosts special events such as a recent Argentinian Wine Dinner. This is another BYOB.

**Bridget's at 8 West $$$
8 West Butler Pike, Ambler
(267) 465-2000
www.bridgets8west.com**
Despite the dark wood decor, this isn't your dad's steak-and-seafood joint. The menu is Pacific inspired, with items such as wok-seared red snapper with cilantro and black bean sauce, Pacific sea bass in puff pastry with sweet corn, and chorizo clams in a garlicky butter broth. We noticed, as you will, the hint of Louisiana that snuck into the dishes. The dining room is intimate and candle-lit, but you can watch the Phillies game in the lounge.

**Coyote Crossing $$
800 Spring Mill Avenue,
Conshohocken
(610) 825-3000**
Have dinner here in warm weather, when you can sip your margarita (selected from a long list of flavors) out on the garden patio, a summer gathering place. The vibrant, colorful decor suits the lively atmosphere and spicy food. Everything we tasted, poblanos to pollo, was excellent, but our favorite was the chunky guacamole.

**Maya Bella $$$
119 Fayette Street,
Conshohocken
(610) 832-2114**
Cheers for another Le Bec-Fin graduate, out on his own: Chef Ken Shapiro opened this two-room BYOB in 2004, teasing every patron's palate with goat cheese ravioli and moving on to such mouth-watering dishes as steamed mussels laced with andouille sausage bits, grilled octopus with cranberry beans and Thai chile oil, and tuna tartare embellished with chopped lavender and watercress. We'll eat here again.

**Shanachie Irish Pub
and Restaurant $$
111 East Butler Avenue,
Ambler
(215) 283-4887
www.shanachiepub.com**
This affordable, friendly pub's menu is a blend of Irish Traditional dishes (farmhouse vegetable and barley soup, bacon-wrapped jumbo scallops) and "New Celtic" cuisine (jumbo lump crab and wild mushroom bruschetta, oak-smoked salmon spring rolls with dill dip). For smaller appetites, the potato leek soup alone is a meal. Entertainment is offered five nights a week, including several evenings of Irish music.

Philly's BYOB Craze

"Cozy restaurants where you can bring your own wine are springing up all over the City of Brotherly Love," wrote a food critic for *Food & Wine* magazine recently. Indeed, BYOBs are Philadelphia's hottest restaurant trend.

In most cities you wouldn't be able to pull it off, but in this city, some of the hardest-to-get-into eateries are BYOBs. Most are smaller, more casual—yet sophisticated—places. Meal prices might be slightly more than you'd find at comparable restaurants, because profits from BYOBs must come from the food, not the wine list, which often is the most profitable aspect of operating a restaurant. But you'll economize on the wine.

We've listed some of the better BYOBs, so grab your favorite bottle of Chilean red from Trader Joe's.

Alison at Blue Bell $$$
721 Skippack Pike, Blue Bell
(215) 641-2660
www.alisonatbluebell.com
If you can visit only one BYOB during your visit to Philly, make it this one. Alison Barshak has been a food sensation here since she was the debut chef at Striped Bass. She loves running her own restaurant in the 'burbs; she considers such places the "town squares" of today for suburbanites, who spend so much time commuting. The menu reflects her international travels; on a given week you might find grilled Haloumi cheese with "Israeli salad" alongside ginger-fried squid with a wasabi drizzle and mango slaw, and selections from France, Greece, and Mexico. Alison's is fun, the food is exceptional, you'll leave happy. (No credit cards accepted.)

Audrey Claire $$$
276 South 20th Street
(215) 731-1222
www.audreyclaire.com
It's easy to graze on small dishes here, such as the grilled flatbreads and marinated shrimp. Big-bowl pastas are another specialty, though we visited in summer and went for lighter fare. We liked the way the huge front windows are thrown open to the street—we hate freezing in air conditioning—and the sidewalk tables. If you insist on drinking from wine glasses, you'll have to bring your own; Audrey Claire only provides clunky water glasses. (No credit cards accepted.)

Cafette $$
8136 Ardleigh Street, Chestnut Hill
(215) 242-4220
www.cafette.com
Every neighborhood wishes it had a Cafette, where the menu isn't terribly ambitious but the food is good, the patio is a great place for an al fresco evening with friends, and the prices aren't out of this world. Vegetarians and vegans get equal billing here; we tried the lemon-peppered tilapia, the black bean cakes with sweet potato, and the "Very Famous Vegetarian Lasagna" and finished every bite.

Django $$$
526 South Fourth Street
(215) 922-7151
Philadelphia magazine called Django the "city's best BYOB," and we wouldn't disagree. The owner and his wife grow much of their own produce in a community garden, so there's no doubt about the freshness of ingredients in such dishes as crab-stuffed zucchini blossoms with crab

broth risotto, sweet peas, and tomato essence. Django's signature is their cheese plate closer with raw honey, fresh blackberries, and nuts. The catch: Make your weekend reservations a month in advance and at least two weeks for weeknights. If you can't get reservations, there's a wait list—but don't stand in line too long; they only get about three cancellations per evening.

Lolita $$$
106 South 13th Street
(215) 546-7100
It's not often that a Mexican restaurant creates a buzz, but Lolita managed when it opened its hip new eatery in the hip new 3B (Blocks Below Broad) neighborhood in Center City. From the 12-foot photo of a calla lily to the exposed brick, open kitchen, and locally designed hanging lights, the space itself is striking. The food lives up to expectation; try the grilled pork chop with Mexican corn and tres leches chocolate cake. Don't forget to bring your favorite tequila; Lolita provides the pitcher of virgin margaritas.

Matyson $$$$
37 South 19th Street
(215) 564-2925
The cooking style at this classy BYOB is "contemporary American"—a label that often means, "anything goes"—and the menu here definitely is diverse. You can indulge in the light potato gnocchi, grilled pork chops, and pan-seared polenta topped with wild mushrooms; or you can turn down the volume with a salad of pink watermelon, feta, red onion, and mint, accompanying a pan-fried trout sandwich. Once a month Matyson serves a prix fixe comprised of a different country's cuisine.

Pumpkin $$$
1713 South Street
(215) 545-4448
Everybody loves Pumpkin—another difficult-to-get-into BYOB. The seafood dishes are most popular; order a stew and you'll find unusual species like walu and hake. Every dish seems brimming with ingredients—raisins, pine nuts, lots of parsley. We loved the mussels with whole-grain mustard and vermouth, and the cookie plate at the end was just perfect—but the menu changes daily, so you might encounter pheasant, rabbit, or gratin of kielbasa instead. (No credit cards accepted.)

Sola $$$$
614 West Lancaster Avenue,
Bryn Mawr
(610) 526-0123
This upscale, American-menu BYOB changed ownership just weeks before press time, so we can't make predictions—but if the food is as luscious as before it was sold, you're in for a treat. Familiar dishes such as cedar-plank salmon and rib-eye steak were the most popular, but they were presented with French or Asian flair. We'll be most interested to see how Sola defines itself in its next life.

NIGHTLIFE 🍸

Ever since Ben Franklin and his cronies tossed back mugs of mead down at the City Tavern, Philadelphians have been socializing in their favorite pubs. Those establishments have evolved over the centuries, but they're still the kinds of friendly watering holes Franklin would have visited.

One major development in Philly is the emergence of the "bottle service" club. These sophisticated nightclubs, in olden days the stomping ground for cigar-smoking bankers, politicians, and industrial tycoons, now host young professionals simply enjoying a night on the town—for a price. These clubs usually are located a floor above less pricey bars, hence are referred to as "upstairs bottle service" clubs. Some will require you to purchase a membership; all sell bottles of liquor for up to 10 times the price you would pay in a liquor store. (That means a bottle of Absolut Vodka will cost $200 or more.) Definitely, the upstairs clubs are places to see and be seen!

From brewpubs to comedy clubs, after-hours Philly has it all. Music is especially important in this town—but of course, the hometown of legendary tenor Mario Lanza, blues immortal Billie Holliday, and "American Bandstand" would be musical. So, regardless of your chosen variety of night spot, chances are you will hear some great music while you're there.

You also will encounter Pennsylvania's quirky liquor laws. For one, there are 30 different kinds of liquor licenses in the state—including one that allows liquor to be served in a nursing home—but every single Pennsylvania bar also has a restaurant license, whether the owners want one or not. A liquor license here *is* a restaurant license, which is why you will find many neighborhood bars selling hot dogs. By law, every bar must provide enough food to serve 30 diners on any given night, so barkeeps will always have something available if you get the munchies.

Another interesting law says that if a bar or nightclub is "private"—that is, if it requires patrons to become members before being admitted or served—then the bar can serve liquor until 3:00 A.M. For that reason, many of the bottle-service clubs sell memberships; the "private club" designation enhances the club's image. It also allows the club to sell its ultra-expensive liquor for a few extra hours, after inhibitions have dissipated.

Some liquor laws, of course, affect everyone who drinks in Pennsylvania. You must be 21 years of age in order to purchase, attempt to purchase, possess, consume, or transport liquor. The legal limit for drinking and driving is .08 BAC (Blood Alcohol Level); above that amount, a person behind the wheel of a car is considered DUI (Driving Under the Influence). Further, a person can be charged with DUI with only a .05 BAC if police have evidence that the person's driving is impaired.

It's worth noting, too, that females reach that legal limit faster than males. A woman who weighs 120 pounds will reach a .08 BAC after only two drinks. (For a woman weighing 180 pounds, it usually takes three drinks to reach the limit.) However, a man weighing 140 pounds typically will not reach .08 BAC until after three drinks, and a 180-pound male probably won't reach it until after his fourth drink. In any case, taxis are everywhere in Philly, and if you've been drinking, the safest plan is to taxi home. For more information on Pennsylvania's liquor laws, go to www.lcb.state.pa.us.

BARS AND BREWPUBS

Bar Noir
112 South 18th Street
(215) 569-9333
www.barnoir215.com

This Rittenhouse Square hot spot is especially fun in summer when the park comes alive. After dark, descend to the bar downstairs, styled after European underground bars. Popular with the after-work crowd, Bar Noir serves light snacks and is a hit with its $1.00 bottled beer during happy hour. The music is slightly cutting-edge; the place is hip but comfy, managing to keep the feel of a neighborhood bar.

Cherry Street Tavern
129 North 22nd Street
(215) 561-5683

Almost everyone stops into the Cherry Street Tavern at some point, so you're likely to run into museum docents, sports fans, teachers, conventioneers, and neighborhood regulars, all at the same time. They come to snack on nachos, down a pitcher, and enjoy some old-fashioned watering hole camaraderie—and while they're at it, they'll admire the vintage bar with beveled glass; it's believed to be original with the tavern. This place itself is an original, operating now for more than a century.

Continental
138 Market Street
(215) 923-6069
www.continentalmartinibar.com

If it's a martini evening, this is the place with the accolades to back it up: *Food and Wine* magazine named it "Best Chef Hangout," and *Playboy* gave it their "Best Bar" award. Martinis come in all varieties, from barely chocolate to rich raspberry, all served in your own personal shaker. Even the decor here is about martinis, down to

the green-olive halogen lamps pierced with a huge toothpick, and pimento-red accented booths. Set in a renovated '50s diner, the Continental was one of restaurateur Stephen Starr's first creations, and the one that first put Old City on the restaurant sizzle-list.

Cuba Libre Restaurant and Rum Bar
10 South Second Street
(215) 627-0666
www.cubalibrerestaurant.com

They don't come any more authentic than this bar that wouldn't dream of using commercial sugar in its drinks: Cuba Libre actually presses hundreds of pounds of its own, fresh sugar cane weekly to extract *guarapo,* the sugar cane juice used in making *mojitos.* More than 60 different rums are poured here, and the drink recipes all originated in Havana bars. We recommend the Watermelon Mojito—or, on a cooler night, the Cafe Cuba Libre, a short shot of Cuban coffee with steamed coconut milk. Between the rum and the decor, you'll believe you are in 1940s Havana.

Glam
52 South Second Street
(215) 671-0840
www.glamphilly.com

Like most upscale bars in Old City, this one has late-night dancing and live music—but the real action is at the Glam Upstairs, where personalized European bottle service is offered to those with swipe cards. The hot pink walls, leatherette love seats, and ottomans are a little chewing-gum sweet, but so are the $200 bottle prices. Bottle service comes with fresh fruits and cheeses and requested attire is "club fashionable."

Independence Brewery
1000 East Comly
(215) 922-4292

This brewpub isn't easy to find, but you'll be glad you made the effort. Tucked into a little side street across from Reading Terminal Market between Market and Arch

Streets, Independence Brewery does a brisk business with the Market Street lunch and after-work crowd. They're known for their pale, herbal-y Kölsch and their dark porter ale. Pints are just $2.00 during Happy Hour, and tours are given Saturday at noon and 2:00 P.M. Take a moment to notice the photos; they show Center City of bygone days and they are a hoot.

Iron Hill Brewery
3 West Gay Street, West Chester
(610) 738-9600
www.ironhillbrewery.com
One of the best places to attend a beer tasting and get educated about beers, is at a brewpub—the info will be as fresh as the ale. With three wheat beers, local brewpub chain Iron Hill is a popular spot. In summer try the crisp raspberry wheat, patterned after the Belgian tradition of incorporating fresh fruit into the brew. Iron Hill is known, too, for its continual participation in charity events, such as designing a signature beer to benefit muscular dystrophy research. Brewpub tours are free.

Library Lounge
Park Hyatt at the Bellevue
Broad and Walnut Streets
(215) 790-2814
www.parkhyatt.com
There's an old-world elegance to this tiny lounge that makes you want to linger. If these walls could talk, the language would be one of quiet elegance, telling stories of momentous political decisions, stolen glances, and secret liaisons. The Art Deco bar and cushy leather chairs awaken the imagination, but the tab will snap you out of it: A snifter of cognac can cost $125 here.

Loie
128 South 19th Street
(215) 568-0808
www.loie215.com
Even on a Sunday night, you can slouch at Loie's outside tables and spend your last weekend hours soaking up the Rittenhouse Square scene. This intimate French bistro was named for the diva of modern dance, and while it's less pretentious than many of its neighbors, Loie's menu is hardly bar munchies, including items like chicken paillard, steak au poivre, and crawfish beignets.

Los Sarapes
17 Moyer Road, Chalfont
(215) 822-8858
www.lossarapes.com
If you've ever wondered what a 60-ounce margarita looks like, you can find out at this Bucks County stop just outside Doylestown. Some 90 tequilas are featured, priced from $4.00 to $90.00 for the finest agave. If it's Thursday, belly up to the bar for $2.00 Mexican beers and some authentic Mexican food. Feeling adventurous? Try a "Vampiro"—tequila, lime juice, and sangrita, served in a salted glass and kissed with a shot of habañero sauce—¡Ay, caramba!

Maggiano's Little Italy
205 Mall Boulevard, King of Prussia
(610) 992-3333
www.maggiano.com
Face it, at some point in your visit to Philadelphia, you're going to get out to the King of Prussia mall for some serious shopping—and we know that's thirsty work. Maggiano's is as good as mall bars get, with a checkered-tablecloth decor straight out of *Big Night,* and drink prices to match, especially during happy hour. On weekends the bar will be crowded with diners waiting up to two hours for a table. Cozy up in the leather banquettes and the piano player will entertain you with bad jokes.

Manayunk Brewery
4120 Main Street
(215) 482-8220
www.manayunkbrewery.com
Housed in an old textile mill, this brewpub might get the prize for the best outdoor deck. It overlooks the Schuylkill River, a great place for sipping a pale lager and

The next time you stop into the Cherry Street Tavern, take a seat at the old, polished bar—and then look down at your feet. That trough was installed when the tavern first opened, in the era when sitting at the bar was strictly an all-male activity. Its purpose was to, um, relieve men of the task of having to leave the room when they had to, um, relieve themselves. Oh, the stories that old DNA could tell. . . .

enjoying a light sushi dinner. If beer makes you crave heartier food, the stone pizza oven should take care of bigger appetites.

Nodding Head Brewery
1516 Sansom Street
(215) 569-9525
www.noddinghead.com
Their motto says it all: "Taking over the world, seven barrels at a time!" Nodding Head's legions of loyal customers count on finding a fresh menu of brews with each visit, from the lemony Bin Ein Berliner Weisse—their version of the tart Weisse made in northern Germany—to the rich, dark Grog and the super-spirited Whiplash I.P.A. Beer here is served with attitude ("Rehab is for quitters," proclaims the Web site), but things mellow out for the 11:00 A.M. jazz brunch on Sunday.

North Star Bar
2639 Poplar Street
(215) 684-0808
www.northstarbar.com
The self-proclaimed "Mighty North Star" doesn't seem too mighty from the outside; it's set in a converted house on a nondescript corner in Northern Liberties—but the crowd is friendly, the beer is cold, and tunes are rock and roll. Drinks are half price during happy hour, 5:30 to 7:30 P.M., and the food is pedestrian bar food—sandwiches and sides—but the music is good. Expect cover charges on live music nights, from $8.00 to $15.00; you'll hear

local talent such as Welcome to My Face, Alo Brasil, and Hydrogen Hellhorses.

Ritz-Carlton Rotunda
10 South Broad Street
(215) 523-8000
www.ritzcarlton.com
Don't you think there's just something special about slipping on the stilettos and hanging out in the lobby of the Ritz? It's something everyone should do once in a while, and this Ritz is a quiet oasis in Philly's often-noisy restaurant and nightlife scene. The Rotunda's grand dome sets the tone. Take a seat and watch for celebrities; you're sure to see at least a senator or two, if not a presidential hopeful, sipping their martinis right down to the blue-cheese-stuffed olives.

Rouge
205 South 18th Street
(215) 732-6622
You don't have to be beautiful to be among the weekend crowd in this tiny French bistro that overlooks Rittenhouse Square, but it does seem that the best-dressed, best-looking Philadelphians all converge here. If you're lucky enough to get a table, the people-watching is great; most local media celebrities and power brokers stop in. The food isn't bad, either: *GQ* named its signature sandwich the "Best Cheeseburger in America" in July 2005.

Standard Tap
901 North Second Street
(215) 238-0630
www.standardtap.com
There is a disappearing breed known as the "bar bar," threatened to extinction by the proliferation of fern bars and stiletto bars—but not if the folks at Standard Tap have anything to say about it. Anchoring the emerging-artsy neighborhood of Northern Liberties, this pub offers a great jukebox, an even better beer selection, and a respectable if slightly ambitious menu. The chicken pot pie will win you over. On Wednesday you can hear live music with no cover charge.

Suede Lounge
120 Market Street
(215) 923–5570
www.suedeloungephilly.com
Furnished with chandeliers, suede lounges and ottomans, a granite bar, and a waterfall wall, this "earth-and-water"-inspired club is upscale and sophisticated, but still offers drink specials ($4.00 Smirnoff Friday, two-for-one drinks Saturday from 9:00 to 11:00 P.M.). Bottle service is available in the VIP Lounge, where the suede is celery green and the carpeting is shag. Couches rim the bar, so there's plenty of seating.

Swann Lounge
Four Seasons Hotel
18th Street and Ben Franklin Parkway
(215) 963–1500
www.fourseasons.com
When you're out to impress a date, this is where you come for dessert and an after-dinner drink. With smooth, marble-topped tables, salmon- and celadon-toned fabrics and an antique baby grand in the corner, the ambience is perfect for romance or sealing a business deal. The cognac and Scotch selection is said to be one of the best in the city. Celebrity-spotting is almost a guarantee at the Swann Lounge, so prepare to be cool.

Tequila's Bar at Los Catrines
1602 Locust Street
(215) 546–0181
www.tequilasphilly.com
With more than 75 tequilas and major emphasis on tequila education, it's no wonder that this bar's name derives from *catrin* a Mexican term used to mock pretentious elegance. Not that Tequila's isn't classy; just steps off the Avenue of the Arts, the sedate marble and carved-wood fireplace in the bar conveys sophistication without snootiness. That space is juxtaposed with the colorful dining room, brilliantly hued baths and "Day of the Dead" entryway, adding up to plenty of personality to go with your gold tequilas.

DANCE CLUBS

32°
16 South Second Street
(215) 627–3132
www.32lounge.com
If 32° were any hotter, it would melt the shot glasses at the bar—and I mean that literally. At this luxe, upstairs bottle-service lounge, premium cocktails and chilled shots are served in glasses made of solid ice. Like other bottle-service clubs, 32° sells bottles of vodka for $200-plus, but at this club the owners at least show a little mercy: They rent personal lockers to clients, who use them to stash their unfinished bottles until their next visit. And if you needed one more clever European twist, you can pay for your drinks here with cash, credit cards—or euros.

Blue Bell Inn
601 Skippack Pike, Blue Bell
(215) 646–2010
www.bluebellinn.com
It's a bit on the kitschy side, but fans who want to dance to Sinatra's greatest hits pack the Blue Bell Inn on weekends. Not all the patrons are oldies, either; many are obviously in their 30s—but this inn's history predates any of its current regulars. First opened in 1743 as the White House Inn, its first and most famous regular was George Washington. More than 50 years later, the name changed to the Blue Bell, and an enormous blue bell, still in place today, was hung on the front door so that thirsty customers who couldn't read would know they were in the right place.

Brasil's
112 Chestnut Street
(215) 413–7000
Order yourself a tall *bebida* and head to this Brazilian nightclub that features jazz, Latin, and Caribbean music—preferably on Wednesday nights, when for $5.00 you can perfect your mambo and samba moves with a dance teacher. The dance floor is upstairs; Thursday is Caribbean night—that's when you can hear the latest

Reggaetone—or come Wednesday for Latin night. If you're a clumsy dancer, blame it on the bossa nova.

Five Spot
5 South Bank Street
(215) 574-0070
www.thefivespot.com

You'll find a bit of everything at this retro dance club: big band music, Latin, swing, hip-hop, reggae—even the occasional appearance by stars the caliber of India.Arie. Check the Web site for a schedule of theme nights, including avant-jazz and swing. Sunday is for the alternative gay crowd. If you get tired of people-watching, help yourself to sweets and board games in the "Candyland" section. Somehow, the beaded curtains and electric fireplace make it all work.

Fluid
613 South Fourth Street
(215) 629-3686
www.fluidnightclub.com

This Old City club is dark and intimate, and you'll hear some of the city's best underground music at Fluid—new electronica, funk, jungle, and hip-hop. Guest DJs make music every weekend; some of the more popular are Cash Money, Prince Paul, Sneak, and Tony Touch. There's a cover charge, but ladies get in free before 11:00 P.M. and pay $7.00 after.

Khyber
56 South Second Street
(215) 238-5888
www.thekhyber.com

"Destroy your liver!" commands the Khyber's Web site, promoting its Sunday "open bar" for $10. That might be the club's best drink special, but there are others, including $1.00 beers every night until 11:00 P.M. in the upstairs bar. This club is known for booking indie bands before they become national names; favorites include Hellshaven, Headkick Rodeo, and Sleepwalkers Union. Need more evidence that this is a cool place? Khyber is the official host of the Philadelphia Rock

Paper Scissors City League Tournament. To learn how to compete, go to www.rpscityleague.com.

Rex's Bar & Entertainment
344 West Gay Street, West Chester
(610) 696-7769
www.rexsbar.com

Depending on the night of the week, you can dance to almost anything at Rex's, from punk to reggae. Dating back to the 1930s, Rex's has hosted the biggest names, including Bruce Springsteen, Tom Petty, and George Thoroughgood. This bar is totally edgy, so bring your attitude with you.

Transit
600 Spring Garden Street
(267) 258-1321
www.transitnightclub.com

If you've ever wanted to get inside one of those grand Spring Garden row houses, Transit is your chance. The club retained much of the building's architectural features, including plaster ornamentation, and they enhance the "urban re-use chic" of the place. You can rent the VVIP suite overlooking the dance floor, or just relax at the vodka bar in the Modpod. Drink specials include "$2.00 Tuesdays."

JAZZ AND BLUES CLUBS

Chris's Jazz Cafe
1421 Sansom Street
(215) 568-3131
www.chrisjazzcafe.com

Ask Philadelphians where you can hear great jazz in an intimate club, and they'll send you to Chris's Jazz Cafe every time. Located in Old City near the Avenue of the Arts, Chris's was named the "Best Casual Jazz Venue" by *Philadelphia* magazine—and this place is definitely casual, down to the grilled cheese sandwiches on the lunch menu. Audience favorites include the Pete Paulsen Quartet, Puzzlebox, the Lars Halle Jazz Orchestra, and guitarist Jimmy Bruno. Come for "$2.00

Tuesday," when you'll pay just a two-spot for lagers, well drinks, appetizers, and cover charge.

Natalie's Lounge
4003 Market Street
(215) 222-5162
This cool spot is Philly's original jazz venue, literally: at 60-plus years, it's the longest-operating jazz house in the city. It's all about the music at Natalie's—no food is served, just the finest jazz, from both amateur and professional performers, in the region, including Latin, downtown jazz, all-female bands—the full range. The best time to come is Saturday night, when drummer Lucky Thompson, who has played with both Big Mama Thornton and Patti LaBelle, hosts a nine-hour show. The music begins at 4:00 P.M.

Ortlieb's Jazzhaus
847 North Third Street
(215) 922-1035
http://ortliebsjazzhaus.com
When Ortlieb's brewery shut down after more than a century, its old lunchroom became the Jazzhaus, named the city's best jazz club by *Details* magazine and awarded multiple "Best of Philly" honors by *Philadelphia* magazine. Regulars include drummer Mickey Roker, who played for years with Dizzy Gillespie's band, and sax master Bootsie Barnes and his Organ Trio. Food here is a blend of Cajun and traditional American.

Warmdaddy's
4 South Front Street
(215) 627-2500
www.warmdaddys.com
At press time, this blues club was temporarily closed; it was moving from Old City to South Columbus Boulevard. Warmdaddy's is the "sister club" to Zanzibar Blue and serves up spicy Creole and Cajun fare along with its traditional Mississippi, Delta, and Chicago blues. Call or watch the Web site for news of relocation and re-opening.

One of the city's most popular jazz "clubs" is the outdoor martini bar at the Philadelphia Museum of Art. Your $10.00 museum ticket admits you to the Friday night jazz cabaret and gives you $2.00 off your first drink. You can enjoy the great skyline view from the portico or wander into the Great Stair Hall with 400 of your closest friends (26th Street and the Ben Franklin Parkway, 215-763-8100; www.philamuseum.org).

World Café Live
3025 Walnut Street
(215) 222-1400
www.worldcafelive.com
Once a cavernous, 40,000-square-foot factory building, World Café Live was converted to a live music center that not only hosts performances, but also enhances the experience for performers as well, for contemporary rock, jazz, world, and folk artists. The three-tiered, downstairs music hall seats 300 as a bistro and holds 650 for standing-room-only concerts, while Upstairs Live, a street-level cafe, seats 100. Both levels are smoke-free and provide full food and beverage service. Opened in late 2005, the Art Deco facility in University City also houses a broadcast studio.

Zanzibar Blue
200 South Broad Street
(215) 732-5200
www.zanzibarblue.com
Located in the historic Bellevue on the Avenue of the Arts, Zanzibar Blue is Philadelphia's only self-proclaimed "upscale jazz club and restaurant," and it has a mission: to make jazz accessible for everyone. Seven nights a week and during Sunday brunch, live jazz is performed, often with no cover charge, and the featured talents often are national acts. At any given time, look for familiar names such as Jimmy Scott, Kenny Rankin, Arturo Sandoval, and Maynard Ferguson to appear on the monthly calendar. Zanzibar's menu

> Will wonders of the Internet never cease? The latest is www.philly karaoke.com, a clearinghouse of karaoke information for the Greater Philadelphia area. Here you will find details about the next "Bucks County Idol" competition, karaoke-related news (such as when rock-and-roll pioneer Chuck Berry sued karaoke music distributors, claiming they sold sing-alongs of his hits without paying royalties or obtaining licenses), a karaoke forum, karaoke podcasts, and even "Philly Karaoke Personals."

of traditional shrimp gumbo, garlic black mussels, delta catfish, and other southern specialties only makes the jazz sound better.

COMEDY CLUBS

Comedy Cabaret
Best Western Hotel
11580 Roosevelt Boulevard
(215) 676–JOKE
www.philadelphia-phl.com/39077.html
This hotel bar takes on a different spin every Wednesday at 8:30 P.M., when amateur jokesters step up to the Open Mic with a four-minute routine. Just be sure you're there an hour early to register. On Friday and Saturday, professional comics take over.

ComedySportz
At the Playground
2030 Sansom Street
(215) 98L-AUGH
www.comedysportzphilly.com
Laughs or athletic competition? You get both at this fast-paced comedy venue, complete with a referee who calls fouls and keeps the action racing ahead. Two teams of "act-letes" compete in this interactive entertainment that always involves the audience, and it's clean family fun. ComedySportz also will come to you; the troupe has customized their routines for

companies including Sunoco, Mattel Toys, Xerox, Procter & Gamble, IBM, Apple Computers, and Tropicana. They'll do team-building comedy workshops for your employees, and even "get your sense of humor back in shape" at their ComedySportz College.

Laff House
221 South Street
(215) 440–4242 (HAHA)
www.laffhouse.com
For classic stand-up routines by touring comics, Laff House is the place. You'll see names that will be familiar to fans of comedy clubs, including Mark Theabold, Coco Brown, and Shaun Jones, performing in a smoke-free showroom. A "lite" menu is offered—and if you want to try your hand at stand-up comedy, the last Wednesday of every month is Laff House's Open Mic night. You won't get 15 minutes of fame, but they'll give you five to seven minutes.

Le Cabaret Mélange, L'Etage
Sixth and Bainbridge Streets
(215) 592-0656
www.creperie-beaumonde.com
Upstairs from the Creperie Beaumonde (home of Philly's most succulent crepes for any meal), is L'Etage, every Thursday an intimate cabaret featuring comedy and other acts. The tin ceiling and rich mahogany woodwork help set the tone that takes you back to the era of the true French bistro. Savory buckwheat crepes make a tasteful accompaniment to the evening's entertainment, just a block (but a world away) from the funky madness of South Street.

KARAOKE

Fergie's Pub
1214 Sansom Street
(215) 928-8118
www.fergies.com
One of several classic Irish pubs in Philly that hosts karaoke, Fergie's offers a warm, wood decor, hot roast beef, and one of

the friendliest crowds in Center City. Monday is Open Mic night, starting at 9:00 P.M. On Thursday the fun takes a different twist with "Quizo," open trivia contests with themes ranging from "Bad Movies" to Shakespeare. Not sure how well you would do at Quizo? Go to Fergie's Web site and take the sample quiz online.

McGillin's
1310 Drury Street
(215) 735-5562
www.mcgillins.com
Tucked into a tiny street in Center City, this historic tavern (circa 1860) claims to be the oldest bar in the city. Since before the Civil War, McGillin's has been serving celebrities of the day, from Tennessee Williams to Robin Williams, and Ethel Barrymore to Ethel Merman. Karaoke starts at 10:00 P.M. every Friday night; hunker down in a dark booth and enjoy a "McGillin's Bloody Mary" with your music: a secret-recipe drink served with olives and a shooter of Miller Light.

Mill Creek Tavern
4200 Chester Avenue
(215) 222-9194
www.millcreektavernphilly.com
Located in the heart of University City, Mill Creek Tavern is set in a "remuddled" century home. Monday nights from 8:00 to 10:00 P.M. are karaoke night, and with 25-cent pints and $1.00 pitchers of beer, it's a great deal for the college crowd. Some 20 taps are drawn; Mill Creek also offers a happy hour, and a late-night drink special after 10:00 P.M., with $2.50 drinks and bottled beers and $6.00 pitchers.

Pontiac Grille
304 South Street
(215) 925-4053
www.pontiacgrille.com
As a bar, the Pontiac has been open since the 1930s, but only began showcasing musical talent in 1975—and what talent has passed through here: Creed, the Indigo Girls, Pere Ubu, Dwight Yoakum, Bo Diddley, the Smashing Pumpkins, and

Courtney Love, just to name a few. Karaoke here is of the punk rock variety, with protein: Pontiac Grille recently opened a full-service steakhouse on the premises.

SPORTS BARS

Bayou Bar & Grille
4245 Main Street, Manayunk
(215) 482-2560
www.bayoubar.com
If 16 TVs are enough for you, then the Bayou Bar is your place for tracking sports action. The bar has three bars on two floors and drink specials most hours. In warmer months, a covered outdoor deck offers respite from TV sports. Popular with the after-work crowd, Bayou Bar has been awarded "Best of Philly" by *Philadelphia* magazine for its spicy buffalo wings, and in 2004 was named Philly's best sports bar by ESPN.com. Come for Wild Wednesday, Thirsty Thursday, Sporty Saturday, or to play in the darts league on Sunday nights.

Buffalo Billiards
118 Chestnut Street
(215) 574-7665
www.buffalobilliards.com
Named the "Best Bar in Old City," Buffalo Billiards is Center City's first pool hall—partly, the award reads, for being one of the "precious few drinking holes near the east end of Market Street that are devoid of muscle-shirted bouncers, Eurotrash, and wannabe VIPs." Ouch. Sounds good to us, with 10 pool tables on two floors, three dart boards, large screen TVs, and happy-hour specials including $3.00 well drinks and half-price appetizers. Even non-sports fans will be comfy here, in four couch-seating areas.

Chickie's & Pete's Cafe
4010 Robbins Avenue
(215) 338-3060
www.chickiesandpetes.com
This small chain of sports bars (three locations) airs sports games seven nights a

week; at this location—the original—two floors and multiple TVs keep everyone tuned to the games. Mussels, cutlet sandwiches, and Old Bay-coated crab fries are the specialties. On game days, flag down the "Taxi Crab" for a free ride to the ballpark. If you prefer a bar within walking distance of the game, head to the South Philly location (1526 Packer Avenue, 215-218-0500).

Drake Tavern
304 Old York Road, Jenkintown
(215) 884-8900
www.draketavern.com

Oversize flat-screen TVs provide game action at Drake's, but if you can't make it to the bar, sign up for the online newsletter. On Sunday mornings, Drake's serves one of the heartiest Irish breakfasts anywhere, including Irish potato cakes and a $2.00 make-your-own Bloody Mary. Curbside takeout is available for dinner, or you can eat on the patio in summer.

J.D. McGillicuddy's
2626 County Line Road, Ardmore
(610) 658-2626
www.jdmcgillicuddys.com

Main Line folks want to watch the games, too, and there's no better place than at McGillicuddy's. Monday you can play Texas Hold 'Em while you watch Monday Night Football, drink $2.00 Yuengling, and eat at the free buffet. Wednesday is "Steak & Cake Nite" ($19.95 filet mignon and crab cake dinner) during Open Mic, and Sunday is for watching the Eagles. On Sunday night, compete for prizes during Quizzo tourneys.

Jon's Bar and Grille
606 South Third Street
(215) 592-1390
www.jonsbarandgrille.com

We always thought the best reason to go to Jon's was because its front patio was so inviting—a great place to take a break from South Street shopping. Now we learn that Jon's is not only one of the neighborhood's most popular sports bars,

but also that Larry Fine of the Three Stooges was born in this building. Naturally, you can buy souvenir T-shirts sporting Larry's mug—just don't poke anyone in the eyes on the way to your table.

Mooney's Pub
2341 South Fourth Street
(215) 463-9781
www.mooneyspub.net

Only a five-minute drive from the Sports Complex, Mooney's is a handy place to celebrate after a Flyers' or Sixers' game—or, you can stay and watch it on one of the pub's three 42-inch HD plasma screen TVs. These guys are into it; you can download the Eagles' fight song from the Mooney's Web site, and if you want a dose of Mummers as backdrop, you can download "Oh, Dem Golden Slippers." Schedules for Eagles' and Phillies' games are posted on the site as well, along with those of the '76ers (pro basketball), Flyers (NHL hockey), and other pro teams. Mooney's also sponsors dart tourneys.

Paddy Whacks Irish Sports Pub
9241-43 Roosevelt Boulevard
(215) 464-7544
www.paddywhackspub.com

Paddy Whacks is one of Philly's relatively newer Irish pubs, opened in May 2004. Already, though, it's a favorite of sports fans who line the bar to watch games on eight TVs, including five digital flat screens, especially during football season. Tuesday through Thursday, local bands play live, and a DJ takes over on weekend nights. The Irish food, shepherd's pie or fish and chips, goes down easily on Sunday when the pub hosts Irish Jam Sessions.

Philadium Tavern
1631 Packer Avenue
(215) 271-5220

No pretense at this old-style sports bar—when the Phillies lose, these guys cry in their beer. There's a kind of comfort in the old, darkened wood and the oval bar; it sets the tone for the sports-memorabilia decor. The menu is as real as the ambience:

burgers, cheesesteaks, roast beef. Unlike some sports bars, this one seems to get busier when the home teams are losing, but it's always crowded at game time and after.

Phil's Tavern
931 West Butler Pike, Ambler
(215) 643-5664
Phil's does double-duty as a sports bar and family restaurant, so this converted house always seems to be packed. The sports bar side—where kids are welcome—specializes in beer, wings, and video games along with multiple TVs for game-watching. For bigger appetites, the cheesesteak sandwiches are enormous. On Monday, wings are 20 cents each.

GAY CLUBS

Bob and Barbara's
1509 South Street
(215) 545-4511
One of the city's true multicultural bars, Bob and Barbara's boasts Philadelphia's longest-running drag show, and you can catch it every Thursday night. Juxtapose that scene with above-Broad-Street regulars during the day, and table tennis showdowns every Tuesday. Drinks are cheap ($3.00 specials some nights) and no fees are charged for table tennis tables. Three nights a week, hear music by local favorite Nate Wiley and the Crowd Pleasers.

Club Libations
231 South Broad Street
Open only on Friday and Saturday evenings, Club Libations is the city's most exclusive club for women of color. It's an upstairs dance club and, because it's upscale, discreet, and open for such limited hours, it's always crowded.

Elevate, at Key West
207 South Juniper Street
(215) 545-1578
www.elevatephilly.com
Key West is one of the city's most open,

If you're more interested in the making of brewski than drinking it, you'll want to visit the Yards Brewing Company, the only surviving brewery within Philadelphia's city limits. Tours are free, and no food is served—but after the tour, you can stop into the tasting room and sample any beer in their line (2439 Amer Street, 215-634-2600; www.yardsbrewing.com).

relaxed, and hip gay-friendly bars, and every fourth Saturday is dedicated to lesbians and their friends. For a $5.00 cover, the young and trendy can enjoy $2.00 pints after 10:00 P.M., two bars, two pool tables, and a busy dance floor.

Girl, at Sal's Restaurant
200 South 12th Street
(215) 574-2110
www.phillygirlparty.com
Like Elevate, Girl is a monthly "circuit party," this one a popular dance party at Sal's. Cover is only $5.00 to join the crowd, many of whom are there from Philly's artist community. Drink specials change every month.

Pure Party Girl First Friday
1221 St. James Street
(215) 735-5772
www.ladies2000.com
What sets apart this monthly lesbian party is its home in Pure, a gay after-hours club. Every first Saturday, the multi-level club opens the Pink Lounge to women-only for karaoke and $2.00 pink drinks from 9:00 to 11:00 P.M. Then the louder music and dancing takes over until the wee hours. Cover charge is $8.00.

Sisters Nightclub
1320 Chancellor Street
(215) 735-0735
www.sistersnightclub.com
Sisters is Philly's largest lesbian club, so its customers drive in from all across the region. If you didn't know better, you

For the best overview of what's happening on the gay scene when you visit Philadelphia, go to www.phillygay calendar.com. This comprehensive Web site offers local, national, and international news of interest to gays and lesbians, plus listings for events, organizations, ads for roommates, and even an online message board.

might mistake it for a sports bar, with its 50-inch TV, 7-foot big screen, and pool tables. Three bars and a full-service restaurant serve patrons in the recently renovated space, along with a lower-level game room, Sunday brunch buffet, and popular DJ dancing. Thursday is the hottest night. Cover charge ranges from $7.00 to $10.00, depending on what's offered that night.

Woody's Bar
202 South 13th Street
(215) 545-1893
www.woodysbar.com
This mostly male gay disco offers a variety of bar experiences, including the "Main Bar," a more intimate Pub Room, a Coffee Bar, and, on the second floor, a dance bar. The nightly themes are just as diverse: Latin night, "La Triviata" quiz night, Karaoke night, Country Two-Step dance lessons, and a DJ dance party. Check the calendar online.

MOVIES/THEATERS

The Bridge: Cinema de Lux Theater
40th and Walnut Streets
(215) 386-3300
www.thebridgecinema.com
The Bridge is what we wish all theaters were—a total evening experience. This movie palace has assigned seating and offers a lounge, restaurant, cappuccino bar, free wireless Internet access, and a media room for local films and shorts,

along with six screens for viewing features. What's more, you can park free with a validated ticket at the garage across the street. With all the competition from view-at-home mail-order movie services, you'd think more theaters would get smart and lure us with such great value!

Film at the Prince
1412 Chestnut Street
(215) 569-9700
www.princemusictheater.org
On selected evenings, this 450-seat stage theater becomes a movie house, showing classics such as *Casablanca* on a 35-mm screen with Dolby Digital Sound. There's a monthly series for children, as well as the monthly "Chumley & Carlotta's" series featuring "good-natured raunchiness." Check the Web site for dates; admission is $8.50; $7.00 for students and seniors, and $5.00 for kids 12 and under.

Marathon on the Square
1839 Spruce Street
(215) 731-0800
www.marathongrill.com
Most evenings, it's a Rittenhouse Square eatery, but on Wednesday the Marathon Grill becomes a movie theater. Several area restaurants offer "movie nights" (Twenty Manning, North Third), and we think it's a great mid-week treat—grab a burger, sip your Tanqueray and tonic, and watch a classic or funny flick.

Movie Mondays at the Trocadero
1004 Arch Street
(215) 922-LIVE
www.thetroc.com
At some point in the venerable Trocadero Theatre's 120-year history, it was a movie house. In fact, the original, full-size screen still hangs behind the stage, and is being put to good use again on Movie Mondays. Admission is only $3.00 and the bar is open, so you can sip a cocktail while you watch a classic flick from the comfort of an old-fashioned upholstered theater seat.

Ritz Theaters
Ritz Five, 214 Walnut Street,
(215) 440–1184
Ritz East, 25 South Second Street,
(215) 925–2501
Ritz at the Bourse,
Fourth and Ranstead Streets,
(215) 440–1181
www.ritzfilmbill.com
With three Ritz Theaters in the Historic
District, and 12 screens between them, foreign and indie films are always accessible
in Center City. If you enjoy watching
movies that depict stories "the way life is
lived," according to one local writer, then
these venues in historic buildings, all with
wide seats and full-size screens, are for
you, and all are in walking distance of Historic District hotels.

WINE BARS

Il Bar
Penn's View Hotel
14 North Front Street
(215) 922–7800
Only part of the elegance here is in the
setting, with mind-arresting *trompe l'oeil*

murals, plush seating, and luxurious win-
dow treatments. The other elegance is in
the wine. One look at the 120-bottle wine
keeper—one of the largest in the country—tells you that this sommelier takes his
wine seriously. The selection is often
regarded as the best in Philadelphia; they
rotate daily and are sold in two sizes, as
well as in flights. Just to be sure no customer is cheated in terms of quality, the
bartenders toss the first pour of the day
from each bottle.

Swanky Bubbles
10 South Front Street
(215) 928–1200
www.swankybubbles.com
Since it's the city's only champagne bar,
connoisseurs of the bubbly always make it
a point to stop here when they visit Philly.
It's also a popular sushi stop for the after-
work crowd (dress code is business
casual), and the interior suits champagne's elegant image, with plush blue
velvet seating and a bar area inspired by
the dream sequence in *The Nutcracker.* If
you're splurging, you can pop a bottle of
Dom Perignon for $500, but you don't
have to spend that much to enjoy the
place: A Kir Royale is just $7.00.

SHOPPING

History may be what drives tourism in Philadelphia, but the city's great stores and boutiques have made it a shopping destination as well. From contemporary and fine art to fashion-forward clothing, Philly's shops are at the front edge of every emerging trend. And one of the most satisfying aspects of shopping here is that Pennsylvania charges no sales tax on clothes! Those extra dollars in your pocket mean even more savings.

Most of the shops included here are in the core city because most visitors to Philadelphia will do their shopping in town—and that encompasses Center City's unique shopping districts: Antique Row along Pine Street (profiled in the Antiques chapter), Jewelers Row, Rittenhouse Row, Fabric Row, South Philly, and South Street (see Close-Up, page 77).

Since shoppers usually plan a day of "retail therapy" in one or two geographic areas, that's how we've organized this chapter. The Philadelphia section is divided into two parts: first Center City, then, because it's an 8-mile drive, Manayunk. Within Center City, we've grouped shops by theme, including Beauty/Health/Spas, Electronics/Gadgets, Gift Shops, Pet Stores, Stationery Shops, and a dozen other types. Since Manayunk shopping all happens along one commercial corridor, it made more sense to simply alphabetize those stores.

We've omitted several shopping categories, for the most part, because they were covered in other chapters: Some of the best antiques shops along Antique Row, for instance, appear in the Antiques chapter. Many of our favorite galleries were included in the Arts chapter, and you will find toy stores and children's clothing boutiques in the Kidstuff chapter. Still, a considerable number of quality shops in those categories didn't make it into those chapters, so we've included some of them here.

Once you get to Philly, you'll hear people mention a handful of shopping destinations—malls and shopping centers—that you should know about:

- **The Bellevue** (200 South Broad Street, 215-875-8350; www.bellevuephiladelphia .com). On the first two floors of the complex where the Park Hyatt Hotel and top-shelf restaurants such as The Palm, Founders, and Zanzibar Blue are located, you'll find high-end boutiques such as Polo Ralph Lauren, Tiffany & Co., Nicole Miller, Origins, and Williams-Sonoma.
- **The Bourse Food Court and Specialty Shops** (111 South Independence Mall, 215-625-0300; www.bourse-pa.com). When it first opened, this restored Victorian stock exchange building housed plenty of small stores and several good restaurants. Then it hit a down-cycle and seemed abandoned, but once again it's near the top end of the curve. A stylish food court makes it a busy place at lunchtime; you'll also see boutiques, souvenir shops, and a movie theater.
- **The Gallery at Market East** (Ninth and Market Streets, 215-625-4962; www.galleryatmarketeast.com). This four-story city mall has seen better days; where Macy's once anchored its western end is now a Kmart. The best part of the mall is good old Strawbridge's, the venerable department store anchoring the eastern end of the mall. Still, if you need a pair of comfy walking shoes, or brought the wrong clothing on vacation, the Gallery is a handy place to pick up whatever you need, with 130 stores and food stops.
- **King of Prussia Mall** (160 North Gulph Road, King of Prussia, 610-265-5727; www.kingofprussiamall.com). You may have heard of this royal mall; after all, it is the second-largest shopping center in the country, with more than 450 stores

and a 126-acre parking lot. King of Prussia offers shopping for every budget, from Neiman Marcus, Hermès, and Gianni Versace to chain drugstores. Obviously, if you're heading to this mall, set aside an entire day.

• **The Shops at Liberty Place** (1625 Chestnut Street, 215–851–9055; www.shops atliberty.com). We admit it; this is our favorite shopping spot. The building itself is a historical footnote: It was the first to inch higher than the statue of Ben Franklin on top of City Hall, inspiring the rest of the city to follow suit and create a skyline. The two lower floors are a shopping mall-in-the-round—fairly small, with just 60 stores, but designed with ambience and comfort. Stores include Nine West, Coach, Ann Taylor Loft, and a list of more affordable shops. Liberty Place, too, has been challenged some years with its share of vacant spaces, but we love the place anyway. Stop here when you're exploring Rittenhouse Row.

• **The Shops at Penn and Sansom Commons** (34th and Walnut Streets/Shops at Penn; 36th and Sansom Streets/ Sansom Commons, 215–573–5290). If you're shopping for a student, this is where you'll find dozens of stores catering to their tastes, since it's so near the University of Pennsylvania. Urban Outfitters, the Gap, and other stores targeting high school and college students are clustered here.

CENTER CITY

Beauty/Health/Spas

Blue Mercury Apothecary & Spa
1707 Walnut Street
(215) 569–3100
Set in a restored 19th-century building, Blue Mercury specializes in hard-to-find, upscale skin and hair care products. If a celebrity is using it, chances are it's one of the 50-plus trendy lines carried by this shop.

Duross & Langel
1218 Locust Street
(215) 735–7075
Every publication in town is singing the praises of this purveyor of all-natural bath and body products. Their Chuck Soaps come in unusual scents, such as pumpkin-oatmeal-spice, and we found a wide selection of unusual balms and oils for massaging and soothing sore muscles.

Groom
1315 Walnut Street, Suite 119
(215) 545–5070
This barbershop is old-school, down to the Al Jolson background music. A cut and shave costs only $25 at this place; look for the cool Art Deco façade.

International Salon
1714 Sansom Street
(215) 563–1141
All of a sudden, your eyebrows look raggedy. Never fear; no appointments are needed at this salon, where a wax costs $8.00. Your brows will be freshly arched and tidy in no time.

Koresh School of Dance
2020 Chestnut Street
(215) 751–0959
www.koreshdance.org
You couldn't find better exercise for toning one's core than belly dancing, and the thighs and arms get attention, too. At $13 per class, visitors to Philly can try out this surprisingly vigorous workout with other beginners; classes are held once a week.

Rescue Rittenhouse Spa Lounge
255 South 17th Street
(215) 772–2766
If you're looking for a spa retreat in the middle of the city, Rescue is the place. Stop first at the "tea bar" for a calming drink, then stay mellow at a candlelit pedicure station. Our favorite treatment is the "Zoom Groom"—a manicure, pedicure, and facial, all at the same time. That is the definition of a sensual afternoon.

School of Hard Knox
112 Chestnut Street
(215) 629-5590
This is where the guy who wants guy-pampering comes for a haircut. Customers at this elegant shop are trimmed while they watch a game on 50-inch plasma-screen TVs. The seating is plush; it's easy to settle in here.

Titus Medical Spa
400 Walnut Street
(215) 413-3738
Forget the Brazilian wax—that's so 1990s—and consider splurging on a French bikini wax instead. We can't imagine a more sensitive (translation: painful) hair removal, but the owner of Titus once worked as an assistant to plastic surgeons, so she is adept. We hear she hasn't lost anyone on the table yet.

Books/Comic Books/Posters

AIA Bookstore and Design Center
117 South 17th Street
(215) 569-3188
www.aiaphila.org
One of the most delightful bookstores anywhere, AIA is the retail arm of the local American Institute of Architects. Jewelry, cards, decorative items—all with a design connection—are sold along with books. Almost any architectural reference is here, including the acclaimed three-volume *Phaidon Design Classics* for $175.

Gift Shops

Manor Home and Gift
210 South 17th Street
(215) 732-1030
www.manorhg.com
Think of Manor Home if you're visiting Philadelphia for a wedding. Here you will find hand-painted china, Italian and

Looking for the city's premier cigar store? Smokers in the know will direct you to the Black Cat Cigar Co. (1518 Sansom Street, 215-563-9850), where you can choose from more than 2,000 kinds of cigars, all at wholesale prices. Black Cat also stocks men's shaving paraphernalia and fragrances.

French place settings, and a large collection of unusual crystal and flatware. European linens and quality vintage items, found at estate sales, also are on display.

Me & Blue
311 Market Street, 2nd floor
(215) 629-2347
www.meandblue.com
You can find pearls, linens, and unique vintage pieces here, but what makes us drool at Me & Blue are the Harvey's seatbelt bags. Made of genuine seatbelts woven together, the bags get pricier by the month, so if you're thinking of nabbing one, do it now.

Simply Cottage
8430 Germantown Avenue
(215) 242-8660
www.simplycottage.com
You can visit the Simply Gift or Simply Home sections of the store; we love to browse in Simply Baby, where luxury rules. The hand-embroidered bed linens, custom-painted room accessories, and handmade, itty-bitty bibs are just precious.

Spirit of the Artist
1022 Pine Street
(215) 627-8801
www.sotagifts.com
We dare you to walk out of this shop empty handed. Contemporary crafts of wood, glass, and ceramics cover the tables and walls; from garden art to jewelry, musical instruments, wall decor, and even cooking utensils, this is a great place to find one-of-a-kind gifts or to treat yourself.

If you want to keep shopping but need a break from the city, head to Peddler's Village in Bucks County (U.S. Route 202 and Route 263, Lahaska, 215-794-4000; www.peddlersvillage.com). More than 70 shops and eight restaurants, all in a Victorian-inspired complex, make for a full shopping day. Consider spending the night at the on-site Golden Plough Inn (215-794-4063); the rooms are spacious and done in a traditional decor.

Town Home
126 South 19th Street
(215) 972-5100
www.townhomephila.com
Anyone could find beautiful items here to "chic up" their home or apartment, and much of it is affordable. From mosaic serving platters to handblown glassware, it's all quietly elegant.

Home and Garden Shops, Florists

Anthropologie
1801 Walnut Street
(215) 568-2114
Yes, it's a chain, but Philadelphia-area Anthropologies were among the first—and this Rittenhouse Square store, housed in a stone mansion, is enhanced by its gorgeous setting. For unusual gifts and decorative home and garden items from around the world, you can't go wrong at Anthropologie.

Evantine Design
The Rittenhouse Hotel
210 West Rittenhouse Square
(215) 790-2576
Beautiful, beautiful flowers in *très*-elegant arrangements. It's fitting that Evantine is located in the posh Rittenhouse. You can also find unusual vases, candles, and other home accessories here.

Fante's Kitchen Wares Shop
Italian Market
1006 South Ninth Street
(215) 922-5557
www.fantes.com
What a great spot for a cookware store—first you absorb the sights and smells of the cheeses, pastries, and meats throughout the Market, then you want to go home and cook something scrumptious. Open since 1906, Fante's is one of the oldest kitchenware shops in the country.

Frugal Frames
1234 Pine Street
(215) 772-1150
Looking for a frame job, but cash flow is at a standstill? Frugal Frames prides itself on its no-frills operation that means savings for its loyal customers—who include local professional sports stars and movie set designers.

IKEA
2006 South Columbus Boulevard
(215) 551-4532
www.ikea.com
No more chain stores, we promise—but how not to include Philly's new IKEA? Truly, Philadelphia has arrived, with 310,000 square feet of inexpensive beige furnishings and more meatballs than South Philly. If you don't have an IKEA in your area, stop here when you visit Philly—but give yourself a few hours.

Linu
1036 Pine Street
(215) 206-8547
www.linuboutique.com
This is no ordinary linen shop. The owner was born in Latvia and buys hand-woven table linens from her native land, then creates flowing wall coverings, hand-sewn tablecloths, and other delicate items for her store.

Matthew Izzo Shop
928 Pine Street
(215) 922-2570
Izzo is one of Philadelphia's hottest young

South Street, "Where All the Hippies Meet"

In its earliest days, South Street was a marketplace—of goods and of ideas—where produce, fish, fabrics, and every imaginable item produced and used by colonists could be bought and sold. Before 1750 it was the southern boundary of Philadelphia and was called New Market, to distinguish it from the Market Street trading center.

Some say that South Street isn't so different today. It's still a corridor of trend-setting commerce, where politics are debated and music is made. It's Philly's edgy, unconventional neighborhood, lined with bookstores, art galleries, sidewalk cafes, import shops, music studios, tattoo parlors, coffeehouses, restaurants, and almost 40 bars—nearly 300 businesses in all.

The range of retail here is amazing. There is Gargoyles (512 South Third Street, 215-629-1700), where you'll actually find a few gargoyles lurking among the displays of architectural pieces—mantels, carousel horses, stained-glass windows, archways, and more. Another favorite is American Pie (718 South Street, 215-923-5333; www.americanpiecrafts.com), with handmade decorative pieces and jewelry—"nice things for nice people." While you're in an artsy mood, stop into the Aphrodite Gallery (704 South Fifth Street, 215-829-4986; www.passional.net)—a departure from American Pie, to say the least; at Aphrodite the art is about eroticism.

Most South Street shops stay open into the evening, so they won't welcome their first customers until 11:00 A.M. or later. The best idea is to have an early lunch somewhere, then plan on spending the rest of the day strolling South Street between Second and Seventh Streets, and the numbered cross streets within a block or so of South. You can browse thousands of posters and art prints in Beyond the Wall (415 South Street, 215-238-1722; www.beyondthewall philadelphia.com), or find a good book on meditation or feng shui in Garland of Letters (527 South Street, 215-923-5946).

Amateur (or professional) magicians will enjoy browsing in Hocus Pocus (523 South Fourth Street, 215-629-8300), while your Wiccan friends will find books and supplies in Morgan's Cauldron (509 South Sixth Street, 215-923-5264; www.morganscauldron.com). If you're interested in Latin American folk art, Eye's Gallery provides plenty of eye candy from Central and South America (402 South Street, 215-925-0193; www.eyesgallery.com). And you can't leave without stopping into the store that has kept South Street's edge since 1980: Zipperhead (407 South Street, 215-928-1123), "where punk is prince but quality is king."

It's a lot to take in. South Street is changing; mixed among the funky elements we now see the Gap and Starbucks. Not everyone is happy with the changes, but as long as shops like Zipperhead persist, South Street will be the marketplace for any age.

interior designers, and he brings other area talents to this bright, airy Antique Row showroom: Plexiglas and rubber chaises by Philly design firm Float, lighting fixtures by Maze, and wall art and accessories by local artists—and always, Izzo's own signature candles.

Open House
107 South 13th Street
(215) 922-1415
www.openhouseliving.com
This is one of Philly's most talked-about new home shops. You might see chenille bath mats, imported mirrors, carved wood vases, and vintage-looking shaving accessories, all working together. Don't miss the garden annex for unusual planters and gardening books.

Phag Shop
252 South 12th Street
(215) 545-5645
www.thephagshop.com
The acronym stands for Philadelphia Home Art Garden Shop, but make no mistake—this is a gay-oriented home accessories store, and it's great fun. Mostly you'll find smaller items, such as candles and throw rugs, along with greeting cards—but relax, it's not over-the-top.

Scarlett Alley
241 Race Street
(215) 592-7898
www.scarlettalley.com
For adding color and pizzazz to your table, this kicky shop will give you lots of options, from polka-dotted glass salad bowls to more sedate, antique-style platters and cake servers. When you're not sure about conversation starters with the new neighbors, you can always count on different-looking tableware to bring fresh energy to the table.

Twist
1134 Pine Street
(215) 925-1242
www.twisthome.com
We shouldn't have lamps, contend Twist's

owners—we should have conversation pieces. The furnishings in our homes should help us feel joyful in those spaces, they say, and that means cashmere, silk, and other luxurious fabrics in our pillows, rugs, and linens. At Twist, opulence is the norm.

Ursula Hobson Fine Art Framing, Inc.
1600 Spruce Street
(215) 546-7889
www.ursulahobson.com
Ursula Hobson not only creates memorable, high-quality frames, its staff also give close attention to conservation of your treasures. Gilded frames are popular here—no surprise—but silver metal leaf and welded steel are also frequent choices. For the budget-conscious, some wood and metal framing is priced at about $10 per foot.

Jewelry Stores

Jack Kellmer Co.
1521 Walnut Street
(215) 627-8350
www.jkellmer.com
After almost 70 years on Chestnut Street, Jack Kellmer moved its exquisite diamond creations to a larger, more prestigious space on Rittenhouse Row. Such high-end brands as Lalique and Judith Leiber continue to be prominent in the display cases.

Linde Meyer Gold & Silver
The Shops at Liberty Place
1625 Chestnut Street
(215) 851-8555
You won't find outrageous, cutting-edge jewelry designs at Linde Meyer—just classic, classy, and enduring. The jewelry is about sophistication and, we're sure, has that same effect on the lady wearing it— we'll let you know exactly how we feel, the next time we purchase a $4,000 set of earrings.

Touches
225 South 15th Street
(215) 546-1221
www.touchesthecatalog.com
If wearable art is your style, you'll enjoy the variety offered by Touches. Not only jewelry, but frames, scarves, gifts, and more are offered here—mostly hand-crafted or limited edition.

Men's Clothing

Boyds
1818 Chestnut Street
(215) 564-9000
www.boydsphila.com
Rarely has *Philadelphia* magazine named any other men's store the "Best of Philly." Boyds is the largest men's clothing store in the United States, and it offers the best designers from A to Z—Armani to Zegna. For high-end formal wear, shoes, even big-and-tall clothes, Boyds has a large selection, and a cafe where you can have coffee while you admire your new suit.

Sparacino
115 South 13th Street
(215) 922-4211
www.sparacinomens.com
Stylish and spacious, the new Sparacino store specializes in casual menswear—Kenneth Cole, Ben Sherman, and its own Sparacino line. Another "Best of Philly" winner.

Stitch
229 Chestnut Street
(215) 923-3910
Classic but fresh is the best way to characterize Stitch, a new Old City menswear store where alterations and delivery are free, the fridge is full of Michelob, and blazers are hip again. Stitch features hot designers such as Joes Jeans, Steelo, and the great Theory line.

Pet Stores

Bone Jour
14 North Third Street
(215) 574-1225
www.bonejourpetsupply.com
For the dog who has everything, a sparkling crystal collar, or vanilla-sandwich cookie treats might be just the thing. For you, a "Pooch Smooch" photography session. And if your pet has been indulging a bit too much, Bone Jour shares info on dealing with pet obesity.

Chic Petique
616 South Third Street
(215) 629-1733
This pet boutique features all-natural treats and foods, and homeopathic pet remedies when they have an ailment. Dog and cat couture are another specialty.

Shoe Stores

Cole Haan
1600 Walnut Street
(215) 985-5801
www.colehaan.com
The soothing neutrals of the Cole Haan store are an ideal backdrop for the classic look of the shoes and handbags. You might spot local news anchors here, several of whom favor Cole Haans for their aching feet behind the news desks.

Decades Vintage
615 Bainbridge Street
(215) 923-3135
Top designers Marc Jacobs and Donna Karan have shopped here to find inspiration for their own clothing lines. Even they love a bargain; one writer reported finding genuine ostrich pumps for just $45.

Souvenir Shops

ArtWorks at Philadelphia Museum of Art
26th Street and Benjamin Franklin Parkway
(215) 684-7966
www.philamuseum.org
One of the classiest souvenirs you could buy is a painting by a true Philadelphia artist. Many of the works sold here are by established artists; you'll also find jewelry and handicrafts by local artists who exhibit in the Museum's annual Art Craft Show.

Portfolio at The Pennsylvania Academy of Fine Arts
128 North Broad Street
(215) 972-2075
www.pafa.org
This is Philly's newest museum shop. Jewelry, glass, and art books are on display and for sale, and they all reflect studies of the Academy—a fine gift to take home.

Souvenir
307 Arch Street
(215) 923-2565
Here's where you'll find Philly mementoes that are different from those crammed into souvenir carts. "LOVE" door mats, interesting soaps and candles, antique postcards, and lots of stars-and-stripes selections are here.

Specialty Food Stores

DiBruno Bros. House of Cheese
930 South Ninth Street
(215) 922-2876, (888) 322-4337
www.dibruno.com
For more than 50 years, this Old World European-style family business has thrived in the same location. Their homemade spreads are famous locally; all 400 cheeses and other food items are available by mail order.

Nuts to You
24 South 20th Street
(215) 677-9520
Whether you like your nuts smoked or coated with wasabi, you can find hundreds of variations on 20 different nuts. Their homemade nut butters are to die for—or, if you're trying to behave, their sugar-free candies are tasty, too. Gift baskets and party trays also are available.

Women's Clothing

Belly Maternity
1600 Pine Street
(215) 985-1169
www.shopbelly.com
There's no reason not to be a sexy dresser if you're pregnant. Belly Maternity carries designer maternity garb, including Liz Lange suits, Bella Dahl jeans, and even maternity thongs! Watch for Belly Maternity's new store to open soon in Manayunk.

bSHEHU
113 South 13th Street
(215) 574-1300
You might wonder if you're in a clothing boutique or an art gallery, the displays at bSHEHU are so beautifully executed, with ancient Indian architectural items juxtaposed with steel and fabrics. You'll be surrounded by cashmere wraps, designer jewelry, and flouncy dresses any woman would feel pretty wearing.

Charles Porter Boutique
212 Market Street
(215) 627-3390
Women's alterations—fast, and affordable? Believe it, at Charles Porter's jeans emporium; as long as you buy the jeans before 3:00 P.M., they'll be shortened, with the original hem reattached, that same afternoon. About 30 brands are on hand, including Seven, Miss Sixty, and Citizens of Humanity, under $200.

Joan Shepp
1616 Walnut Street
(215) 735-2666
www.joanshepp.com
Women's suits for day and evening are Joan Shepp's claim to fame, with fashion-forward designs by Ghost, Marni, Dries Van Noten, Yohji Yamamoto, and Lilith. The shop also sells casual clothing for both men and women, and kids' clothes by Fitigues.

Knit Wit
1721 Walnut Street
(215) 564-4760
www.knitwitonline.com
With fashion and accessories by designers such as Miu Miu, Max Mara, and Anna Molinari, it's no wonder Knit Wit has been a Rittenhouse Row icon for more than 30 years. From resort wear to formal gowns, Knit Wit covers any fashion need—including shoes, in its small designer-shoe boutique.

MANAYUNK

Artesano
4443 Main Street
(215) 483-9273
www.artesanoironworks.com
Every piece is one-of-a-kind here. You can buy a small wrought-iron sconce or an entire balcony; a candle holder or a dining room table or armoire; all are handcrafted and can be custom-built.

Bendi Fine Jewelers
4339 Main Street
(215) 508-5220
www.bendijewelers.com
Using a computerized three-dimensional design system, Bendi's master designer works with customers to create original, handmade jewelry based on their own ideas. You can also purchase international art of Murano glass, needle art, and imported works from the Greek Isles.

Bias
4442 Main Street
(215) 483-8340
In this slick, modern boutique, clothing by established designers is sold alongside wearable pieces by local designers. Four times a year, the interior of the store is totally revamped, so that new styles will be shown in their optimal, most fresh light.

Events in Style
4329 Main Street
(215) 509-6400
www.eventsinstyle.com
More great wearable art: We don't think arty dressing could be any more comfortable than the cotton jersey pieces by No Blu, or Japanalia's microfiber cropped pants. You'll find jewelry here, too, so you can leave with a complete outfit.

Mainly Shoes
4410 Main Street
(215) 483-8000
The *New York Times* called this shop an "ultra-hip boutique for cutting-edge shoes . . ." Prada, Puma, all the best designers are here in this sleek, silvery-toned shoe store. We could spend a lot of money here.

Nicole Miller Philadelphia
4249 Main Street
(215) 930-0307
www.nmphilly.com
From casual handkerchief dresses to bridal gowns, Nicole Miller brings her entire line to Philadelphia at last. Her contemporary sportswear is almost as fun to browse as her handbags, and her upbeat designs fit the Manayunk sensibility perfectly.

Rugmaven
4335 Main Street
(215) 483-1321
In Philadelphia's only discount Oriental rug gallery, you can view an extensive collection of tribal, traditional, contemporary, and antique rugs at more affordable prices than at many higher-end rug galleries. If you're interested in rugs, the quality and value here are worth a stop.

ANTIQUES

What's the first thing that comes to mind when we hear the word, Philadelphia?

It's history, of course. Philadelphia's image is overwhelmingly about history. The past shapes the city's tourism, it defines its neighborhoods and it is, in short, everywhere you look. So, in a place where history is so alive it practically talks to you, can anyone be surprised that antiquing is one of Philadelphia's favorite pastimes?

The region is a mecca for antiquing, a treasure trove of old stuff. It stands to reason; immigrant families lived in these parts long before the country existed. They came with their family heirlooms, and then they put their skills to work and produced and acquired more. Philadelphia still is home to descendants of those earliest settlers, and as longtime residents depart, their possessions often become antiques to be rescued by the rest of us.

Since the 1700s, Philadelphia has been a furniture-making center. This tradition evolved over the centuries and today, those locally produced chairs—as well as fine desks and furnishings brought from England, France, and Sweden—are found in more than 100 shops from Antique Row in Center City to emporiums in Lambertville and West Chester.

It isn't only the upper crust, however, who provide the most desirable antiques. Pennsylvania is an agricultural state, and one of the largest Amish settlements in the United States is just two hours west of the city, in the Lancaster area. Country-based antiques are immensely popular everywhere, and southeast Pennsylvania is no exception; flea markets and shops throughout the region are packed with such collectibles as McCoy pottery, vintage kitchen gadgets, '40s linens, and old farm tools.

Whether you can strike a good deal depends partly on your haggling skills. Do not hesitate to bargain, even in the most upscale shops; if an item is priced over $20, it's always acceptable to ask, "Can you come down? What's your best price?"

But it's important to remember: This is still the East Coast. A lucite purse you can pick up for $75 at a flea market in Indiana might cost $200 in a Philadelphia shop. If you are accustomed to paying *real* bargain prices for antiques in another part of the country, then prices in Philadelphia will seem somewhat inflated.

But the selection and sheer volume of antiquing opportunities in Philadelphia make up for paying a bit extra. And, not only do Philadelphians buy and sell antiques, they've also developed expertise in repair, refinishing, and restoration. From early electric and gas lighting to fine jewelry, restoration of antiques is part of the shopping landscape here, and specialists are easy to locate.

Pine Street, or "Antique Row," is a walkable, enjoyable place to start your hunt (see the Close-Up in this chapter). If you start at Broad Street and head east on Pine, you'll only walk about 2 blocks before antiques shops start appearing, and they'll continue for the next 4 blocks.

Lambertville, New Jersey, is the other remarkable antiques center. Located just across the Delaware River from New Hope, Lambertville's antiquing—especially combined with a few hours in eclectic New Hope—make for a great shopping excursion.

And no antiques buff should miss the Philadelphia Antiques Show, one of the longest-running and most acclaimed antiques expos in the country. A preview gala launches the four-day show every April at the historic 33rd Street Armory, and renowned authorities, such as Leigh Keno of "Antiques Roadshow" fame, give lectures on art, decor, history, and antiques.

ANTIQUES

If time is limited, here's a strategy for shopping Antique Row: Combine it with an edgy afternoon on South Street. Start at Pine and 12th Street at noon and slowly work your way east. Antique Row's shops end at about Ninth Street, so head over to South Street, 2 blocks south. The best of South Street begins at about Seventh and continues east; your only challenge will be deciding how to criss-cross the street to see everything!

Our sampling of antiques shops and emporiums is grouped by region, then alphabetized for easy shopping reference. Because they travel to expos and arrange private consultations, some shop owners keep scant or odd hours, so be sure to phone before you visit the shop.

ANTIQUE ROW AND CENTER CITY PHILADELPHIA

Architectural Antiques Exchange
715 North Second Street
(215) 922-3669
www.architecturalantiques.com
Prepare for sensory overload: With three packed floors and 30,000 square feet, the Exchange isn't a store; it's an extravaganza. Some of its inventory is reclaimed from French and Belgian castles, others from churches, mansions, saloons, and pubs worldwide. The majority of pieces are from the Victorian period, but others date from as early as the late 1700s through the 1930s, representing Gothic, Colonial, French, English, Art Nouveau, Art Deco, and Victorian styles. Whether you're drawn to ornate armoires, French advertising, limestone mantels, stained-glass doors, or bars of any size, you will find examples here.

Calderwood Gallery
1622 Spruce Street
(215) 568-7475
Catering to true collectors, this Ritten-

house Square establishment specializes in French Art Deco, Modernist and '40s furniture, glass, bronzes, and rugs. Their display of more than 800 pieces features exotic woods and fine craftsmanship, all by top names in the decorative arts: Dufrene, Montagnac, Arbus, Ruhlmann. Calderwood has been featured in *Architectural Digest, France Magazine,* and *Art & Antiques.*

Classic Antiques
922 Pine Street
(215) 629-0211
www.classicant.com
This Antique Row fixture is a direct importer of French and English antiques from the 18th and 19th centuries. One fine example we noted is a circa-1935 Art Deco rosewood vanity from France; it sat among armoires, chests, mirrors, tables, buffets, desks, and lighting. Be sure to call first.

Dollbox.com
1825 East Passyunk Avenue
(888) 465-6111
www.dollbox.com
This Philadelphia-based dealer only sells online, but since they're one of the few area vendors who specialize in dolls, we wanted to include them. Madame Alexander, Annalee, Adora, and Lee Middleton are all here—as their motto says, "for the kid in all of us."

H. A. Eberhardt & Son Inc.
2010 Walnut Street
(215) 568-4144
www.eberhardts.com
Anyone looking for a long-established shop and restorer of fine antiques need look no further than this Rittenhouse Row firm. Billing themselves as Philadelphia's largest antiques dealer, they also are America's oldest restorers; records date back to 1869, but the restoration studio operated in Europe long before that date. H. A. Eberhardt became a partner in 1888 and gave the business his name; they deal in jade, glass, European

porcelain, Japanese cloisonné and Satsuma, Lladro, Wedgwood, Staffordshire, and other quality pieces. Wednesday, they say, is the best day to schedule appraisals. Their Web site includes a page on what to do (and what *not* to do) if a piece gets broken, and all are advised: "Save *all* the pieces."

Freeman's
1808 Chestnut Street
(215) 563-9275
www.freemansauction.com

Freeman's had a monumental year in 2005. It not only was the auction house's 200th anniversary, but they also acquired a copy of the first public printing of the U.S. Constitution. (The pre-auction estimate was $80,000 to $120,000.) It's not Freeman's first important document; in 1968 they auctioned one of the original fliers carrying the Declaration of Independence that was posted across the city, for $404,000. They also have auctioned rare books, such as a first edition of *Winnie the Pooh*, signed by A. A. Milne. Other specialties include 20th-century design, fine paintings, and American and European furniture.

Moderne Gallery
111 North Third Street
(215) 923-8536
www.modernegallery.com

Moderne Gallery is another emporium that deals in the works of top-name designers such as Sam Maloof, Wendell Castle, and George Nakashima. Its specialty is Deco (it was bestowed a "Best of Philly Award" for Deco furniture from *Philadelphia* magazine in 2000) and participated in the rediscovery and sale of a 1930 Viktor Schreckengost "Jazz Bowl," widely regarded as the most important American Art Deco ceramic. The gallery is known for staging major exhibits and has been profiled in *Architectural Digest, House Beautiful, The New York Times,* and other national publications. Another claim to fame: Pieces from the Moderne Gallery have played significant roles in many

The best browsing along Antique Row (Pine Street) is between 10th and 12th Streets, and the best time is after 11:00 A.M., when most shops open. Don't make the mistake we made and go on Monday; that's the universal day of rest for antiques dealers.

movies, including *Philadelphia* and *The Hudsucker Proxy.*

Niederkorn Silver
2005 Locust Street
(215) 567-2606

As the name and Rittenhouse Row address imply, Niederkorn Silver is a dealer of fine antique silver. Jewelry, desk items, napkin rings, Judaica, and tea balls are all offered, along with books on silver collecting. This is where you will find that silver baby rattle.

Reese's Antiques
(215) 922-0796
www.reeseantiques.com

Reese's Antiques is another Philadelphia-based, online-only antiques outlet. It's one of the oldest antiques outlets in the city—founded in 1905—and there's a bit of glamour in its history. In the 1920s, when Calvin Coolidge was U.S. president, owner Dorrance Reese's grandfather built a Chippendale secretary for the White House, and in 1960, his parents sold a pair of 18th-century andirons now displayed in Independence Hall. The business also has provided set decorations for movies produced in Philadelphia and today deals in quality furniture, porcelain, paintings, silver, jewelry, pottery, and clocks.

Schwarz Gallery
1806 Chestnut Street
(215) 563-4887
www.schwarzgallery.com

The business was born in 1930 on Atlantic City's boardwalk and moved to its Rittenhouse Row location during World War II, prompting an emphasis on Philadelphia

ANTIQUES

CLOSE-UP

Antique Row Evolves

It's the oldest continuously operating antique district in the nation, and Antique Row lives up to the expectation—even if it does embrace many businesses unrelated to antiques.

Technically, the Historic Antique Row Business Association centers on Pine Street, running from Broad (the equivalent of 14th Street) east to Ninth Street, and includes businesses on the corresponding blocks of Spruce Street, which runs parallel to Pine on the north, of Lombard Street to the south, and the numbered side streets connecting them.

Expanding the scope of Antique Row beyond Pine means that such businesses as Uhuru Furniture & Collectibles (1220 Spruce, 215-546-9616), a non-profit secondhand store, and Chartreuse (1200 Spruce, 215-545-7711; www.chartreuse flowers.com), a custom-design flower shop, are brought into the corridor. Retailers such as Neat Stuff Toys & Memorabilia (341 South 13th Street, 215-545-6883); urban decor, whose "intelligent mix" of tra-

ditional and contemporary furnishings includes prints, potter, plants, and more (238 South 11th Street, 215-574-8552); and Rustic Music (333 South 13th Street, 215-732-7805), all benefit from the association's collective promotion of the area.

Accommodations here, including the Alexander Inn and four B&Bs, make it easy for visitors who view Antique Row as a destination of its own. Eateries in the district include at least three coffeehouses, and the smattering of music and video stores, casual and elegant restaurants, and even hair salons and pharmacies, remind us that Antique Row isn't just a tourist spot; it is a neighborhood where people live.

Along Pine Street, though, most of the businesses deal in antiques and collectibles, with some contemporary galleries blending in. Some are larger than they look; Eloquence Antiques and Decorative Arts (1034 Pine, 215-627-6606) has three sizable showrooms of traditional china, porcelain, silverware, and jewelry. The familiar names—Limoges, Dresden,

arts. That interest continues today, as owner Robert D. Schwarz Jr., the third generation to lead the gallery, focuses on 19th- and 20th-century American paintings. The gallery's collection includes the era's most renowned artists, including Mary Cassatt, Thomas Eakins, Winslow Homer, John Singer Sargent, and Andrew Wyeth.

South Street Antiques Market
615 South Sixth Street
(215) 592-0256
Prepare to gasp when you enter this antiques mall, Philadelphia's only indoor

antiques market. Vintage fabrics, cupboards you wish you hadn't thrown away, plastic purses, kidney tables, paintings, jewelry, stained glass, and '50s collectibles of all kinds fill the stalls of some 25 vendors. This place is pure fun, just a few doors off funky South Street. It's closed Monday and Tuesday, so plan your visit for later in the week.

Vintage Instruments
1609 Pine Street
(215) 545-1100
www.vintage-instruments.com
Vintage Instruments says they specialize in

Minton, Waterford—are all represented, alongside timeless Asian and European embroideries and tapestries.

Another neighborhood anchor is M. Finkel & Daughter (936 Pine, 215–627–7797), the country's leading dealer of antique samplers and needlework, with some dating from the 17th century. The father-daughter team of Morris and Amy Finkel do deal in antique furniture as well, but samplers and needlework are the cornerstone of the business, and Amy lectures and consults across the country. Their schoolgirl samplers tug at the heart ("when this you see, remember me . . ."). They also tug at the pocketbook: Samplers featured at any given time run to $8,000 and higher, and prices for the most rare pieces can top $25,000.

Another unique shop is Antique Design, Inc. (1102 Pine, 215–629–1812), specializing in antique stained and leaded glass. In addition to selling rescued old windows, the shop also offers glass restoration and custom-designs for entryways and windows.

Some of the most intriguing shops along Pine Street, however, deal in con-temporary goods. SOTA/Spirit of the Artist (1022 Pine, 215–627–8801) deals in 100-percent American handmade gifts, such as one-of-a-kind carved wooden bowls, and was named, "the best reasonably priced cool gift shop in Philadelphia" by City Paper. Sophie's Yarns (918 Pine, 215–925–5648; www.sophiesyarns.com) is a knitter's nirvana, with designer yarns and classes offered. Show of Hands Gallery (1006 Pine, 215–592–4010) is part of the national organization of contemporary crafts guilds, and sells jewelry and gifts of textiles, glass, ceramic, metal, and paper, all crafted by juried professional artisans. And the Mathew Izzo Shop (928 Pine, 215–922–2570; www.mathewizzo.com) offers Izzo's own line of interior and product designs, from progressive furniture to unique home accessories, as well as a Jonathan Adler boutique.

In all, more than 70 shops and restaurants inhabit Antique Row, along with dozens more service businesses, all in a historic, tree-lined setting. For more information, contact the Historic Antique Row Business Association, (215) 731–1709; www.antique-row.org.

vintage Martin and Gibson guitars, banjos, and mandolins, but as America's largest shop dealing in antique acoustic musical instruments, their scope reaches much further: They also deal in 18th- and 19th-century woodwinds and brass, fine violins and cellos, and any category of instrument with historical interest. The above address is for the office and guitar shop, which has a separate phone number (215–545–1000), and the violin shop is so extensive it operates out of a different address, 1529 Pine Street (215–545–1100). On occasion, they're able to offer instruments that are most rare and collectible, such as the two tárogatók we found in the woodwind section.

CHESTNUT HILL

Antique Gallery
8523 Germantown Avenue
(215) 248–1700

The specialty of the house is estate jewelry, but Antique Gallery is fairly eclectic. Its offerings include art pottery, art glass, sterling, English and French porcelains, Chinese exports, and desk accessories.

Your (former) best friend sets her hot coffee on your pricey end table, burning a nasty ring into the finish—who you gonna call? Try the Restoration Studio, who apply magic to damaged furniture, giving it a second chance. (Whether you give that friend a second chance is up to you.) Best of all, Restoration Studio makes house calls (376 Shurs Lane, Manayunk, 610-834-4995; 1932 Route 212, Pleasant Valley, 610-346-7551; www.werefinish.com).

Corkscrew lovers can always find a good selection here, and the shop is a resource for reference and pricing books on decorative arts and collectibles.

Chestnut Hill Resale
7830 Germantown Avenue
(215) 248-6033
Chestnut Hill Resale is the kind of second-hand shop that everyone loves: clean, big, and packed with bargains. The selection includes every kind of everyday item, from antiques, glassware, china, and other collectibles, to dining room tables, chairs, furniture, books, chests, beds, loveseats, and lamps.

John Alexander Ltd.
10-12 West Gravers Lane
(215) 242-0741
www.johnalexanderltd.com
Set in historic Chestnut Hill, the John Alexander gallery is spacious—almost 3,000 square feet of exhibition space—with plenty of room for the more than 500 pieces on display. It is regarded as one of America's premier venues for period Arts and Crafts furnishings in the British tradition, and also deals in significant works in Reformed Gothic, Aesthetic, and 20th-century British handcrafted furniture and decorative pieces, most from 1860 to 1920.

Philadelphia Print Shop
8441 Germantown Avenue
(215) 242-4750
www.philaprintshop.com
Collectors of antique prints could spend a day in this shop. The natural history section is our favorite, with gorgeous examples of botanicals, fish, shells, and foodstuffs from herbs to elaborately fashioned sweets. Americana is likewise intriguing, with extensive collections of Winslow Homer and Currier & Ives. Book conservation is a specialty. The shop also offers a large selection of print and map reference books. These works are mesmerizing, and it's not flea-market stuff: Look to spend an average of $100-plus for a print.

WEST CHESTER

Acorn Cottage
14 West Gay Street
(610) 430-3316
One of the intimate shops that has turned West Chester into one of Greater Philadelphia's hottest shopping destinations, Acorn Cottage carries an eclectic assortment of high-quality antiques from around the world—but because they're all beautiful, it works. You'll find porcelains, antique and contemporary art, and antique French textiles in the same display as transferware pottery, embroidered pillows, and French iron garden benches. Browsing here is a comfortable pleasure.

Brandywine River Antiques Market
Route 1
(610) 388-2000
Look for the big white barn just down the road from the Brandywine River Museum. It's filled with treasures sold by 50 vendors, from estate furniture to accessories, from 10-foot farm tables to a Victorian wardrobe. Not all of the pieces are large; old milk cans, ornate picture frames, and doll clothes are displayed, as well as

dishes, postcards, and antique sleds. Expect to see a little of everything here.

J. Palma Antiques
Route 202
(610) 399-1210
To say that J. Palma deals in 18th- and 19th-century American country furniture and accessories doesn't begin to do justice to the carefully selected inventory in this store. One might find a rare walking toy of a Native American with hatchet in hand, made of sheet metal in the early 1800s, or an 18th-century Pennsylvania walnut coffin that was converted for the storing of alcohol. This is an unusual shop with a fine reputation.

DELAWARE COUNTY

Briggs Auction, Inc.
1315 Naamans Creek Road (Route 491), Boothwyn
(610) 566-3138
www.briggsauction.com
Briggs Auction is a family business in historic Booth's Corner, and the best day to go is Friday for the weekly Estate Absolute Auction. They might include primitives, oriental carpets, and other hard-to-find items, and usually there are pottery, crystal and glassware, tools, toys, country antiques, sterling, coins, and books being auctioned. Photographs and extensive listings are posted on the Web site.

William H. Bunch Auctions & Appraisals
One Hillman Drive (Routes 202 and 1), Chadds Ford
(610) 558-1800
www.williambunchauctions.com
Although Bunch Auctions caters to serious collectors of high-quality American and Native American crafts, don't expect a somber experience here. Auctions are entertaining, and staff are happy to explain the background of various pieces to new collectors and the simply curious. Typical items include Rookwood, Roseville, and Weller pottery, Coors

One of the most appealing features of the revered Philadelphia Antiques Show is where it sends its profits: Proceeds are donated every year to special programs at the University of Pennsylvania Health System (UPHS). In the 45-plus years it has been operating, the show has raised more than $12 million toward patient care at UPHS.

Golden Colorado pottery, Navajo textiles, Hopi Kachina figures, Hopi wedding jars, and elaborately designed seed pots. Bunch is known as an "interactive retailer"—come and enjoy.

LAMBERTVILLE/ STOCKTON, NEW JERSEY

Mix Gallery
17 South Main Street, Lambertville
(609) 773-0777
www.mix-gallery.com
Uncluttered as Lucy Ricardo's kitchen, Mix Gallery's display style matches the vintage inventory: clean and sleek. The "mix" is handbags and furniture, from Gucci classics and super-architectural bakelite wonders, to 1940s chests and swirly lamps. Birch and alabaster abound here, melding easily with alligator and Noguchi. This shop was a great idea, and they carry it off beautifully.

Morten-Monberg Antiques
19 Bridge Street, Stockton
(609) 397-7066
www.morten-monberg.com
Some would characterize Morten-Monberg as "intimidatingly classy." Their featured pieces, such as a Swedish faience tile wood-burning stove, are sumptuous and beautiful. Many items are Asian—a bamboo console, a Chinese kitchen counter—and most, but not all, are imported. Classic modernism is a specialty. The shop is not crowded; the air is one of selection and restraint.

VALLEY FORGE

The Warehouse at Urban Artifacts
2702 Roberts Avenue
(215) 951-9343
www.urbanartifactswarehouse.com
For more than 20 years, Urban Artifacts has been selling antiques from its wholesale warehouse west of Philadelphia. Most of the furniture is American, French, and Victorian, and all of it is offered at auction on eBay as well as in the warehouse. This is a good first stop for anyone who needs to fill a house with quality furniture for a reasonable price—furnishing an inn, for instance, or model homes.

ATTRACTIONS

This chapter might as well be titled "Historic Attractions," because history is the major driver of tourism in Philadelphia—but that doesn't mean it has to be dry, or boring.

In the Betsy Ross House, for instance, visitors see—many for the first time—that Ms. Ross was no wimpy little seamstress; she was an assertive, take-charge lady who persevered and thrived in spite of terrible tragedies in her personal life. The home of another favorite daughter, famous African-American opera star Marian Anderson, likewise has been beautifully restored. And no historic places could be more dynamic than the bustling Reading Terminal Market and, in South Philly, the Italian Market!

Walking the streets of Philadelphia, the thought occurs that one would be hard-put to find a home in this city that *isn't* historical. You do come upon the occasional contemporary condo building, juxtaposed with beautifully maintained homes that have graced the streets for 200 years or longer, accented with flower boxes and boot scrapers. And, not surprisingly, the housing stock is progressively newer as you venture farther from Center City.

There's no escaping history in Philadelphia's attractions—but, that said, you also cannot overlook the vibrancy and liveliness of it all. Sure, the Mummers Museum has been around for decades—but no one parties like the Mummers do! And attractions like Edgar Allan Poe's house and Boat House Row do represent slices of history, but any scholars observing from the shadows are far outnumbered by curious students and families having fun.

Then there are the more contemporary attractions, like Linvilla Orchards, River Rink, and Temple University's Shoe Museum. They remind us that, while Philadelphia is a place of momentous history for our country, it's also a busy city with a lot going on!

Many attractions appear in other chapters. No one should visit Philly without lingering at the Philadelphia Museum of Art, which you'll find in the Arts chapter; or South Street, in the Shopping chapter. And, since most of the city's historic churches still operate with active clergy and parishioners and regular services, you can read about those "attractions" in the chapter on Worship.

Your first stop should be at the new visitor center, described below. As you skim through the following pages, you will note that many attractions in Philly do not charge admission, or they ask for voluntary donations. For those that do charge admittance, the following price code will give you an idea of what you can expect to pay. Price ranges refer to one adult admittance.

PRICE CODE

$	$5.00 and under
$$	$6.00 to $9.99
$$$	$10.00 to $14.99
$$$$	$15.00 to $19.99
$$$$$	$20.00 and over

VISITOR INFORMATION

Independence Visitor Center   **Free**
Sixth and Market Streets
(215) 965-7676, (800) 537-7676
www.independencevisitorcenter.com
Most people skip the visitor centers when they travel because so often they are dreary little road stops with a few racks of brochures, staffed by low-paid workers who can't even give directions or answer basic questions about their hometowns.

Not so in Philly's state-of-the-art Independence Visitor Center! Here, you can learn about more than 4,000 attractions and events; how you want the info delivered is up to you—by touch-screen computers, videos, exhibits, and brochure displays—or you might just want to stop Ben Franklin or one of his colleagues as they're roaming the halls, ready to assist.

The Visitor Center is the gateway for travel to this region, not only to Philadelphia proper but also to Bucks County, Chester County, Delaware and Montgomery Counties, and southern New Jersey. You can buy admission tickets here to museums and other attractions, get directions and maps, and even make hotel and dinner reservations. And if you aren't sure just what you want to do while you're visiting, the concierge staff will help you plan your trip. A message board above the reception desk displays an up-to-the-minute events schedule, and rangers from the National Park Service are on hand to answer questions about federally maintained museums, historic homes, and other sites in their domain.

For a special treat, the family can enjoy Saturday breakfast with Ben Franklin himself. Kids can ask him questions, pose for photos, and hear Ben talk about his inventions and life in colonial America. Everyone takes home a souvenir goodie bag; the breakfast is $19 for adults, $12 for kids, and reservation

---

We don't always think of bridges as tourist attractions, but we'll make an exception with the Ben Franklin Bridge, built in 1926. At 1.8 miles, it's the longest single-span suspension bridge in the world, and at night, with every cable illuminated, it makes a gorgeous photo op. And if it looks as if it's "shimmying," your eyes aren't playing tricks on you: As trains barrel across the bridge, they trigger sensors that light each cable, one after another, that make the bridge appear to be doing a little dance over the Delaware.

---

forms are available at the center's Web site.

Underground parking is available at the center. While you're there, stop into the gift shop—one of the largest souvenir shops in town, stocking unusual and classy goods—and relax with some Bucks County Coffee and a Tastykake in the cafe.

HISTORIC HOMES

Marian Anderson Residence Museum $$$
762 South Marian Anderson Way
(215) 732-9505
www.mariananderson.org
She stopped performing decades before her death in 1993, so legions of Americans never heard Marian Anderson's voice. Start by visiting the great opera singer's Web site, where her deep, moving contralto is the backdrop for every page. Ms. Anderson debuted with the New York Philharmonic in 1925. Although she made history in 1955 as the first African American to perform with the New York Metropolitan Opera, her most famous performance was on the Mall in Washington, D.C., during FDR's tenure.

William Brinton 1704 House $
21 Oakland Road, West Chester
(610) 399-0913
www.brintonfamily.org
Located on part of a 450-acre land grant from William Penn, this house was first occupied in 1704 by William Brinton Jr., called "William the Younger." William and his parents fled Britain to escape religious persecution; one notable Brinton descendant is former President Richard M. Nixon. Preservation buffs will have a field day touring this house, with its 22-inch-thick walls of stone from a nearby quarry, original flooring, leaded casement windows, indoor bake oven, and a colonial herb garden. The house is maintained today by a family association, which offers tours May through October.

Cliveden of the National Trust $$
6401 Germantown Avenue
(215) 848-1777
www.cliveden.org
Philadelphia's only Revolutionary War battle was fought on the grounds of Cliveden, which British soldiers occupied during the Battle of Germantown. Benjamin Chew, suspected to be a British loyalist, built Cliveden as a summer home in the 1760s. He was away in September 1777 when British troops took over the home and used it as a stronghold against Washington's soldiers. Six generations of Chews lived in Cliveden; it is open for tours and special events April through December.

Deshler-Morris House   Free
5442 Germantown Avenue
(215) 596-1748
www.ushistory.org/germantown/lower/deshler.htm
George Washington really did sleep here—twice. The first time, in 1793, he was there with his family, trying to escape the Yellow Fever epidemic; a year later it was again his temporary home while he met with his cabinet—Alexander Hamilton, Thomas Jefferson, Henry Knox, and Edmund Randolph—in the "Germantown White House." The owner, Colonel Isaac Franks, charged Washington $131.56 that first summer, which sum included Washington's furniture and bedding, traveling costs between Philly and Bethlehem, three ducks, four fowl, a bushel of potatoes, 100 bales of hay, four plates and the loss of a flatiron. Washington disputed the costs but returned the following year anyway.

Johnson House   Free
6306 Germantown Avenue
(215) 438-1768
www.johnsonhouse.org
Four generations of the abolitionist Johnson family have owned this Quaker house, once a stop on the Underground Railroad, now a museum. You'll find artifacts of slavery displayed, along with an outstanding selection of educational materials. Art shows and history lectures are continually featured; the home is also used for special events such as Jazz in the Garden (August), a Book Fair (May), and many events during Black History Month (February). Check the calendar on the Web site.

Thaddeus Kosciuszko National Memorial   Free
301 Pine Street
(215) 597-9618
www.nps.gov.thko
A Polish engineer living in Paris when the Revolutionary War broke out, Kosciuszko joined the rebels at a colonel's salary of $6.00 per month, and became a war hero. He planned forts along the Delaware River; after Fort Ticonderoga fell (partly because higher officers disregarded his advice), Kosciuszko blocked roads with trees and flooded fields to slow the Brits' advance. His strategy gave him time to plot the battle of Saratoga, his great victory that prompted the French to join the colonists in their fight. After the war, he returned to Poland to fight the Russians and was wounded 17 times. Returning to Philadelphia, Kosciuszko lived for a time in the boarding house that is preserved as his national memorial.

Physick House $
321 Fourth Street
(215) 925-7866
www.ushistory.org/tour/tour_physick.htm
He's known as the "Father of American Surgery," though the aptly named Dr. Philip Syng Physick wasn't the first in his family to make it into the history books. His grandfather, silversmith Philip Syng, designed the inkstand that was used in the signing of both the Declaration of Independence and the U.S. Constitution, and which is still displayed today in Independence Hall. Dr. Physick learned his trade by slicing open cadavers, and practiced it largely through bleeding his patients. His 32-room, Federal-style Society Hill mansion features a ballroom and numerous fireplaces with Valley Forge marble surrounds—just two of the architectural

features worth noting. It was built in 1786 by an importer of Madeira. Dr. Physick died in 1798 of the yellow fever—a cruel irony, as he had built his reputation fighting the disease in his patients.

Edgar Allan Poe
National Historic Site   Free
Seventh and Spring
Garden Streets
(215) 597-8780
www.nps.gov/edal

The raven, who was created in Philadelphia by Poe, the master of dark literature and creator of the detective story, stands guard over the home where Poe lived with his family for two years. While here (he lived in Philadelphia six years in total, the most prolific of his life) he also penned "The Fall of the House of Usher," "The Pit and the Pendulum," and "The Masque of the Red Death." Poe's tragic life and literary legacy are presented here in film and talks by Park Service employees. Hours vary with the season, so call ahead.

Powel House $
244 South Third Street
(215) 627-0364
www.powelhouse.com

Called "The Patriot Mayor" because he was mayor of Philadelphia when the country declared Independence, Samuel Powel was the city's last mayor under British rule and the first as part of the new republic. He was respected and well liked, and with his wife Elizabeth entertained Adams, Franklin, and Washington in his parlors. The home was built in 1765; as you tour, note the Gilbert Stuart portrait of Powel in the front room.

Among the personal tidbits you might pick up while touring Betsy Ross's house is the fact that this lady was great at multitasking: An upholsterer by trade, she eloped with her sweetheart, made ammunition for the colonial troops—and just happened to sew a flag in her spare time.

Betsy Ross House $
239 Arch Street
(215) 686-1252
www.betsyrosshouse.org

In 1776 George Washington and two members of the Continental Congress walked into Betsy Ross's upholstery shop and asked her to sew a flag for the new country. A year later Congress passed the Flag Resolution, adopting Betsy's flag. The home she rented from 1773 to 1786 is now a museum, thanks to two million Americans who, beginning in 1898, donated dimes to help save the little house and upholstery shop. More than 250,000 people visit the Betsy Ross House each year, making it Philadelphia's third-most popular tourist attraction, after the Liberty Bell and Independence Hall.

Fairmount Park Houses $
Fairmount Park
(215) 763-8100
www.philamuseum.org/collections

Out in William Penn's suburban "Liberty Lands" stand a scattering of stately, 18th- and early-19th-century homes, fashionable retreats for the city's gentleman merchants. As the city gradually acquired land to establish Fairmount Park, it also gained the beautiful homes, orchards, and farms in the vicinity.

The first acquisition was Lemon Hill, the 350-acre estate owned by Robert Morris, signer of the Declaration of Independence and good friend to George Washington. Morris was a financier, but apparently not such a good one, for he was sent to Debtors' Prison in 1798. The land was sold to Henry Pratt, son of a portrait painter, who built the elegant home now standing.

In all, seven Fairmount Park mansions have been restored and are open to the public as museums. Different civic and private organizations maintain the historic homes, all under the umbrella stewardship of the Philadelphia Museum of Art. For more information regarding specific homes, go to www.philamuseum.org, click on "Collections," then click on "Museum

Collections." The links for individual Fairmount Park Homes appear along the right-hand side of that page.

HISTORIC MUSEUMS AND SITES

Boathouse Row   Free; fee for events
Kelly Drive

Look to your left as you're driving along Interstate 76 into the city: Boathouse Row is your introduction to Philadelphia; to rowers, it is the hub of their athletic lives. Site of numerous high-level triathlons and national rowing competitions, Boathouse Row consists of 10 Victorian boathouses, each representing a rowing club. Collectively they comprise the Schuylkill Navy, founded in 1858—the country's oldest amateur athletic association. The big competitions, including the Stotesbury Cup, the Regatta, and the Dad Vail, happen May through July. That stretch of Kelly Drive also is a popular spot for jogging, rollerblading, and dog walking. If you drive past in the evening, you'll see the houses lit up year-round, a real postcard shot.

City Hall   Free
Broad and Market Streets
(215) 686-1776
www.geocities.com/Athens/Delphi/2115/Mainframeset.html

It took 30 years to build this temple to local politics, and it's easy to see why. Hundreds of statues grace its walls, the tallest being William Penn, looking down on his city from 510 feet, atop the center spire. Until 1987 Philly followed the "gentleman's code" that no building in Pennsylvania should rise higher than Penn's statue, but the code eventually was broken by a hard-fought vote of the people, who wanted a skyline. Penn himself chose the location, in the exact geographic center of Philadelphia, for an office of "publick concerns." Today his townspeople either adore the building's Second Empire Mode of French Renaissance-Revival architectural style, or they find it grotesque.

The City Hall at Broad and Market wasn't Philly's first house of governance. Adjacent to Independence Hall on the corner of Fifth and Market Streets stands Old City Hall, the second administrative center. (The first was on Second Street near the Delaware River.) Built in 1791, the Hall also housed the U.S. Supreme Court, which shared first-floor space with the Mayor's Court until 1800, when the feds moved to Washington, D.C. Justices during those years included John Jay, John Marshall, and Alexander Hamilton. There is no admission charge.

Fort Mifflin on the Delaware $$
Island Avenue and
Fort Mifflin Road
(215) 685-4167
www.fortmifflin.com

The country's oldest fort in continuous use (1771 to 1954), Fort Mifflin was the site of the biggest bombardment of the Revolutionary War. Today it's the popular site of battle reenactments, not only regarding the Revolution but also other wars, including World War II. Members and those who study hauntings enjoy the "Sleep with the Ghosts Events," with lectures by ghost researchers; visitors are invited to take photos or record unusual sounds.

Liberty Bell   Free
Entrance on Market
between Fifth and Sixth Streets
(215) 965-2305
www.nps.gov/inde/liberty-bell.html

It's the centerpiece of Independence National Historic Park and the city's biggest draw, though it hasn't rung in more than a century. In the late 1800s, as a way to heal leftover resentments from the Civil War, the Liberty Bell traveled to fairs and expos across the country, but it made its last trip in 1915. Today it stands silent in its own glass hall, an icon to freedom. The famous crack first appeared in 1846—no one knows why—and was repaired, but the crack remains, as does its inspiring inscription: "Proclaim LIBERTY throughout all the Land unto all the inhabitants thereof" (Leviticus 25:10).

Independence Hall   Free
Chestnut Street between
Fifth and Sixth Streets
(215) 965-2305
www.nps.gov/inde/indep-hall.html

Built between 1732 and 1756 as Pennsylvania's State House, Independence Hall made a handy meeting place when the Second Continental Congress needed to gather and plot the Revolution. George Washington was appointed Commander in Chief of the Continental Army in the Hall's Assembly Room—the same space where the Declaration of Independence was signed on July 4, 1776, and the design of the American flag was approved in 1777. The Articles of Confederation also were adopted here (1781), and it's here that the U.S. Constitution was drafted in 1787. Most of the furnishings are period pieces from other sources, but the "rising sun" chair, where George Washington sat as he directed the Constitutional Convention, is the original.

Masonic Temple $$
1 North Broad Street
(215) 988-1917
www.pagrandlodge.org

This circa-1868 headquarters of the Fraternal Order of Freemasons, of which George Washington and Ben Franklin were members, is a must-see for students of historic architectural styles. Guided tours take visitors through seven grand, elaborately furnished halls, each representing a different style: Corinthian, Ionic, Italian Renaissance, Norman, Gothic, Oriental, and Egyptian. Tours are offered Tuesday through Saturday, but call first because tours are suspended if a Masonic function is scheduled.

Reading Terminal Market   Free
12th and Arch Streets
(215) 922-2317
www.readingterminalmarket.org

First the aromas hit you, then the visual spectacle. Come hungry to this food, crafts, and flower market, because you'll want to taste everything: Amish butter, succulent nut strudels, plump fruits, dark chocolates, sizzling-hot horseradish, and poultry so fresh you expect it to start squawking. If you don't feel like grazing, more than 30 restaurants and food stands will serve up lunch. (For breakfast, the heartiest fare and best people-watching happens at the Down Home Diner.) Almost 80 vendors, some descended from the original tenants a century ago, serve 80,000 locals and tourists every week at this noisy, eclectic farmers' market, considered one of the best in the country.

Saint Katharine Drexel
Mission Center and Shrine   Free
1663 Bristol Pike, Bensalem
(215) 244-9900, ext. 314
www.katharinedrexel.org

Katharine Drexel (1858-1955) was an affluent Philadelphian, daughter of a prominent banker and philanthropist, whose parents raised her to believe that wealth should be shared. Starting at an early age, Katharine devoted her life to poor Native Americans and African Americans as a nun in the Sisters of the Blessed Sacrament. The center honors Katharine, who was canonized as a saint in 2000, and operates an online gift shop, selling handicrafts and artwork from Haiti, Guatemala, and the American Southwest, the three areas most actively served by her Order. You also can purchase books and memorabilia about Saint Katharine.

Vietnam vets weren't overlooked by the City of Brotherly Love. The Philadelphia Vietnam Veterans Memorial, dedicated in 1987, honors the 80,000 Philadelphia-area men and women who served, and the 646 who made the ultimate sacrifice. The Memorial, which has been recognized for its architectural style, is in a beautiful spot overlooking the Delaware River. No admission charge (Columbus Boulevard and Spruce Street).

Touring Philly's Wine Trails

With the right climate, great things are possible—and southeast Pennsylvania is blessed with a microclimate that's ideal for winemaking: Warming breezes from the Chesapeake and from the Atlantic Ocean bestow moderate temperatures on the region year-round. Rain is plentiful. Marry such kindly weather conditions with fertile, rocky, fast-draining limestone soil, bring in the best vines from the homeland, and *voila!* You've got grapes.

Home-grown grapes distinguish Philadelphia-area wine trails in an important way. In most states, grapes sometimes are grown elsewhere—even out-of-state—and shipped to the wineries to be made into wine. Almost all of the wineries on the Bucks County and Brandywine wine trails, however, grow their own. The winemaker has intimate knowledge of the fruits because he or she grew them, and the batch is predictably exquisite. When the winemaker uses grapes from his own vines, there is no guesswork.

Another distinction that makes southeast Pennsylvania wine trails special: The wine choices here surpass those in most other winemaking regions. The Brandywine Wine Trail alone offers more than 30 varieties, a testament to the compatible soil and climate. It makes perfect sense that American commercial winemaking began in Pennsylvania.

Wine-touring is a self-guided activity. As you move along between wineries, don't try to hit all of them in one day. Take your time; many encourage you to bring lunch—or they might even serve food in their own cafes. Visit their Web sites, look at their wine lists, and target three or four whose offerings intrigue you.

Taste, learn, and enjoy the vino—and if you plan to drink more than one glass, be sure to invite a designated driver.

BRANDYWINE VALLEY WINE TRAIL

Chaddsford Winery
632 Baltimore Pike, Chadds Ford
(610) 388-6221
www.chaddsford.com
This is the countryside that captivated three generations of Wyeths. Set in a renovated 17th-century colonial barn, Chaddsford, a large winery by Pennsylvania standards, produces 30,000 cases of award-winning wine each year. The Pinot Noir recently took top honors in the Tasters Guild International Wine Competition, and the Chambourcin is a repeat winner in the Pacific Rim International Wine Competition.

Folly Hill Vineyards
700 Folly Hill Road, Kennett Square
(610) 388-5895
www.follyhillvineyards.com
Wouldn't you love it if your workplace property was adjacent to the renowned Longwood Gardens! The scenery makes a beautiful backdrop for sipping award-winning Chardonnay, Vidal Blanc, Cabernet Franc, and Chambourcin in the winery's 200-year-old Quaker farmhouse. At 4,000 cases annually, this winery is relatively small.

French Creek Ridge Vineyards
200 Grove Road, Elverson
(610) 286-7754
www.frenchcreekridge.com
Set in a converted farmhouse and log cabin, French Creek Ridge is, at this writing, the only American winery to win a gold medal at the celebrated Vinalies Internationales Competition in Paris, for its

Blanc de Blancs. They specialize in dry champagnes and dry vinifera table wines.

Kreutz Creek Vineyards & Winery
553 South Guernsey Road, West Grove
(610) 869-4412
www.kreutzcreekvineyards.com

Another award-winning winery in the 4,000-case range, Kreutz Creek is one of the wineries with a lovely picnic area. It's only open to the public on weekends; this is a winery for white-wine lovers, as its most notable selections are the Chardonnay and the Gewurztraminer.

Paradocx Vineyard
452-464 Chesterville Road, Landenberg
(610) 255-5684
www.paradocx.com

This small-batch winery produces more unusual varieties under its PDX label. The Viognier is a deep, golden color, while the Pinot Grigio is more subtle. The Carmine and Petit Verdot are a bit sharp and often used in blends. Our recommendation: the lovely, dry white Auxerois.

Stargazers Vineyard
1024 Wheatland Drive, Coatesville
(610) 486-0422
www.stargazersvineyard.com

Located near the "Stargazers Stone"—the spot where Mason and Dixon drew the line—Stargazers makes an effort to run a "sustainable" winery, using rainwater to wash down the vines, mowing between rows so that weeds and grass become a natural compost for the vines, and fermenting in cellars with no additional heating or cooling. Their Pinot Noir is deep and just fruity enough; we also enjoyed their Pinot Gris.

Twin Brook Winery
5697 Strasburg Road, Gap
(717) 442-4915
www.twinbrookwinery.com

On land granted to the Society of Friends by William Penn's brother more than 300 years ago, this estate winery grows 30 acres of vines, 10 of which are French hybrids. The history in this soil can't help but lend character to the long list of reds and whites produced here. If you can, come for a Saturday summer concert and sip while you listen to great blues, Caribbean, or Zydeco. Check the Web site for the concert schedule.

Va La Vineyards
8822 Gap Newport Pike (Route 41),
Avondale
(610) 268-2702
www.valavineyards.com

When we start a vineyard, we want a Web site as cool as Va La's. "Our joy is for food," they write, "and we specifically design our wines, as we design our whole lives, to pair with foods." Start pouring the Vino Vala, we say: We'll start with Zafferano ("Saffron," an unoaked blend of Pinot Grigio and Viognier, 100 to 190 cases); then move on to La Prima Donna, "she is a slightly rare and unusual thing . . . " (200 to 290 cases); and finish with Nebbiolo, "the grape that marches completely to its own drummer" (49 to 90 cases, by reservation only). All wines are micro-produced and paired with local artisanal foods while you taste.

BUCKS COUNTY WINE TRAIL

Buckingham Valley Vineyards
1521 Route 413, Buckingham
(215) 794-7188
www.pawine.com

One of the first farm wineries in the state, Buckingham also is one of the largest, producing almost 50,000 cases annually. Their wines range from deep, oak-aged reds (Chambourcin, Cabernet) to light whites (Vidal Blanc), using vinifera, hybrid, native, and fruit vines. They're one of the few where tours are self-guided.

Crossing Vineyards & Winery
1853 Wrightstown Road, Washington Crossing
(215) 493-6500
www.crossingvineyards.com

With its first vintage in 2002, Crossing Vineyards became the newest addition to the Bucks County trail. The old and new are beautifully juxtaposed in this 200-year-old-estate, less than a mile from the spot where George Washington crossed the Delaware in 1776. The contemporary tasting room overlooks 25 active vineyards, and this high-tech winery uses a computerized weather station to collect data on its microclimate. Eight grapes are grown here, including Steuben, Vidal Blanc, Concord, and Chambourcin. Young as they are, Crossing collected six medals in a recent Finger Lakes International Wine Competition.

New Hope Winery
6123 Lower York Road, Route 202
New Hope
(215) 794-2331
www.newhopewinery.com

Housed in a 17th-century bar, this winery sells gourmet food gifts and while-you-wait custom labeling in its gift shop, along with its wines and wine accessories. It's a short drive to both Peddler's Village and New Hope, and the winery also produces fruit wines.

Peace Valley Winery
Old Limekiln Road, Chalfont
(215) 249-9058

High on a ridge in central Bucks County, this winery overlooks Peace Valley Park. More than two dozen grape varieties are grown here for their sparkling wines, hybrid cuvées, fruit wines, and European varietals. Ninety percent of Peace Valley's wines are estate-bottled.

Rose Bank Winery
258 Durham Road, Newtown
(215) 860-5899
www.rosebankwinery.com

Rose Bank's history seems to suit its romantic setting: The circa-1719 house and three-story stone barn, built in 1835, sit on land that William Penn gave to his daughters. The wines produced here are mostly fruity and on the sweeter side; sip them on the second-story deck, overlooking the vineyards and pastures where a herd of Baby Doll sheep graze.

Rushland Ridge Vineyards
2665 Rushland Road, Jamison
(215) 598-0251
www.rushlandridge.com

At least 12 estate-grown, handcrafted wines make it to Rushland Ridge's shelves each year—Chardonnay, Chambourcin, and Villard, among 17 varieties of grapes—produced from this boutique winery's four acres of vineyards. The ambience here is one of down-to-earth friendliness, and those who prefer sweeter wines will like Rushland Ridge's selection.

Sand Castle Winery
755 River Road, Erwinna
(800) 722-9463
www.sandcastlewinery.com

Vintner Joseph Maxian brought his craft from Bratislava, Slovakia, more than 20 years ago, and his passion for his craft shows in the 14 current labels. Some 60,000 Johannisberg Riesling, Chardonnay, Cabernet, and Pinot Noir vines bask in the sun high atop a knoll overlooking the Delaware River, producing 12 to 14 wines each year. During tours, visitors descend into the 30-foot-deep wine cellar—inside the hill—while upstairs, tastings are complimentary.

SPECIALTY MUSEUMS AND SPECIAL PLACES

African American Museum in Philadelphia $$
701 Arch Street
(215) 574-0380
www.aampmuseum.org

The contributions, culture, and traditions of African Americans, both local and from other regions, are presented in this museum's collections and programs. More than 400,000 artifacts, images, and documents, including fine art, folk art, memorabilia, and furnishings, are housed here, celebrating the African-American experience relating to sports, medicine, architecture, law, technology, entertainment, the arts, the Civil Rights movement, and family, religion, and politics. The archives are widely used for research. Among the museum's programs are a distance learning initiative, and on-the-job training for students pursuing museum-focused careers.

Blue Cross RiverRink $$
Columbus Boulevard at
Market Street, Penn's Landing
(215) 925-RINK
www.riverrink.com

RiverRink is the destination outdoor skating rink for Philadelphia and environs. Once it opens in November, it stays open seven days a week, including holidays, until the season ends February 15. For kids who are physically or developmentally challenged, RiverRink provides "sled

If you visit Philly in mid-February, be sure to come during the African American Museum in Philadelphia's all-night jazz jam, "Jazz 'Til Sunrise." For eight hours, musicians from across the region play, including such top names as Jimmy Heath, Shirley Scott, Jimmy Oliver, and Ted Curson. Call the museum for details (701 Arch Street, 215-574-0380; www.aampmuseum.org).

skates"—sleds equipped with regulation skate blades. Sled skaters can propel themselves along the ice with specially designed poles, or be pushed by skaters using handlebars attached to the sleds. The rink also hosts special events such as "Reels at the Rink," free special screenings of newly released DVDs. Rental skates are available; download a $1.00-off coupon at the Web site.

Eastern State Penitentiary $$
22nd Street and
Fairmount Avenue
(215) 236-3300
www.easternstate.org

This crumbling hulk is guaranteed to give you the willies. Once home to notorious bad guys Al Capone and "Slick Willie" Sutton, Eastern State Penitentiary is massive, the world's first real "penitentiary"—designed, literally, to inspire penitence for the crime—with vaulted, skylit cells, and an architectural style that's haunting, yet strangely beautiful. Be sure to take the audio tour (free with admission) and meander down Cell Block 15—Death Row.

Fabric Workshop and Museum $
1315 Cherry Street, Fifth Floor
(215) 568-1111
www.fabricworkshopandmuseum.org

The only non-profit arts organization in the United States devoted to the fabric arts, this museum will immerse you in gorgeous textiles. Fashioned from elegant silks, sleek satin, or down-home calico, garments and other art pieces are displayed. Of particular interest are the "Artist Boxes," containing samples, swatches, prototypes, and other items that represent the creative process for those whose work is in the museum's collections.

Headhouse Square Free
Second and Pine Streets

Most tourists come upon Headhouse Square when they've been shopping on South Street and, eventually, make their way down to Second Street, where the stores end. Even then, they usually don't realize they've arrived anywhere distinctive; there are no signs, and the street pretty much opens up to become a mini-parking lot and taxi stand. Headhouse Square is the historic marketplace in Old City. The cobblestone street surrounding the market area has been preserved, and several restaurants and shops rim the square. It gets busier on summer Saturdays, when a farmers' market is staged in the square, and during occasional craft fairs.

Italian Market   Free
South Ninth Street Corridor,
Wharton to Fitzwater Streets

Mama Mia! Prepare for sensory overload at the Italian Market, the oldest and largest outdoor market in the United States. It's an entire neighborhood, with two pasta manufactories, four poultry shops, four cheese stores, three spice houses, two bread bakeries, two pastry bakeries, seven meat markets, four fish merchants, and more than 40 produce vendors—now, *that's* amore! They're joined by two cafes, five luncheonettes, two delis, two pizza shops, and small stores selling antiques, dry goods, linens, luggage, and other necessities, all surrounded by a close-knit neighborhood where neighbors have carried on South Philly's Italian legacy for more than a hundred years.

Longwood Gardens $$$
Route 1, Kennett Square
(610) 388-1000
www.longwoodgardens.org

On 1,050 acres once owned by William Penn—and later by Pierre S. du Pont—Longwood Gardens is a showcase for some 11,000 different types of plants in 20 outdoor and 20 indoor gardens. The greenhouses alone cover four acres. Eight hundred events are held here each year, including flower shows, concerts, musical theater, famous holiday displays, and horticultural training programs. George Peirce, who first acquired the land from

Penn, developed the estate's original arboretum; du Pont, who owned Longwood from 1907 to 1954, personally designed most of the gardens. A $25-million renovation, completed in 2006, includes the redesigned Children's Garden and a new Organ Museum.

Mario Lanza Museum   Free
712 Montrose Street
(215) 238-9691
www.mario-lanza-
institute.org/museum.htm

The great tenor still is one of South Philly's favorite sons, and this neighborhood museum is a tribute with a mission: Admission is free, but donations are accepted to help fund the Mario Lanza Institute's scholarships for young opera students. Inside the museum, many of Lanza's costumes, photos, movie posters, clippings, telegrams, and other memorabilia are displayed, and vintage films are shown during the day. Each November a special Mass is celebrated at St. Mary Magdalene de Pazzi Church (next door to the museum) where Lanza sang "Ave Maria" as a young boy. Visitors can purchase CDs, photos, and books in the gift shop.

Mummers Museum $
Second Street and
Washington Avenue
(215) 336-3050
www.mummersmuseum.com

You haven't been to Philly if you haven't watched the Mummers Parade on New Year's Day—a celebration that started in South Philly in 1901 and now is an all-day spectacle involving 10,000 participants in elaborate costumes, dancing down the street, singing and playing "Oh, 'Dem Golden Slippers." But if you're not visiting on the holiday, the museum is the next best stop; you see the prize-winning costumes, learn to dance the "Mummers' Strut," and hear some great banjo music. Stop by Tuesday evenings at 8:00 P.M., May through September, and hear a free outdoor string band concert.

Museum of Mourning Art   Donation
2900 State Road, Drexel
(610) 259-5800
www.fieldtrip.com/pa/02595800.htm
Exhibits in this unusual museum explore
the ways in which we express grief, and
the symbols we've devised throughout
history. A fine horse-drawn hearse is displayed, symbolizing the soul's journey into
eternity. Also shown are dozens of pieces
of "mourning jewelry," bequeathed to
loved ones. One ring on display was
ordered by George Washington, to be
given to friends " . . . as mementos of my
esteem and regard." Also here is a rare
"cemetery gun," rigged to shoot grave
robbers; unfortunately, the gun sometimes
was triggered by mourners simply visiting
graves, so it soon was outlawed. Visitors
who arrive with some self-doubts can
peruse a 400-year-old instructional book-
let on getting into heaven.

Mütter Museum $$$
19 South 22nd Street
(215) 563-3737
www.collphylphil.org/mutter.asp
If anatomical specimens floating in fluids
are your thing, then you've come to the
right place. More than 20,000 medical
anomalies and treasures are housed here,
including President Grover Cleveland's jaw
tumor, the largest colon on record, and a
collection of 2,000 objects removed from
people's throats. The conjoined livers of
conjoined twins Chang and Eng are here,
along with a noted skull collection. Named

For one of the best views of the city,
take the elevator to City Hall's outdoor
observation deck, just below the statue
of William Penn. Admission is free, but
it's best to call that morning for reservations. If you were to climb up inside
Penn's hollow statue—which you must
not—you would find a child-sized hatch,
just 22 inches across, at the top of his
hat (Broad and Market Streets,
215-686-2840).

for the surgical professor who in 1858
donated his personal collection of materials and specimens to the College of Physicians of Philadelphia (who still administer
the museum), the Mütter is fascinating,
but it's not for everyone.

National Constitution Center $$
525 Arch Street
(215) 409-6600
www.constitutioncenter.org
Celebrating the freedoms behind the document, this center is as fun as history
gets. Visitors can stroll down a 1787 street,
listening to "citizens" discussing their lives
and issues; be sworn in as President; wear
the robes of a Supreme Court Justice and
decide constitutional cases; even sign the
Constitution. It is an unexpectedly emo-
tionally moving place where more than
100 interactive and multimedia exhibits
will engage you as you personally connect
with the Constitution and what it means
for your life.

National Liberty Museum $
321 Chestnut Street
(215) 925-2880
www.libertymuseum.org
Honoring heroes of liberty is the National
Liberty Museum's mission, from inspiring
figures such as Nelson Mandela and
Anne Frank, to U.S. presidents. One
major exhibit presents more than 100
fine art works in glass, including Dale
Chihuly's two-and-a-half-story "Flame of
Liberty," showing the fragility of freedom.
In "From Conflict to Harmony," visitors
can use a "shredder" to destroy cruel
words, just one way in which the
museum demonstrates peaceful ways of
resolving conflicts.

Philadelphia Doll Museum $
2253 North Broad Street
(215) 787-0220
www.philadollmuseum.com
More than 300 black dolls portray the
lives and perceptions of people of color,
now and throughout history. The collection of the museum, whose aim is to

preserve doll history and culture, includes African, European, and American folk arts. Workshops and seminars on doll making, doll heritage, and doll research are offered.

QVC Studio Park $$
1200 Wilson Drive, West Chester
(800) 600-9900
www.qvctours.com
Want to try selling the doodad you invented to millions of television viewers? First, you would have to attend "QVC School." QVC is the world's largest electronic retailer, and a tour through its studios shows how it's done. You'll learn how studio officials decide which products to sell, how they're tested, and you may even be able to view QVC programs in progress. Tours start on the hour, 10:00 A.M. to 4:00 P.M. daily, and reservations are not necessary except for groups of 10 or more. You can join the studio audience free of charge, but advance reservations are required.

Shoe Museum Free
Temple University School of
Podiatric Medicine
Eighth and Race Streets
(800) 220-FEET
http://podiatry.temple.edu/shoe_
museum/shoe_museum.html
This offbeat museum runs the gamut from Egyptian burial sandals to the 6-inch blue satin platform sandals Sally Struthers wore on the TV sitcom "All in the Family." A collection of tiny Chinese "lily shoes" is here, with drawings contrasting the deformed foot of a woman with bound feet and a foot allowed to grow normally. (The ideal was a 3-inch "Golden Lotus" foot.) Malaysian clogs, a circus giant's size 18 shoes, and shoes donated by celebrities, including André Agassi's 1990 pink and black Nikes, are included in the collection's 900 pairs. Call for an appointment.

While you're touring Eastern State Penitentiary, look for the mug shots of Inmate No. c2559—a black labrador named Pep. In 1924 the poor mutt was sentenced to life in prison by Pennsylvania Governor Gifford Pinchot for killing his wife's cat—though one newspaper speculated that the governor donated Pep to the warden to boost prisoner morale. His cell is a tour stop (2124 Fairmount Avenue, 215-236-3300; www.easternstate.org).

Shofuso Japanese House and Garden $
West Fairmount Park,
off Montgomery Drive
(215) 878-5097
www.shofuso.com
The first Japanese structure and landscaping on this beautiful site was the Japanese Bazaar and garden of the 1876 Centennial Exposition. Later a 17th-century gate from a Japanese Buddhist temple stood here until it burned down in 1955. The current Japanese House, a gracious replica 17th-century Shoin mansion, was built in 1953 in Nagoya and reassembled in Fairmount Park five years later; today, renovations of the house, manicured gardens, and koi pond are carried out by the Friends of Japanese House and Garden.

MADE IN PHILADELPHIA

Crayola Factory $$
30 Centre Square, Easton
(610) 515-8000
www.crayola.com
Don't pass up this plant tour thinking it's just for kids, though dozens of interactive exhibits will be fun for kids of any age. Watching how Crayola crayons and markers are made, and learning about the crayons' century-plus of history, sparks

Okay, not that we advocate visiting strip joints . . . but "Sopranos" fans already have discovered that Satin Dolls, a real-life strip club about 90 minutes from Center City in Lodi, New Jersey, is their beloved "Bada Bing." The club's owners make the most out of their unexpected notoriety by selling Bada Bing T-shirts, sweats, and tote bags. And, lest gentlemen curiosity-seekers be disappointed, the dancers here wear cover-ups; New Jersey law forbids topless dancing in bars (230 Route 17 South, Lodi, New Jersey, 201-845-6494).

both memories and new creative ideas. Themes and activities change monthly, but some—such as "Crayola Meltdown," where youngsters paint with melted crayon wax— are ongoing. Our favorite: coloring on both sides of a glass wall to watch how colors combine and form new shades.

**Herr's Snack Factory Tour   Free
Route 272 and Herr Drive,
Nottingham
(610) 932-9330
www.herrs.com**
If you've ever wondered how pretzels get

that brown color, or how cheese curls get that shape, you'll enjoy touring Herr's Snacks. Since 1946 Herr's has been a popular Pennsylvania munchies brand, including snacks from potato chips to tortilla chips. And don't worry about getting hungry on the one-hour drive back to the city; everyone taking the tour gets free samples of chips, fresh from the oven.

**United States Mint   Free
151 North Independence
Mall East
(800) USA-MINT or 872-6468
www.usmint.gov**
Exhibits and audio-visual stations inform visitors about the history and current programs of the U.S. Mint at Philadelphia, but the real fun is in watching those massive sheets of copper becoming amazingly detailed pennies—1,625,600,000 of them, in fact, turned out at this mint every year. That's more than two-thirds of the total coins produced here; the other 558,200,000 are quarters. The list of prohibited items is long; it includes aerosol cans, make-up, hair brushes, umbrellas, cameras, and hand lotions. Tours are self-guided, take about 45 minutes, and no reservations are required.

ARCHITECTURAL AND HISTORIC PRESERVATION

In older cities the aging housing stock and public buildings can become a community crisis if city leaders aren't on their toes.

Fortunately, that's not the case in Philadelphia. Literally dozens of public and private societies, associations, and other entities band together to protect and preserve the city's important buildings—its most visible heritage.

When visitors stroll the streets of Society Hill and other historic neighborhoods, they find themselves surrounded by brick and stone row homes, many more than two centuries old. Brickyards and stone quarries were among the colonies' first industries; thanks to the abundance of these natural resources, the historic structures of Philadelphia are sturdier than in many other cities built primarily of wood.

Still, all old buildings deteriorate, and the hard work of preserving Philadelphia's architectural heritage is ongoing. Most of the significant, preserved sites are covered in Attractions and other chapters; in this town, virtually every block features one or many historic homes, inns, restaurants, or museums. In some instances, entire streets appear on the National Register of Historic Places. Those buildings are protected from demolition, and any remodeling or changes to fixtures must be approved by the Philadelphia Historical Commission.

Another unique aspect of architectural and historic preservation in Philadelphia relates to the owner of many of the historic sites: it is you, Mr. and Ms. American Taxpayer. From the Liberty Bell to the Edgar Allan Poe House to Ben Franklin Parkway, the National Park Service of the

U.S. Department of the Interior keeps the sites clean and in top shape.

Dozens (possibly hundreds) more historic sites across the region, especially house museums, are owned and maintained primarily by smaller non-profit organizations devoted exclusively to the preservation of that specific property, such as the Pearl S. Buck House in Bucks County. In many Greater Philadelphia communities, those small societies work alongside local organizations such as the Chadds Ford Historical Society, Delaware County Historical Society, or Chester County Historical Society, to encourage and facilitate preservation.

Preservation is more than an initiative in Philadelphia; it is part of the culture of the place, inherent in every development or economic plan. A number of major organizations drive that continual movement. The following are among them.

PHILADELPHIA SOCIETY FOR THE PRESERVATION OF LANDMARKS

Great stories are always grounded in the extraordinary efforts of one individual, and

The entire downtown area of West Chester is listed on the National Register of Historic Places. The architect who designed the Chester County Courthouse, Thomas U. Walter, is the same man who designed the U.S. Capitol building.

the Philadelphia Society for the Preservation of Landmarks is no different. In 1931 Frances Anne Wister and some supporters organized around the news that the historic Powel House—home of Philadelphia's mayor, Samuel Powel, when America declared independence from England—was to be demolished. It's a home where George Washington and Ben Franklin danced, held court, and debated the issues of the day, and in spite of the Great Depression, Wister and her group succeeded in saving it from the wrecking ball.

A decade later the same group purchased the Grumblethorpe, the Wister family's circa-1744 summer retreat, built from native stone quarried on and oak cut from the property. In the late 1960s Ambassador Walter H. Annenberg restored the Physick House, home of Dr. Philip Syng Physick, "Father of American Surgery" and physician to President Andrew Jackson, Dolly Madison, and other notables of the day, and donated it to the Society.

Since then, the Landmarks Society has acquired additional properties and restored them as museums open to the public. Their membership is open to anyone interested in preserving and celebrating Philadelphia's heritage (215-925-2251; www.philalandmarks.org).

Among its many roles, the Landmarks Society sponsors all Philadelphia-based Elderhostel programs, hosting hundreds of adults 55 and older for in-depth, affordable visits and learning opportunities. Programs are customized by theme— art, music, history—and go "beyond the Liberty Bell" to places such as the Barnes Foundation, Gettysburg, and the Philadelphia Flower Show. To learn more, e-mail landmarks.elderhostel@verizon.net; or call (215) 925-2423.

PRESERVATION ALLIANCE FOR GREATER PHILADELPHIA

Perhaps more than any other group, it is the Preservation Alliance for Greater Philadelphia that leads in setting the agenda for preservation issues that affect the entire region, and in advocating strong public preservation policies. Its members include local historical districts, regional and federal preservation agencies, and heritage tourism organizations, as well as individuals and preservation-related companies.

The Alliance also provides technical assistance and educational materials, in its ongoing effort to preserve and restore historic buildings and sites. Its online directory includes appraisers, fabric and millwork specialists, organizational development and "smart planning" consultants, architectural salvage companies, scaffolding and steeple experts, and three pages of architectural historians.

In its outreach to the community, the Alliance regularly distributes "Preservation News," with stories ranging from reports on federal preservation budget issues to announcing a new architectural salvage store opening in a Philadelphia neighborhood. Not all of the conservation news relates to conventional-historic buildings; in one story, for instance, the Alliance was describing a new Neighborhood Conservation District ordinance that would enable residents of city neighborhoods "with notable character" but not qualifying for historic-preservation status, to protect the integrity of their neighborhoods from broad-brush development. One of the neighborhoods seeking such protection was Queen Village, adjacent to South Street, where working-class row homes are distinctive but not protected by the National Register.

Another coup for the Alliance was saving a 19th-century farm on the

Carpenters' Hall: Philly's Best-Kept Secret

It doesn't appear at the top of every tourist's itinerary, but perhaps it should: Carpenters' Hall is one of the most historically important buildings in the city.

Since 1770, the Hall has been owned and operated by the Carpenters' Company of Philadelphia, the nation's oldest trade guild. For years, the Hall was the largest building in the city that could be rented—a distinction that inadvertently made it the site of choice for some of the city's (and America's) most pivotal events. Some of its most famous "tenants" include:

- Ben Franklin's Library Company, the first free-lending library in the United States, moved into Carpenters' Hall in 1773 before the building was even complete. The library remained for 17 years and served as the Congressional library.
- From 1776 to 1778, the Hall served as a military infirmary, first for American soldiers, then British.
- For about a year in 1778, the U.S. War Office used the Hall as an arsenal and outfitted its expeditions from the building.
- America's first scientific organization, the American Philosophical Society, met in the Hall for five years beginning in 1780.
- Carpenters' Hall was America's first "Pentagon" in 1790, when General Henry Knox, who advised George Washington in battle strategy, set up headquarters here.

- The Bank of the United States, the first central bank not owned by a monarch, operated in the hall from 1794 to 1797, organized by Secretary of the Treasury Alexander Hamilton. It signaled the beginning of our Federal Reserve system.
- The Philadelphia Customs House was located in the Hall from 1801 to 1817.
- The Philadelphia College of Pharmacy—the first pharmaceutical college in the world—was established in the Hall in 1821.
- The Franklin Institute held the country's first trade expo here from 1824 to 1826, with more than 300 displays of American-made goods.
- In 1833 the Carpenters' Company School of Architecture began holding classes on the third floor of the Hall.
- Its greatest claim to fame: In 1774 Carpenters' Hall was the site of the First Continental Congress. After the Boston Tea Party, and in response to taxes and other "Intolerable Acts," all of the colonies except Georgia agreed to send delegates to a "congress." Delegates' opinions ran the spectrum from rebellion to loyalty to the Crown, and Carpenters' Hall was selected for the Congress because it was viewed as neutral territory. After seven weeks of debate, delegates adopted 10 resolutions on October 26, declaring the rights of British citizens in America.

Schuylkill River, adjacent to the Schuylkill Environmental Center, that had been zoned for 200-plus single-family homes and threatened to become, according to an Alliance news writer, an "antenna farm."

One of the Alliance's most successful preservation programs is its nationally recognized Historic Easement Program, in which individuals or organizations donate a building, or its interior or façade, to protect it from future demolition, neglect, or insensitive alterations (215–546–1146; www.preservationalliance.com).

HERITAGE CONSERVANCY

Charged with protecting the natural and historic resources of the region, Heritage Conservancy—formed in 1958 as the Bucks County Park Foundation—partners with other conservation groups, participates in community planning, and oversees historic architecture evaluations.

Some of Heritage Conservancy's projects involve assessments of historic homes and districts, such as the Richard Leedom Homestead or the Delaware and Lehigh Heritage Corridor Market Towns projects. Others focus on natural resources, such as protection of the Nockamixon Cliffs and Little Neshaminy

Creek Rivers Conservation. Planning is a major initiative of the Conservancy; projects include the Kohler Park Streambank Restoration and the Musconetcong River National Wild & Scenic River Study.

One of Heritage Conservancy's most successful initiatives is "Lasting Landscapes," a program of uniting "open space protection and historic preservation comprehensive at the landscape level." The process involves four steps: research, planning, implementation, and stewardship; its projects have included the Bushkill Creek Watershed, the Forks of the Neshaminy, and the Quakertown Swamp.

The Conservancy is based in Aldie Mansion in Doylestown (215–345–7020; www.heritageconservancy.org).

HISTORICAL SOCIETY OF PENNSYLVANIA

The Historical Society has been in the preservation business since 1824, longer than almost any other conservation organization in the country. Keepers of more than 19 million manuscripts, the Society holds one of the largest family history libraries in the country, is the top archive for Pennsylvania and regional history, and, since merging with the Balch Institute for Ethnic Studies in 2002, is one of the country's most respected centers for study and documentation of ethnic communities and immigrant experiences.

Nearly 600,000 books, pamphlets, serials, and microfilm reels are housed in the Society, along with 20 million manuscripts and more than 300,000 posters, ads, and other graphic items spanning our country's history from the 17th century onward.

And it is the repository for many national treasures, including the first draft of the United States Constitution. An original printer's proof of the Declaration of Independence, and the earliest surviving American photograph also are in the collection (1300 Locust Street, 215–732–6200; www.hsp.org).

Carpenters' Hall is known as the "Birthplace of Pennsylvania" because, in late June 1776, 103 delegates elected from across the state met there to chastise the colonial Assembly for doing too little in the quest for independence. Delegates pronounced Pennsylvania an independent state and sent their proclamation to the Second Continental Congress, which was meeting at the State House (now Independence Hall). Apparently, Pennsylvania's act of defiance was just what the Congress needed to hear: several days later, on July 4, the Declaration of Independence was adopted.

THE PHILADELPHIA SHIP PRESERVATION GUILD

Their motto is, "Two Ships, One Mission"— but in reality, their mission is twofold: to maintain and operate historic vessels, while they also educate the public on marlinspike seamanship and maritime culture.

The Guild owns two vintage vessels: the 1883 barkentine *Gazela Primeiro,* and the 1902 tug *Jupiter,* built in Philadelphia. Both ships are maintained largely by volunteers; when they are not sailing, both welcome visitors at their Penn's Landing berth. On occasion Guild members and guests ride the *Jupiter* and help with routine maintenance (801 South Columbus Boulevard, 215–238–0280; www.gazela.org).

TOURS

Driving into Philadelphia isn't like driving into any other city. After a lengthy prequel along the Schuylkill River, with a surprise view of the historic boathouses at water's edge, the Museum of Art and skyline suddenly, finally, appear on the left. It's a dramatic introduction to Penn's City of Brotherly Love—and, once you enter the core city, the architecture and appearance on every block is distinctive.

Philadelphia simply *looks* different, because its heritage is unique. The city was shaped in colonial times, right along with America's independence, and consensus long ago was to retain that flavor on every level, in every aspect. From Independence Hall to the row homes of DeLancey Street and westward into University City, one knows that these buildings, these surroundings, are historically significant.

That sense of importance developed as Philadelphia grew, so that it's not only the colonial-era sites that are maintained. Migrations from the American South and all points of the world are honored in their cultural environments. Important moments in music, art, and philosophy all are protected on one tour or another. Even Count Dracula is given a nod at the Rosenbach Museum & Library, where Bram Stoker's notes and outlines for *Dracula* are archived.

There's no escaping it: Touring Philadelphia is about historical touring, and in this tourism destination, it is its own industry. Most historic and other attractions offer tours of their sites; those are covered in the Attractions chapter. This section is devoted to those tours that are not of single sites; here we present tours of neighborhoods, clusters of attractions, and "theme" city tours.

They are offered in a range of formats: walking tours, riding tours (including two

that take you into the Delaware River), walking/bicycling tours, and even a Segway tour. Many offer wheelchair access; together they accommodate all ages and ability levels. You will notice a bit of overlap between sections: Several walking tours, for instance, are included among the Ethnic and Neighborhood Tours rather than with the Walking Tours because their focus is on one specific ethnic group.

We should also note that a diverse selection of tours are organized and hosted by the Neighborhood Tourism Network, a coalition of community-based organizations dedicated to the economic and cultural development of their areas through cultural and heritage tourism. Most of those tours are offered just twice a year, in spring and fall, and all leave from the Independence Visitor Center. Prices vary according to the tour, but all are about three hours long. Because they are not all clustered together in this chapter, we have repeated the contact information with each tour.

ETHNIC AND NEIGHBORHOOD TOURS

**Fishtown and Kensington:
Traditions of Art and Industry
Neighborhood Tourism Network
Independence Visitor Center,
Sixth and Market Streets
(215) 599-2295
ntn@gophila.com**
You can feel the vitality in these two comeback neighborhoods. Tour behind-the-scenes operations and enjoy Philadelphia-made goods at the Yards Brewery, one of the oldest remaining brewery buildings in the city, then browse and buy at the farmers' market at Greensgrow Farms' hydroponic garden. At the Rocket Cat Cafe, visit the cafe and studios of local artists. This bus tour aims to create

If you're thinking of taking a horse-and-carriage sightseeing tour, let the weather be your guide. Summer heat can be brutal for the horses, and once the temperature reaches 90 degrees, the tours stop for the horses' well-being. Your best bet: take your buggy tour in the morning, when temps are still relatively cool.

awareness of renewed commercial interest in the neighborhoods; prices range from $30 for adults to $20 for children 8 to 12.

From Farm to Table
Neighborhood Tourism Network
Independence Visitor Center,
Sixth and Market Streets
(215) 599-2295
ntn@gophila.com
To kick off Buy Local Week in July, NTN offers a tour of Somerton Tanks, a well-known urban farm inside Philadelphia. Learn about farming as you "follow" the path of your food from field to table by traveling from Somerton Tanks to a restaurant in South Philadelphia that buys its foods only from local family farms. You can learn more about Buy Local Week activities at www.buylocal.org.

Immigrant Jewish Philadelphia Tours
(215) 918-0326
www.boonin.com/tours.htm
Led by Harry D. Boonin, author of *The Jewish Quarter of Philadelphia: A History and Guide, 1881-1930,* these two-hour walking tours start on Spruce Street and include immigrant synagogues in Society Hill and Queen Village. They take in the Kratchman bathhouse, the Talmud Torah, the Hebrew Literature Society, and other Jewish icons, and often begin or end at one of the neighborhood's two delis. Boonin also includes a slide lecture, covering the same sites as the walking tour, on request.

Latin Soul, Latin Flavor
Neighborhood Tourism Network
Independence Visitor Center,
Sixth and Market Streets
(215) 599-2295
ntn@gophila.com
Feel the rhythms during your visit to El Centro de Oro, the heart of Philadelphia's Latino community. Learn about the roots of Latin American music, performed live for you at AMLA, and sample authentic Caribbean coffees and pastries during this bus tour to North Fifth Street. You'll also have the chance to browse the art gallery, crafts, and bookstore at Taller Puertor-riqueño. Prices range from $30 for adults to $20 for children 8 to 12.

Philadelphia's Civil Rights Struggle
Neighborhood Tourism Network
Independence Visitor Center,
Sixth and Market Streets
(215) 599-2295
ntn@gophila.com
Philadelphia's civil rights struggle was centered in North Philadelphia, and this bus tour takes visitors through the era as it unfolded here. At Girard College, they learn about the dramatic protests that brought about the integration of this school that once admitted only poor, white, orphan boys. Then they take in the renowned murals at the Church of the Advocate, and celebrate the leadership of local civil rights leaders. Prices range from $30 for adults to $20 for children 8 to 12.

Shalom Philly Tour
(215) 635-3494
www.shalomphillytours.com
Inspired by letters written by Philadelphia Jews during the colonial and Federal periods, the Shalom Philly Tour takes visitors throughout Old City to such landmarks as the Mikveh Israel Cemetery and the grave of Haym Salomon, a financier of the Revolutionary War. They also learn about how the creation of the U.S. Constitution relates to the Jewish notion of "Tikkun

Olam" (repairing the world) and the Jewish families who lived in Elfreth's Alley. Tours can be conducted in Hebrew or English and can be customized.

The Sound of Philadelphia
Neighborhood Tourism Network
Independence Visitor Center,
Sixth and Market Streets
(215) 599-2295
ntn@gophila.com
Always a sellout, this riding tour slides through Philadelphia's impressive musical legacy, from bee-bop to hip-hop to rock 'n' roll and rhythm and blues. Visit Philadelphia International Records where musical pioneers Kenny Gamble and Leon Huff "laid the tracks" that defined a generation. Tour the American Bandstand studio that had the attention of teens across the country every Saturday afternoon during the 1950s and '60s, and meet some of "the regulars" from the show. Prices range from $30 for adults to $20 for children 8 to 12.

Taking a Stand for Freedom
Neighborhood Tourism Network
Independence Visitor Center,
Sixth and Market Streets
(215) 599-2295
ntn@gophila.com
The Underground Railroad, and the bravery of those who participated in that perilous network, is the focus of this moving bus tour. Visit historic Mother Bethel AME Church and the Johnson House Historic Site, where you will witness first-person accounts evoking the moral and spiritual battles of conscience with which black and white Philadelphians struggled—station masters in the Railroad—as they risked their lives and personal liberty. Prices range from $30 for adults to $20 for children 8 to 12.

University City: Ethnic Dining
Neighborhood Tourism Network
Independence Visitor Center,
Sixth and Market Streets
(215) 599-2295
ntn@gophila.com
Ride to this busy neighborhood of nearly

60 ethnic restaurants for a dine-around to three very different eateries (a different selection for each tour). Learn about the history of University City and why many consider it Philadelphia's most lively cultural "melting pot." Experience the cultures through the cuisine that spans the globe. Prices range from $30 for adults to $20 for children 8 to 12.

University City: Left of Center
Neighborhood Tourism Network
Independence Visitor Center,
Sixth and Market Streets
(215) 599-2295
ntn@gophila.com
Aren't most suburbs conventional, quiet places? Not this one. It's in the city now, but University City was Philadelphia's first suburb and evolved to become one of its funkiest neighborhoods. Visit the Institute for Contemporary Art, Spiral Q Puppet Theater, and the studios of WXPN, home to "World Cafe," public radio's most popular program of contemporary music. Prices range from $30 for adults to $20 for children 8 to 12.

Urban Oases: the Gardens of West Philadelphia
Neighborhood Tourism Network
Independence Visitor Center,
Sixth and Market Streets
(215) 599-2295
ntn@gophila.com
You wouldn't believe where some of Philadelphia's most beautiful community gardens are hidden—tucked between row houses, claiming corner lots, and dotting city parks, their perseverance and grace in a concrete environment are inspiring. Ride to Aspen Farms, one of the city's most enduring and award-winning community gardens since the 1970s, and hear from local residents who work together to stabilize and beautify their neighborhoods through gardening. Prices range from $30 for adults to $20 for children 8 to 12.

Voices of Chinatown
Neighborhood Tourism Network
Independence Visitor center,
Sixth and Market Streets
(215) 599-2295
ntn@gophila.com
On this walking tour, immerse yourself in Asian-American culture during a visit through Chinatown. Learn about the political and social forces that shaped this bustling community while you stroll its busy streets. You will sample some of the neighborhood's best dim sum as you enjoy the artistry of music played on traditional Chinese instruments. Prices range from $30 for adults to $20 for children 8 to 12.

Wok 'N Walk Tour of Chinatown
1002 Arch Street (10th and Arch)
(215) 928-9333, (215) 782-2258
www.josephpoon.com/toursWokWalk.htm
Featured on "The Tonight Show" and "The Ellen DeGeneres Show," Chef Joseph Poon's tour illuminates the history, culture, and food of Chinatown through a real insider's eyes. You get a bit of everything: The tour includes a full lunch or dinner at Joseph Poon Asian Fusion Restaurant, followed by a tai chi demonstration, a Chinese vegetable carving lesson, and a walking tour of Chinatown, with stops at a fortune cookie factory, Chinese herbal medicine shop, Chinese place of worship, Chinese bakery, and Asian grocery store and fish market. The cost is $45 plus tax and tip, and worth every penny.

RIDING TOURS

American Heritage Landmark Tours
14 Anthony Drive, Malvern
(610) 647-4030
www.ahltours.com
Specializing in custom-designed cultural and historic tours of Philadelphia, Valley Forge, Brandywine Valley, Lancaster (Amish Country), and Bucks County, American Heritage tours focus on such themes as colonial taverns, medical history, the Underground Railroad, local gardens, and others. Call for a list of specialty tours.

Big Bus Tours
Sixth and Market Streets
(866) 3BIG-BUS
www.bigbustours.com
London isn't the only town with double-decker coaches. Big Bus Tours offers 90-minute tours of Philadelphia with about 20 stops at city sights and hotels, plus complimentary hotel shuttle service. From the Betsy Ross House to Logan Circle, passengers have on-off privileges at any stops. Tour prices range from $10 to $27, and buses depart every half-hour.

Carriage Tours
76 Carriage Company
Fifth and Chestnut Streets,
Sixth and Market Streets
(215) 925-TOUR
www.phillytour.com
Visitors can see Philadelphia the way many colonial residents did, by horse-drawn carriage, on these day and evening tours. No reservations are needed during the day; just go to one of the two departure points listed above. Tours are planned according to your own time constraints: Short tours (15 to 20 minutes) cover Independence National Historical Park, the nation's most historic square mile. Medium tours (30 to 35 minutes) add Society Hill, America's largest collection of original 18th-century homes and churches, and long tours (1 hour) add more Old City attractions such as the Betsy Ross House. Prices range from $25 for up to four people, to $70. Reservations are needed for evening tours.

Ride the Ducks
Sixth and Chestnut Streets
(215) 227-DUCK
www.phillyducks.com
See the city and cruise the Delaware River near Penn's Landing, all in one wacky vehicle. Ducks tours have taken off in numerous cities including Philadelphia; the 80-minute adventure takes in Independence Hall, the

Liberty Bell, South Street, Society Hill, the National Constitution Center, City Tavern, and more. Tickets can be purchased at the Independence Visitor Center or the Ducks kiosk at Sixth and Chestnut; prices range from about $23 for adults to $13 for kids age 3 to 12, and include a free "wacky quacker."

Super Ducks and River Loop
Docked at the Hyatt Regency at
Penn's Landing
(215) 923-4778, (866) 577-LOOP
www.riverboatqueenfleet.com,
www.riverloop.com
Replicas of luxury paddle wheelers leave on one-hour scheduled tours of the scenic Philadelphia and Camden waterfronts. River Loop also offers two- and three-hour tours, showcasing the skyline, bridges, Museum of Art, Navy Yard, and other attractions. All boats have beverage service and snack bars.

Trolley Tours
Philadelphia Trolley Works
The Bourse, Fifth & Chestnut Streets
(215) 925-TOUR
www.phillytour.com
Choose from a 90-minute, fully narrated City Tour ($23.00 adults, $5.00 children) with on-off privileges at 20 stops across the city, or the Fairmount Park Trolley Tour ($20 adults, $13 children and seniors), an escorted tour through the country's largest city park with stops at two historic mansions (admission included). For a small additional charge, City Tour passes can be used a second day. Both tours depart every 30 minutes starting at 9:30 A.M., April through November, and hourly during the off-season.

West Chester Railroad
Market Street Station, West Chester
(610) 430-2233
www.westchesterrr.net
A specialty railroad, the train runs between the Market Street Station in West Chester, through the Chester Creek Valley to Glen Mills Station and back, a 90-minute trip.

Philadelphia's edgy South Street is the same "South Street . . . where all the hippies meet . . . " in the famous song recorded by the Orlons.

Various tours operate throughout the year, including Sunday Summer Picnic Specials, Foliage Express and Harvest Express in the fall, and other seasonal trips. A snack bar is available on board; times and prices vary with the trips. The train also is available to charter for private parties.

Your Philadelphia Tour
500 South 25th Street
(215) 272-TOUR (8687)
www.yourphiladelphiatour.com
If Your Philadelphia Tour doesn't offer the specific tour you want, they'll research it and custom-design a themed tour just for you. Most tours feature history, contemporary city life, the arts and architecture, and focus on special locations not included on the larger group tours.

WALKING TOURS

Centipede Tours
1315 Walnut Street
(215) 735-3123
www.centipedeinc.com
A colonial-costumed guide escorts visitors on a stroll through historic Society Hill, weather permitting. The company specializes in custom packages, as well as Candlelight Strolls, Saturday evenings beginning in late May through early October. Call for reservations; strolls start at Welcome Park, Second and Walnut Streets.

The Constitutional Walking Tours of Philadelphia
Independence Visitor Center
Sixth and Market Streets
(215) 525-1776, (800) 537-7676
www.TheConstitutional.com
In just 75 minutes, these guided walking tours take visitors in the footsteps of our Founding Fathers, past the Liberty Bell

Center and Independence Hall, Declaration House, Signers' Walk, Christ Church Burial Ground, and other historic sites, rain or shine. Tours are offered seven days a week from Memorial Day through Labor Day, at $15 for adults or $12.50 for kids ages 3 to 12. Tickets can be purchased online or at the Visitor Center.

Historic Philadelphia AudioWalk™
Sixth and Market Streets
(215) 965-7676
www.ushistory.org/audiowalk

Travel Holiday magazine called this tour, "the best way to see historic Philadelphia." It's certainly hassle-free: Just pick up a lightweight CD player and map at the Visitor Center and follow the prompts, touring the historic section at your own pace. Stroll cobblestone lanes, linger in an 18th-century garden and mail postcards from a colonial post office—a clever way of showing visitors life in the 1700s. Renting the CD player is $10.00, with discounts for additional participants, and you can take home a CD for $14.95. (The map is yours to keep after the tour.)

Poor Richard's Walking Tours
(215) 206-1682
www.phillywalks.com

You might call Poor Richard's the "thinking person's tours." They go beyond sightseeing to help visitors understand how the colonial town became the contemporary metropolis. They also offer customized and specialized tours, including Literary Philadelphia, Ethnic Marketplaces, the Footsteps of George Washington, and the Quaker City:

Benjamin Franklin was not a Quaker, but he did believe everyone should be able to worship as he or she wished and contributed to many churches and temples besides his own, the Christ Church. The Free Quaker Meeting House, on Arch Street between Fifth and Sixth, is one that benefited from Franklin's support.

Beacon of Religious Toleration. These tours leave visitors not only more informed, but with a deeper appreciation of the city's evolution over four centuries.

Walking in Benjamin Franklin's Footsteps
www.gophila.com/itineraries/i_itinben.htm

This one-hour, self-guided tour was developed for Ben's birthday in 2006. The complete itinerary is online, beginning at the Independence Visitor Center, and includes sites such as the Federal Reserve Bank (during his career as a printer, Franklin printed currency for several colonies) and City Tavern, where Franklin and his colleagues dined and debated hot issues of the day. Most attractions are free.

UNIQUE AND NOVELTY TOURS

Creepy Crypts and Criminals
Neighborhood Tourism Network
(215) 599-2295
ntn@gophila.com

Get creeped out this Halloween by touring two of Philadelphia's scariest historic spots. First, visit the abandoned Eastern State Penitentiary, the prison where some of America's most notorious criminals did time, then an after-dark visit to Laurel Hill Cemetery. Everyone who lives there is dead . . . we think.

Famous Criminals of Philadelphia
Second and Market Street,
Northwest corner
(215) 525-1219
www.phillycrimetour.com

Gangsters, pirates, and other bad guys are the stars of this 90-minute candlelight walking tour. Learn how all the gold from America's largest bank was smuggled away, and which world-famous pirate was in such a hurry to leave Philadelphia that he left his treasure behind! The Bible Riots of the 1840s, a plot against the governor, and America's first bank robbery—all true stories—will have you keeping one eye on the shadows along the waterfront and narrow alleyways. Reservations are required; prices and times vary.

Ghosts of Philadelphia
Fifth and Chestnut Streets
(215) 413-1997
www.ghosttour.com

Peek through the cobwebs and discover the "other side" of Philadelphia's history. Featuring burial grounds and potters' fields, haunting tales of plague and pestilence, this tour brings traitors and heroes alike back to life. Reservations are required for the 75-minute candlelight walking tour, April through November, that "materializes" each night at 7:30 P.M. and takes you through Independence Park and Society Hill.

I Glide Tours'
Segway Tour of Philadelphia
(877) GLIDE-81
www.iglidetours.com

"Why walk," asks the literature, "when you can glide?" Indeed, once you try touring on a Segway, you may never want to use your legs again. The escorted tours begin with hands-on training at Eakins Oval, just across the street from the Philadelphia Museum of Art, and glide for up to three hours past some of Philadelphia's best attractions. "The tour . . . mostly provides a respectable excuse to spend $69 to screw around on the Segway," wrote a *Philadelphia* magazine writer. Team building and other group tours can be arranged; reservations are a must.

Mural Arts Program (MAP) Tour
1729 Mount Vernon Street
(215) 685-0750
www.muralarts.org

Since 1984, when MAP began as an anti-graffiti initiative, more than 2,000 mural projects have been completed, making Philadelphia home to the largest collection of public murals in the country.

Storytellers are not born, they're taught—and the "ambassadors" working Philadelphia's storytelling benches got their education at the Benstitute, a three-week certification program where they learned the finer points of local history, the art of storytelling, and customer service. Inspired by the legacy of Ben Franklin, the Benstitute aspires to Ben's lifelong goals of engaging the mind, serving the public, and improving society.

Those first artists were adjudicated kids whose artistic energies were redirected into making art that would enhance, rather than damage, their neighborhoods. Visitors can walk, bicycle, or drive the self-guided tour; MAP's brochure shows routes for all three options—but unless you're walking, take a navigator to point out approaching art. All tours begin at the Visitor Center on Sixth and Market Streets.

Once Upon A Nation
Various Historic District Venues
(215) 629-5801
www.onceuponanation.org

Storytelling is the vehicle for Once Upon A Nation, which installed thirteen new storytelling benches—at the Betsy Ross House, Christ Church, and other locations—so that visitors can learn "firsthand" about Philadelphia's past. The stories continue into the evening with readings by such illustrious figures as Edgar Allan Poe, who spent some of his most prolific years in Philadelphia; George Washington; and Thomas Jefferson. One "adventure tour" will allow residents to eavesdrop on the heated argument over independence, and whether Americans should take up arms; in another, youngsters can join their colonial ancestors as they play hoops, marbles, and hopscotch. See the Web site or call for a fact sheet on current offerings.

Philadelphia Hospitality
123 South Broad Street, Suite 1330
(215) 790-9901, (800) 714-3287
www.philahospitality.org
For a quarter-century, Philadelphia Hospitality has provided distinctive cultural programs for special groups visiting the city, by "opening the doors of private Philadelphia"—taking visitors behind the usually closed doors of beautiful homes, elegant private clubs, and antiques and art collections. The programs are designed to suit the interests of clients, which have included historical societies, museum and horticultural groups, and professional associations and corporate groups.

KIDSTUFF 👫

Finding kid-friendly attractions is easy in a city like Philadelphia, where the economy is largely rooted in tourism and the city itself is a family tourism destination. The challenge is in isolating those attractions that are specifically aimed at kids, just because the city as a whole *is* so kid-friendly.

Philly is the birthplace of democracy, so literally every block is historically significant, from the Christ Church Burial Ground, where Ben Franklin and so many of the country's founders are laid to rest, to the cherished Liberty Bell. These and dozens more attractions are informative and entertaining not only for kids, but for their entire families.

To avoid cross-referencing virtually every museum and attraction listed in this chapter, we are including here *only* those places and activities aimed directly at children. Most of those included in the Attractions chapter welcome kids, but also will be fun for their parents. You also will find many kid-friendly destinations and activities in the Parks and Recreation chapter.

Many Kidstuff attractions are free of charge. For those that do charge admission, we have instituted a price code; the code refers to adult prices. Children's admission typically is less.

PRICE CODE

$	Less than $5.00
$$	$5.00 to $9.99
$$$	$10.00 to $14.99
$$$$	$15.00 to $19.99
$$$$$	$20.00 and over

PARKS AND AMUSEMENT PARKS

Camden Children's Garden $
3 Riverside Drive, Camden, New Jersey
(856) 365-TREE
www.camdenchildrensgarden.org

Interactive exhibits bring the greenery alive in this kids' garden, with more than four acres of fun: If they're brave, they can even approach the giant apatosaurus in the Dinosaur Garden—and discover that it's made of recycled car parts! They can go on to the sandpit to unearth old dinosaur bones, wander through the upside-down *Alice in Wonderland* garden, and work their way through the maze garden to the Butterfly house. The garden is open every day.

Giggleberry Fair $$
Routes 202 and 203, Lahaska
(215) 794-4000
www.peddlersvillage.com

A short drive outside the city is Peddler's Village, a Bucks County complex of shops, restaurants, and bed-and-breakfast style lodging. Giggleberry Fair is the always-popular kids' section, crowned by the spectacular Grand Carousel. Kids can romp freely on Giggleberry Mountain, a six-story indoor obstacle course, and test their skills in the Game Room. In Discovery Land they can harvest "produce" from the garden, operate a waterway with canal locks, and climb aboard a full-size wooden pickup truck, then eat a snack at the Painted Pony Cafe.

Ben Franklin might have been the most inventive person in history: He invented the odometer (so that, as the nation's first postmaster, he could keep track of how far he traveled to deliver mail), bifocals, Daylight Saving Time, the Franklin Stove, and the single-fluid theory of electricity (you can see one of his lightning rods on display at the Franklin Institute). But he wasn't Philly's only inventor; bubble gum, licorice, ice cream, and the Girl Scout cookie all were created here.

Kids' Castle   Free
425 Wells Road, Doylestown
www.discover-doylestown.com
It takes a child to raise a village . . . and in this case, they built a playground. A local contest challenged kids to design and name the playground, and the outcome was the 35-foot-high, eight-story wooden castle with a tree house, swings, twisty slides, and picnic shelter nearby.

Sesame Place $$$$$
100 Sesame Road,
Langhorne
(215) 752-7070
www.sesameplace.com
It's an amusement park, but the biggest fun at the 14-acre Sesame Place happens in the water park section. On a hot day, even the names of the water attractions are irresistible, from Sesame Streak to the Slippery Slopes and, for younger kids, the Teeny Tiny Tidal Wave. You'll find bigger thrills in the Sky Splash and a watery challenge in Mumford's Water Maze. Little ones can mix and match totem poles, crawl through toddler-size mazes, and play at a variety of activity tables. Sesame Place is a 30-minute drive north of Philly. For an extra fee ($12.95 to 26.95), kids and their parents can have breakfast or dinner with Elmo or Big Bird. Find directions on the Web site, or call.

THEATER FOR KIDS

Arden Theatre Company $$$
40 North Second Street
(215) 922-1122
www.ardentheatre.org
What sets Philadelphia children's theater apart from other cities, is that the actors and designers meet the same high standards for kids' shows as for adult productions, and Arden Theatre is a great example. Its mission is "to bring to life the greatest stories of the greatest storytellers of all time," and the shows always end with an after-show Q&A session so the kids can meet the cast. Every youngster

gets a poster of the show to take home, and if they catch the acting bug, parents can sign up for the "Family Usher Network" (FUN), where kids can take a backstage tour and help seat the audience.

Mum Puppettheatre $$$$
115 Arch Street
(215) 925-7686
www.mumpuppet.org
Both puppets and live actors are featured in Mum Puppettheatre's productions, geared for both younger and older audiences. Kids' shows include great stories such as *The Velveteen Rabbit, Jack and the Beanstalk,* and *The Adventures of a Boy and His Dog in Outer Space.* The theater sponsors a "Mum Puppet School" as well.

**The People's Light and
Theatre Company** $$$$$
39 Conestoga Road,
Malvern
(610) 644-3500
www.peopleslight.org
People's Light features a three-play season aimed at kids each year, including old favorites such as *Jason and the Golden Fleece, A Christmas Carol, The Little Prince,* and *Yemaya's Belly.* Performances are held in the 380-seat Mainstage and 200-seat Steinbright Stage; discussions follow each show, and People's Light also operates a theater school. Tickets for the three-play series cost $71.50 for adults and $44.00 for children.

ATTRACTIONS AND MUSEUMS

Academy of Natural Sciences $$$
1900 Benjamin Franklin Parkway
(215) 299-1000
www.acnatsci.org
Ever climbed inside the skull of a tyrannosaurus rex? Now is your chance, in the Academy's Dinosaur Hall, where you can try on claws and horns, dig for fossils, and let a time machine take you to the Mesozoic Era. In the hands-on Nature Center,

you can crawl under a pond, get up-close to a beehive, and, in the "rain forest," stand still while hundreds of butterflies from Kenya, Costa Rica, and Malaysia flit about your head. Opened in 1812, the Academy is the oldest continually operating nature museum in this hemisphere. Ask about the "Safari Overnight" program, for about $40 per child.

American Helicopter Museum $$
1220 American Boulevard,
West Chester
(610) 436-9600
www.helicoptermuseum.org
Climb aboard—and feel free to play with the switches and dials! The Helicopter Museum gives a hands-on experience—the only museum in America devoted exclusively to the science of "rotary wing aviation." Since two of the three major helicopter manufacturers began in the Philadelphia area, this is the perfect place to showcase the first mass-produced helicopter, along with many experimental aircraft, artifacts, films, documents, and memoirs. The Toddler Learning Area features a control tower with knobs to turn, a radar screen, a voice-activated LED screen, and puzzles. You can even create a once-in-a-lifetime family memory with a helicopter ride, $35 per person for six to eight minutes.

Lights of Liberty $$$$
Sixth and Chestnut Streets
(877) GO2-1776
www.lightsofliberty.org
Billed as the "first ambulatory sound and light show in the world"—meaning, you walk along historic city streets to see and hear this show—Lights of Liberty tells the story of America's independence through beautiful hand-painted images, some up to 50 feet high, projected at night onto the buildings where the events actually happened more than 200 years ago. Wearing a lightweight headset, you follow a costumed guide along cobblestone streets, listening to a soundtrack performed by the Philadelphia Orchestra and narrated by familiar voices

such as Charlton Heston and Walter Cronkite. Whoopi Goldberg narrates a special kids' version. The $12-million show covers 5 city blocks. Come on a weeknight when it's less crowded; reservations are recommended.

Fairmount Water Works
Interpretive Center Free
640 Waterworks Drive
(215) 685-0723
www.fairmountwaterworks.org
It's been nearly a century since the Water Works stopped pumping water in 1909, but it now thrives in its new life, focusing on how our land-locked behaviors impact our water. In these unique exhibits, kids can make it rain, look inside a 48-inch water main, re-route historic waterways, follow their "flush," and pilot a helicopter up the Delaware River—all while learning that we drink the same water the dinosaurs drank. Closed Monday; admission is free.

Franklin Institute
Science Museum $$$
222 North 20th Street
(215) 448-1200
www.fi.edu
The granddaddy of all hands-on science museums, the Franklin Institute never gets boring. The exhibits are eclectic and fun: the giant heart—15,000 times life-size—with crawl-through arteries and a blood fountain; "Space Command," where you can pilot a state-of-the-art flight simulator; the "Sports Challenge," where kids of

The best remedy for kids' "museum fatigue" is a stop in the CoreStates Science Park, the 38,000-square-foot greenery located between the Franklin Institute and the Please Touch Museum. Kids can swing on a 12-foot tire, tell time on a sundial, harness up to ride a tandem bike on a high-wire, or just nap in the grass. Admission is free with Franklin Institute tickets (210 North 21st Street, 215-448-1200; www.fi.edu).

all ages can balance on a surfboard; or "Island of the Elements," where the under-eight crowd can board a sailing ship and climb to the top of a lighthouse. The 20-foot statue of Big Ben in the rotunda is an attraction in itself. First opened in 1824 to honor Ben Franklin and his creative genius, the Institute houses three floors of please-touch exhibits, the Fels Planetarium, and the Tuttleman IMAX Theater.

Please Touch Museum $$
210 North 21st Street
(215) 963-0667
www.pleasetouchmuseum.org
"Please Touch" is the country's first museum for children seven years and under, with exhibits designed to make the most of their imaginations. In the Sendak section, kids can frolic with a "Wild Thing" and make a cake with the "bakers who bake until dawn." Then they can move on to the "Supermarket," the "Kids Construct," the "Move It!" area, and, for children under three, the "Barnyard Babies," where they can drive a tractor, dress a scarecrow, and feed the baby chicks. When they wind down, the kids can hear a storyteller—or you—in the Story Garden.

ANIMAL TIME

Adventure Aquarium $$$$
1 Riverside Drive, Camden,
New Jersey
(856) 365-3300, (800) 616-JAWS
www.adventureaquarium.com
When they say "adventure," they mean it. Located just across the river from Penn's Landing on the Camden Waterfront, this aquarium specializes in thrills—as in, swimming with the sharks. Kids over 12 can suit up and swim among stingrays, while sharks glide below you in a separate tank—with all of their hungry eyes, following the intruder's every move. More than 850 animals live in the "shark realm," while dozens more, including a Nile hippo and carnivorous crocodiles, reside along the West African River Experience. A penguin island, shipwreck, and two-story waterfall add to the entertainment.

Elmwood Park Zoo $$
1661 Harding Boulevard,
Norristown
(610) 277-3825
www.elmwoodparkzoo.org
Visitors are sometimes surprised to find this tranquil haven in the middle of a busy suburb about 20 miles northwest of Philadelphia. More than 80 species (about 200 animals) make their home here, from jaguars and timber wolves to snakes, beavers, bison, and a bald eagle. A barn exhibit features domesticated burros, goats, and sheeps for younger kids. Owned by a local zoological society, this 16-acre park is dedicated to conservation. In summer Elmwood Park hosts an overnight "Zoosnooze" ($38 per person), including dinner, breakfast, and snacks.

Gateway Stables $$$$$
949 Merrybell Lane,
Kennett Square
(610) 444-1255
www.gatewaystables.com
When the little ones need a break from the concrete, think about a pony ride along the gorgeous trails at Gateway Stables in the Brandywine Valley. This riding center near the Pennsylvania–Delaware border offers trail guides and certified instructors. If you'll be in the area for more than a few days, the kids can take lessons or attend holiday or summer camp—or even have their friends join them for a "pony party." The price of $35 to $40 per person includes the guide.

Once Upon A Nation

This is not your parents' history of the colonies: On the sidewalk outside Christ Church, one might overhear stories of ministers who whisper plans of treason, and women whose behavior can only be described as rebellious. Around the corner, you might "meet" a young brewer named Timothy Matlack whose handwriting was so tidy, he was recruited to pen the Declaration of Independence. And what kind of woman was Betsy Ross anyway?

All across the Historic District, costumed storytellers share their tales of America's heroes and their friends, in the places where the history actually happened. Ben Franklin is there, along with Betsy and George and Thomas. They give tours, too, including Colonial Kids' Quest ($15)—in which kids search for a missing copy of the Declaration of Independence—and the Tippler's Tour, a tavern tour of colonial watering holes ($30 per person, including tastings), including the Plough & the Stars, Old Original Bookbinders, and City Tavern. A colonial barkeep offers insights about drinking traditions from the era, and leads guests in colonial drinking songs and toasts.

Mostly, though, Once Upon A Nation is about telling good stories. Thirteen storytelling benches are placed throughout the District; in some spots, visitors also can watch period crafts being created, or musical numbers played on the Glass Armonica, Ben Franklin's favorite musical invention. Kids can participate in a military muster and be "recruited" into the Continental Army, and everyone can listen to neighborhood gossip along Harmony Lane, one of Philly's first streets. If you're out walking in the evening be on the alert as you pass the Christ Church Burial Ground: You might spot Edgar Allan Poe, wandering among the graves by candlelight.

Linvilla Orchards
137 West Knowlton Road, Media
(610) 876-7116
www.linvilla.com
The family who bought this farm in 1914 are still running it, offering the total farm experience: Small children will have fun with the farm animals, including white-tailed deer, horses, sheep, goats, pigs, turkeys, and even a few ostriches and emus. The family can join a hayride out to the raspberry fields or peach orchards, and on weekends you can all go fishing for rainbow trout in the well-stocked pond, for $9.00 per person for anyone 11 years and older, or $5.00 for younger kids. Linvilla rents fishing rods and sells bait; no license is required. After you've worked up an appetite with the animals and fishing, you can buy homemade candy, pastries, preserves, and honey in the farm market.

Newlin Grist Mill   **Free**
219 South Cheyney Road,
Glen Mills
(610) 459-2359
www.newlingristmill.org
A commercial grist mill until 1941, this historic mill sits on land that Nathaniel Newlin's father bought from William Penn in the early 1700s. Even today, corn is ground here for visitors to sample. Most will

visit the "Historic Water Walk," the hand-dug mill race, along with the circa-1710 spring house and reproduction blacksmith shop. A summer nature program opens the world of tadpoles and forest creatures to kids ages 4 to 12, and pond or stream trout fishing is available for $3.00 per person. Admission to the grist mill is free.

Philadelphia Insectarium   **$$**
8046 Frankford Avenue
(215) 338-3000
www.insectarium.com
It's all about bugs at the Insectarium, where you can see them, hold them, play with them, and even eat an insect or two. Exhibits are fascinating, from the tank of glow-in-the-dark scorpions to the working beehive, the termite mound, Arachnid Alley, and hundreds of exotic butterflies. The only insect museum in the tri-state area, Insectarium is the brainchild of an exterminating company owner who loved to tease his neighbors by displaying his "catch of the day." Thousands of live and mounted creepy-crawlies reside here; hundreds of them live in Cockroach Kitchen. Don't leave without tasting a chocolate-covered cricket or mealworm.

Philadelphia Zoo   **$$$$**
3400 West Girard Avenue
(215) 243-1100
www.philadelphiazoo.org
In the nation's oldest zoo (1874), exhibits are placed throughout a 42-acre Victorian garden with sculpted shrubbery, ornate iron cages, and historic architecture—including the country home of William Penn's grandson. But the kids won't care about that; they come to see the elephants, zebras, bears, and giraffes. They can ride in a giant "swan boat" on Bird Lake, or cuddle with bunnies in the Tastykake Children's Zoo. Rare species housed include white lions, pygmy marmosets, coati, and blue-eyed lemurs; for an extra $12.00, kids of any age can take a thrilling ride in the Zooballoon, or ride a camel for $5.00.

HISTORIC SITES

Independence Seaport Museum   **$$**
211 South Columbus Boulevard
and Walnut Street
(215) 925-5439
www.phillyseaport.org
For a glimpse at what the Delaware and Schuylkill Rivers have meant to Philly's development, the Seaport Museum is the best place—and great fun for kids, who can wiggle through the hatches of the submarine USS *Becuna*. Inside the museum itself are displays showing Philadelphia's role in maritime history, along with exhibits showing what makes boats float and other vital questions. Berthed near the *Becuna* is the *Olympia*, the country's oldest warship (1892) and Admiral Dewey's flagship for his Manila Bay victory in the Spanish-American War. To watch artisans building and restoring wooden boats, visit "Workshop on the Water," a working boat shop. On Sunday from 10:00 A.M. to noon, admission is free.

Mercer Museum   **$$**
84 South Pine Street, Doylestown
(215) 345-0210
www.mercermuseum.org
It's easy to spot Mercer Museum in little Doylestown, as this castle towers over all its neighbors. Rooms are themed—tools, folk art, home gadgets—and full of artifacts used in America before everything

Heading across the Delaware River to visit Adventure Aquarium or other riverside attractions? Save yourself the hassle of traffic congestion and parking fees, and take the Riverlink Ferry from Penn's Landing, Walnut Street, and Columbus Boulevard. The first ferry leaves at 9:40 A.M. and ferries run every 40 minutes, May to September. For the complete schedule and other details, call (215) 925-LINK or visit www.river linkferry.org.

was mechanized. From log sleds to leather-working hammers, more than 40,000 items are stored here—even a Conestoga wagon and whaling boat, hanging from the ceiling of the four-story central court! Mercer built the museum in 1916 to house his private collection of pre-industrialization everyday items, so this bit of history wouldn't be lost. Kids can dress in colonial-era garb and try many of the activities represented in the collection, including driving a team of horses.

Pennsbury Manor $
400 Pennsbury Memorial Road, Morrisville
(215) 946-0400
www.pennsburymanor.org
Kids love being greeted by "Sir William Pea," one of the resident peacocks at William Penn's 17th-century Bucks County estate. Though he founded this wonderful city, Penn fervently believed that life in the country was more wholesome. That sense of grace seems to follow visitors as they tour the elegant Manor House, brew house, blacksmith shop, and other buildings, watching costumed interpreters portray life in 1683. Penn only lived in his dream home for two years, but the kitchen garden remains as he planned it, and Pennsbury staff brew their own beer with the same methods used 300 years ago. Resident animals, too, are true to the era—South Down sheep, Red Devon oxen, horses, and chickens. Watch for reenactments of witch trials, weddings, and festivals.

Valley Forge National Historical Park   Free
North Gulph Road and Route 23, Valley Forge
(610) 783-1077
www.nps.gov/vafo/index.htm
For kids and their families, visiting Valley Forge is an eye-opener: For six months, George Washington and his soldiers camped here, with rationed supplies and severe weather. It was so bad that, though not a single shot was fired, some 2,000 men died here that winter. The exhibit in the Welcome Center, "Determined to Persevere," portrays life during that encampment with artifacts. Some of the outbuildings are original, including Washington's headquarters; together, the displays bring to life the struggles of the Continental Army. In the "Saturday Morning Kids Corner," youngsters can join in unusual aspects of Revolutionary War activities, such as being a recruit in Washington's army, preparing the foods the soldiers ate, and learning the role of women and children in the camp. Admission to the park is free; admission to Washington's headquarters is $3.00.

SHOPS AND TOY STORES

Born Yesterday
1901 Walnut Street
(215) 568-6556
You would expect nothing less of a Rittenhouse Square boutique: upscale clothing lines like Petite Babeau, Malina, and Deux par Deux; Laura Lynn's vintage print bibs and rompers; and the shop's own line of hand-knit sweaters. For baby's room, drool over handmade one-of-a-kind quilts, dollhouse bookshelves, and mobiles made of tiny stuffed Gund bunnies. Baby needs accessories? Pick up some handmade barrettes and a pair of itty-bitty calfskin shoes.

Character Development
209 Haverford Avenue, Narberth
(610) 668-1545
http://characterdevelopment.net
Once you know this children's bookstore

When you really want the kids to feel at home, take them to a drive-in movie—the country's oldest, in fact, about 60 miles north of Center City near the city of Bethlehem. Shankweiler's is the closest drive-in to Philadelphia and shows a double-feature seven nights a week. Admission is $6.00 for adults, $3.00 for kids (4540 Shankweiler Road, Orefield, 610-481-0800; www.shankweilers.com).

is owned by a child psychotherapist and her graphic designer husband, you want to say, "Yeah, it shows." Care was taken with the hip design, and the book selection ranges from soft cloth books for infants, to Thich Nhat Hanh books for teens. Music, art, stationery, scrapbooking supplies, and CDs, all related to emotional and intellectual development, pack the shelves in this light, uplifting space.

Children's Boutique
1702 Walnut Street
(215) 732-2661
http://echildrensboutique.com
If your baby girl craves a necklace of freshwater pearls with 18-karat gold accents ($80), or a hand-knitted hooded baby cardigan ($90), then this Rittenhouse Square fixture is the place to shop. The stuff here is so cute that you'll wish you had a baby to cuddle inside the cashmere baby blankets, or to dress in a $90 firefighter's uniform. Several of the European and domestic lines are customdesigned for sale exclusively in Children's Boutique—and if you aren't sure what to get the baby who has everything, the shop's Personal Shopper service will be happy to advise.

Five Below
147 East Swedesford Road, Wayne
(610) 964-1925, and six other locations
This is a classy discount store for teens, where every item costs $5.00 or less (hence the name). Created by Zany Brainy founder David Schlessinger, Five Below is the perfect store when kids just *have* to take home a purchase but don't have much to spend. Computer games, hair trimmings, books, sporting goods— nothing they need is overlooked in this can't-resist shop.

Hey Little Diddle
123 North Narberth Avenue,
Narberth
(610) 664-1228
www.heylittlediddle.com
From prettily painted toy bins to coordinated Maddie Boo bedding, Hey Little Diddle is, in their words, a "luxurious lifestyle boutique for you and your baby." Posh cribs, designer diaper bags, and colorful clocks are featured alongside clothes and accessories. Owned by two sisters, this cottage-style shop is worth a look if you want unusual items both for baby and baby's room.

Marcella Soret's
845-47 West Lancaster Avenue,
Bryn Mawr
(610) 527-2700
www.marcellasoret.com
Out here on the Main Line, Marcella's is *the* place to shop for kids' shoes. They also carry clothes, but the footwear selection is impressive, from sporty wear such as Teva and Puma, to dressier brands— Nimi, Elefanten, Primigi, and more, to kids' size seven. And for your youngster's mystifying sneaker requirements, the Skechers wall should answer any questions.

Oxford Circus
15 West Avenue, Wayne
(610) 293-0321
As Marcella Soret's is to shoes, Oxford Circus is to toys for Main Line families. Their selection is refreshing, featuring familiar favorites like Erector sets and old-fashioned paper dolls. Jewelry-making kits, pull toys, trains, and rockets, they're all here.

ANNUAL EVENTS

Philadelphia loves a good party! The city started celebrating in 1776 and it hasn't stopped yet—and Philadelphians are great hosts. The music at every event is superb; how could it be otherwise in the home of American Bandstand? With nine four- and one five-star restaurants in the city, the food is destined to be scrumptious. And with so many pristine historic sites as the backdrop, the setting is ideal for any festivity.

Sports fans, film buffs, garden enthusiasts, and art lovers all can find major events—parades, cultural festivals, competitions, and expos—to keep them busy all year long. Some, such as the outrageous Mummers Parade, are legendary, and no city celebrates July 4 like Philadelphia—they stretch *that* party into to a week-long escapade of concerts, barbecue, film fests, dancing, and the best fireworks anywhere.

Most events have Web sites, and we've noted those below. For dates and other information, the best one-stop source is the Greater Philadelphia Tourism Marketing Corporation (GPTMC), (215) 599-0776, www.gophila.com. GPTMC's Web site is massive, and it's constantly updated.

JANUARY

Blue Ball Weekend (various sites)
(267) 514-2088
www.blueballphilly.com
The National Constitution Center, clubs such as Bump and Shampoo, and elegant ballrooms at the Ritz-Carlton and Loews have all hosted this extravagant weekend that benefits the gay and lesbian communities. From black-tie donor receptions to dances with the hottest DJs, the weekend signals three days of celebration and support.

Chinese New Year
Chinatown
(215) 922-2156
One of the most dazzling observances of the year is the Chinese New Year in Chinatown. It begins at midnight on Chinese New Year's Eve, the night of the new moon, when every door and window of every home is open to allow the old year to leave. Festivities continue until the full moon, 15 days later, welcomed with a Lantern Festival. Dragon parades and fireworks highlight each Sunday—a way of putting the old year firmly behind, and launching the new with a bang!

Mummers Parade
Along Broad Street
(215) 683-3622
www.mummers.com
If you haven't watched a Mummers Parade, you haven't been to Philadelphia. More than 30,000 outrageously garbed strutters parade down Broad Street, some of their dazzling costumes taking up two traffic lanes. The Mummers' merrymaking can be traced to the 19th century, when thousands of costumed characters crowded the streets, tooting noisemakers in a "Carnival of Horns." Southern plantation life contributed to today's tradition, especially with the parade's theme song, "Oh! Dem Golden Slippers." Bands compete, drink, strut, and put on a show that makes other parades pale in comparison.

FEBRUARY

Mardi Gras Carnivale
Hyatt Regency at Penn's Landing
201 South Columbus Boulevard
(215) 928-1234
www.hyatt.com
For more than 100 years, the Alliance Française de Philadelphie, whose mission is to promote all things French, has staged a magnificent soirée on Fat Tuesday, the evening before Ash Wednesday. The organization's mission is to promote all things French, and an elegant French dinner is presented along with a silent

auction and dancing. Carnival attire is optional, but Mardi Gras beads are a must.

Philadelphia International Auto Show
Pennsylvania Convention Center
One Convention Center Place
(610) 758-9691, (800) 999-6810
www.phillyautoshow.com
More than 700 classic, luxury, and exotic vehicles are on display at this mega-expo, produced by the Automobile Dealers Association of Greater Philadelphia. Wander among trucks, convertibles, sports cars and dream cars of the future. The Tuner Salon, added in 2005, provides an extra 20,000 square feet of exhibits featuring celebrity cars, racers, and more. From each admission ticket, $1.00 is donated to the Children's Hospital of Philadelphia.

MARCH

KitchenAid The Book and The Cook Festival
Fort Washington Expo Center
1100 Virginia Drive, Fort Washington
(215) 545-4543
www.thebookandthecook.com
This is the event that helped fire up Philadelphia's lively restaurant scene more than two decades ago. The fest pairs more than 100 elite cookbook authors and celebrity chefs with local restaurants in over 125 cooking demonstrations, food tastings, and other activities at a Culinary Market and Kitchen Showcase. Bring your appetite; the food-enthusiasm here is contagious.

Philadelphia Flower Show
Pennsylvania Convention Center
One Convention Center Place
(215) 988-8899
www.theflowershow.com
Every garden professional and hobbyist knows about the Philadelphia Flower Show; it's the granddaddy of them all—the largest indoor flower show in the world and over 175 years old. Plant lovers from across the country come to see floral demonstrations,

lectures, and other presentations by celebrities and experts on topics from container and deck gardening to Ikebana, growing orchids, and more. Local celebrity chefs give culinary demos, and participants can buy tickets online for the twice-daily Garden Tea. Nearly 150 vendors showcase their wares on the convention floor.

APRIL

Penn Relays
Franklin Field, 235 South 33rd Street
(215) 898-6122
www.thepennrelays.com
This legendary competition, in which high school and college track stars compete in multiple events, is the longest uninterrupted collegiate track meet in the nation. In the 110-plus years since the Relays were first held, more than 100,000 athletes from high schools, middle schools, colleges, sports clubs, and the armed services have competed. Today, more than 425 races are run, including at least two dozen distance races.

Philadelphia Antiques Show
33rd Street Armory
(215) 387-3500
www.philaantiques.com
For more than four decades, the Philadelphia Antiques Show—one of the longest-running antiques shows in the country, as well as one of the most acclaimed—has wowed dealers and collectors from across the country. Private tours of notable collections are on display, and experts in various realms of collecting offer seminars. The finest vintage jewelry, furnishings, art, and quality pieces from pendulum clocks to rare manuscripts will be for sale, with proceeds going to the University of Pennsylvania Health System.

Philadelphia Film Festival
In theaters across Philadelphia
(267) 765-9700, festival hotline
www.phillyfests.com
From Italy to Estonia, Lebanon, and South

Africa, filmmakers' new works are show-cased for two weeks. Nearly 300 features, documentaries, shorts, and animation from 50 countries are viewed by some 61,000 movie buffs. Watch for stars here to pick up awards; in past years, honorees have included Steve Buscemi, Malcolm McDowell, Mary-Louise Parker, and Jill Clayburgh. Aspiring screenwriters get feedback, too, in the "Set in Philadelphia" screenplay competition.

**Philadelphia Furniture &
Furnishings Show
Pennsylvania Convention Center
1 Convention Center Place
(215) 832-0060
www.pffshow.com**
What distinguishes this show from other furniture expos is that all pieces are designed by artisans and built by hand. More than 200 juried exhibitors showcase their one-of-a-kind works, all for sale. Thousands of collectors, designers, and other individuals come to buy home items from hand-printed placemats to sleek shelving or a dining room suite. In the Design Smart Seminars, experts from woodworkers to solar energy profession-als answer homeowners' questions. A popular new section, Art of the Home, is devoted to residential and high-end prod-ucts relating to architecture and home design.

**Somewhere Over the Rainbow:
New Hope, PA Celebrates!
Village of New Hope
(215) 639-0300, (888) 359-9110
www.experiencebuckscounty.com**
This weekend celebration of the gay, les-bian, bisexual, and transgender communi-ties attracted more than 1,000 guests in its first year, 2004, and organizers expect it to keep growing every year. Local busi-nesses of the borough host the festivities with a variety of entertainment and activi-ties. Look for special packages at gay-owned B&Bs that might combine a room, dinner, shopping discounts, and some activity like a balloon ride.

If you're looking for gay- and lesbian-owned shops, restaurants, and lodging, Bucks County eliminates the guesswork! Visit www.GayBucksCounty.com, where you also can find info on same-sex com-mitment ceremony packages and week-end getaways.

MAY

**Bell to Bell Bike Ride
Schuylkill River Trail
(610) 834-1550, (866) VF-VISIT
www.womenadvancing.org**
From the Liberty Bell in Philadelphia—the symbol of American freedom— to the Jus-tice Bell in Valley Forge, symbol of women's freedom, the scenic 22-mile route takes participants along the Schuylkill River to celebrate women get-ting the vote. Pennsylvania was the eighth state to ratify the law in June 1919, which went into effect a year later.

**Blue Cross Broad Street Run
Broad Street, from Olney to South
Philadelphia
(215) 235-7481
www.broadstreetrun.com**
For one Sunday morning each May, 10 miles of Broad Street, Philadelphia's main thor-oughfare, are devoted to nearly 14,000 rac-ers, both top competitors and recreational runners. The race is an official Mid-Atlantic USATF Grand Prix event, with proceeds going to the American Cancer Society; over the past decade the Society has received more than $200,000 from participants' pledges. Kids can join the "Fun Miler," a 1-mile race, and families can check out the "Not for Runners Only" Health and Fitness Expo at the Navy Yard, Friday and Saturday.

**Dad Vail Regatta
Schuylkill River/Kelly Drive
(215) 542-1443
www.dadvail.org**
Named for University of Wisconsin crew coach "Dad" Vail—the oldest in the country

when he died in 1928—the Regatta was founded in 1934 to encourage rowing competition among small colleges. Today more than 3,300 rowers from large and small schools, from tiny Bowdoin College in Maine to the giant Ohio State University, compete each year. The 2,000-meter course is Olympic-length, with six lanes, and spectators can purchase programs and heat sheets during the races. Easy directions are on the Web site.

Devon Horse Show and Country Fair
Devon Show Grounds, Route 30 West, Berwyn
(610) 964-0550
www.thedevonhorseshow.org

Every day's events are different in this week-long horse show. One morning features pony hunter, equitation, and junior hunters; another might showcase hackney pony, friesian, and fine harness exhibitions. Purses are generous; the Devon Grand Prix alone offers $75,000—yet it's an affordable choice for spectators, with single tickets up to about $16. The kids' pavilion keeps them busy with beading and other crafts projects.

Peddler's Village Strawberry Festival
Route 202 and Street Road
Lahaska, Bucks County
(215) 794-4000
www.peddlersvillage.com

Guess what the favorite dessert is at this festival? The agenda is predictable, but the Strawberry Festival is still great fun, with live entertainment, pie-eating contests, and craftspeople demonstrating their skills and selling their wares. Strawberries are front and center—dipped in chocolate, baked in pies, sold in jams, fritters, and alone, and, of course, in delectable strawberry shortcake.

Rittenhouse Row Spring Festival
Along Walnut Street from Broad to 19th Street
www.rittenhouserow.org

This is your chance to experience Rittenhouse Row at its best, and indulge in some

of the best shopping and dining in the city. Businesses along the Row ease the way with special promotions—in past years, five-star Le Bec-Fin has given complimentary champagne with an entree, AIA Bookstore gave a free T-shirt with a $10 purchase—even Tiffany & Co. joined the fun with lessons on tying a necktie. Entertainment from ballet to jazz, Shakespeare to magicians, happens on stages along the corridor. Park at the Bellevue or Liberty Place.

Student Exhibition
Pennsylvania Academy of the Fine Arts
(215) 972-7600
www.pafa.org

For more than a century, this annual, month-long tradition has showcased the works of third- and fourth-year art students in all media. Winners are awarded scholarships; works that won in past years are displayed on the Web site.

JUNE

Bloomsday
Rosenbach Museum and Library
2008-2010 DeLancey Place
(215) 732-1600
www.rosenbach.org

Fans of James Joyce line up each June to celebrate Bloomsday—the day in which Leopold Bloom, the hero of Joyce's novel *Ulysses,* made his fictional odyssey through Dublin. Hundreds of people are drawn to the event, which includes a series of readings outside the small library and a special exhibition of Joyce materials. It's worth dropping by just to get the feel of DeLancey Street, one of the tiny historical streets of row homes where the houses still have boot scrapers at the door.

First Person Festival of Memoir and Documentary Art
Various venues across Philadelphia
(267) 402-2057
www.firstpersonfestival.org

No other event in the nation is dedicated to art based on real-life experiences, and for 10 days, the First Person Festival features more than 25 performances, screenings, and interactive workshops by local and nationally known artists. Participants can attend classes in storytelling, learn about the "fluent body" moves, talk about journaling and its role in storytelling—and, naturally, hear plenty of great stories.

Gay and Lesbian Theatre Festival
Various theatres across Philadelphia
(215) 627-6483
www.philagaylesbiantheatrefest.org
One aspect of Gay Pride Month that has grown tremendously is the Theatre Festival. For 10 days each June, venues across the city host new plays, musicals, and revues by or about members of the gay, lesbian, bisexual, and transgender community. Tickets are sold for single performances, in three-packs, or special festival passes that include admission to all shows.

LGBT Pride Parade and Festival
1315 Spruce Street, Suite 227
(215) 875-9288
www.phillypride.org
June is International Gay Pride Month, and the highlight is the annual Pride Parade and Festival, always held on Pride Day on Penn's Landing. What began as an impromptu party in the late 1980s has evolved into a major celebration—one of several during the year in which the lesbian, gay, bisexual, and transgender communities join together—that now attracts more than 25,000 people each year.

Manayunk Arts Festival
Main Street, Manayunk
(215) 482-9565
www.manayunk.com
More than 275 artists exhibit their work in this juried art show, the largest outdoor arts show in the Delaware Valley. More than 300,000 visitors come to buy ceramics, paintings, glass works, jewelry, and more in this National Historic District tucked into the banks of the Schuylkill River and the Manayunk Canal. A

"Clothesline Art Exhibition" shows 600 artworks by Philadelphia schoolkids, and aspiring artists of any age can enter the Chalk Art Competition. See the Web site for parking and shuttle information.

Odunde African American Street Festival
South Street
(215) 732-8510
www.odundeinc.org
Beginning in the late 1970s, Odunde is one of the oldest African-American street festivals in the country. The first fest was held at 23rd and South Streets to celebrate the New Year of Yoruba, a Nigerian culture in which rituals commemorate both special occasions and everyday life. Today a spiritual procession to the Schuylkill River begins the celebration that ends with the street fair.

Philly is Grilling!
Belmont Picnic Grove,
Belmont Mansion Drive
(800) 537-7676
www.americasbirthday.com
Kicking off the nation's most spectacular July 4th celebration is a late-June barbecue fest, showcasing Philadelphia's best chefs for lip-smacking barbecue. This cook-off is one of the dozens of Independence Day festivities in the Sunoco Welcome America Philadelphia gala; it's followed over the next week by such events as a showing of one of the *Rocky*

While most of us are taught to "keep our hands to ourselves" when we're around expensive antiques, organizers of the annual Philadelphia Antiques Show take a different tactic: They encourage patrons to touch the artifacts. They believe touching the beautiful objects creates a deeper appreciation, even affection, for the exquisite craftsmanship. It also enables people to more closely assess the objects' value, and to get a feeling for the history.

movies on the steps of the Philadelphia Museum of Art (the steps Rocky ran up when he was training); gospel, R&B, and salsa concerts; an opera in Rittenhouse Square; an open-air arts fest along Broad Street; and a concert by the world-renowned Philadelphia Orchestra on the Delaware River waterfront at Penn's Landing. Several events require tickets but most are free; the Web site lists times and places.

Wachovia USPro Championship/Wachovia Cycling Series
Ben Franklin Parkway, Kelly Drive
(866) 4-CYCLING
www.wachoviacycling.com
Ten times the cyclists have to cycle the grueling 14.4-mile circuit, along Ben Franklin Parkway to scenic Kelly Drive and the bone-breaking, 17-percent-grade Manayunk Wall. But when they finish, the reward is great: The winner is the U.S. Professional Road Champion. More than 500,000 spectators line the streets to watch this exciting race every year, along with the 57.6-mile women's Wachovia Liberty Classic, held the same day. This is the longest-running and richest one-day cycling race in the country, the culmination of the Wachovia Cycling Series, and attracts more than 140 of the world's best professional cyclists. Bring your lawn chair; these thrills are free.

World's Largest Garden Party
Greater Philadelphia gardens
(215) 247-5777
www.greaterphiladelphiagardens.org
A collaborative of 32 arboreta and public gardens in Greater Philadelphia celebrate summer with more than 40 events that are as varied as the gardens themselves. Guests can take a guided walk with a naturalist through Bowman's Hill Wildflower Preserve, explore hundreds of manicured, lavish acres at Longwood Gardens, learn about botanical watercolor at Jenkins Arboretum, or sip tea on the cherry blossom–shaded veranda at Shofuso Japanese House and Garden. Hikes, workshops, and gala events usher in the blooming season.

JULY

Let Freedom Ring
Liberty Bell Center, Independence Mall
(215) 965-2305
www.let-freedom-ring.org
At 2:00 P.M. every July 4, the bells of freedom are heard, literally, throughout the land. At that moment, four young descendants of the signers of the Declaration of Independence, tap the Liberty Bell in a symbolic "ringing," setting off a nationwide bell ringing ceremony. The bells are rung 13 times to honor the 13 states those signers represented.

Sunoco Philadelphia Freedom Concert, July 4th
Benjamin Franklin Parkway
(800) 537-7676
www.americasbirthday.com
In 2006, Lionel Richie was the headliner, joined by "American Idol"'s Fantasia Barrino. It's the biggest concert of the summer, and it's a blockbuster, culminating in the best fireworks show (we think) on the Eastern seaboard. Come early; the concert doesn't start until about 8:30 P.M.—with fireworks following two hours later—but tens of thousands of people will spend the day on the Parkway, watching the parade and having fun at the Parkway Festival. Music, food, games, and fun begin at 2:00 P.M.

AUGUST

Philadelphia Folk Festival
1323 Salford Station Road, Schwenksville
(610) 287-7818
www.folkfest.org
This mini-Woodstock has been rocking Old Poole's Farm every year since the early 1960s. It's the longest-running folk fest in the country; local and national acts perform, but bring the kids because they keep busy with juggling classes, candle-making, dolls, puppets, storytelling, crafts clinics, and, of course, some terrific music.

SEPTEMBER

Fringe Festival
Venues across Philadelphia
(215) 413-1318
www.pafringe.com
Once you attend a few avant-garde performances, you'll know why this two-week performance extravaganza is called Fringe Festival. One evening in past years, you might have attended *If Coffee Could Talk*, in which two women evolve onstage, alternately being snooty, fun, and vicious, waxing on love, art, aging, and even taking questions from the audience. The next evening you might have gone to a light show at The Bourse. Dance, comedy, improv, song, and poetry appear on various nights—all edgy, all the time.

Sippin' by the River
Penn's Landing, Columbus Boulevard at Chestnut Street
(215) 396-9100
www.sippinbytheriver.com
If a town can't decide whether to stage a wine-tasting, beer-tasting, or food-tasting festival, what's the solution? Combine them into one mega-event, of course. Compare wines and beers, then sample foods from area restaurants in the Taste of Philly Alley, all for one admission price (at press time, $25 in advance, $30 at the gate). Festivalgoers also can stop by the German and colonial Philadelphia pavilions to taste authentic beers and food, and watch cooking demonstrations. Live music entertains throughout the four-hour party, and proceeds benefit the Crohn's and Colitis Foundation of America.

OCTOBER

OutFest Festival Weekend
In the GAYborhood (Pine Street to Walnut, Juniper to 11th)
(215) 875-9288
www.phillypride.org
Part of a nationwide coming-out celebration, Philadelphia's OutFest—the largest in the country, with more than 20,000 people participating each year—happens the Sunday before Columbus Day. National Coming-Out Day not only celebrates and encourages coming out, it also serves to showcase the many aspects and services of Philadelphia's lesbian, gay, bisexual, and transgender communities.

Peddler's Village Scarecrow Competition
Route 202 and Street Road
Lahaska, Bucks County
(215) 794-4000
www.peddlersvillage.com
You think scarecrow-building is kid stuff? Well, yes, some of it is, and kids are definitely not overlooked at this competition. But nearly $5,000 in cash prizes gets their parents' attention, too. Bigger-than-life scarecrow entries are displayed across the landscape and the public votes to pick winners in various categories: Extraordinary Contemporary, Traditional, Amateur, Whirligig—and a new category in 2006, Kids Only! Scarecrow.

Terror Behind the Walls
Eastern State Penitentiary
22nd Street and Fairmount Avenue
(215) 236-3300
www.easternstate.org
Could there be a better setting for Halloween horror than an old prison? Ranked as one of the top 10 "haunts" in the country, this spooky place has been home to plenty of evil. The aim is scary-without-gore, enhanced with high-scream special effects. "Night Watch," the creepiest section yet, opened in 2006. Visitors explore this section on their own, in complete darkness, armed only with a flashlight. In "Intake," visitors are marched through the de-lousing chambers, into an interrogation with the Warden. Those who survive march single-file into the prison yard where "good" and "bad" prisoners are separated—all while insane, blood-loving guards scamper and taunt on the catwalks above.

USArtists: American Fine Art Show
33rd Street Armory
(800) 455-8312
www.usartists.org
The world's largest show of American art, USArtists always takes place during the third weekend of October. It was created as a fundraiser by the Women's Board of the Pennsylvania Academy of Fine Arts and has been praised by critics as "the premier American art fair." The Board's aim was to introduce the Academy to a larger audience; they envisioned the show as an artistic "walk across America," showing both historic and contemporary works from a cross-section of galleries across the country. More than 50 dealers now participate.

NOVEMBER

Peddler's Village Apple Festival
Route 202 and Street Road
Lahaska, Bucks County
(215) 794-4000
www.peddlersvillage.com
One of the best parts of autumn is making all sorts of concoctions with fresh, sweet, and tart apples. This traditional celebration is the place for finding the best of the season. Apple treats of every variety are available, from apple butter to cider, dumplings, fritters, and apples dipped in caramel. Craftspeople, live entertainment, and pie-eating contests add to the fun, and admission is free of charge.

When you register to run in the Philadelphia Marathon, leave the iPod at home; no headphones are allowed. Also taboo are baby joggers, roller blades, or scooters. One more restriction: Although the marathon is open to all runners and no qualifying time is required, you must maintain a pace of 12.5 minutes per mile to go the distance.

Philadelphia Marathon
4231 North Concourse Drive
(215) 685-0054
www.philadelphiamarathon.com
The race begins and ends at the Museum of Art—and for 26 miles in between, nearly 10,000 runners get to tour some of the most historic scenery in America. At this time of year, the average temperature is a runner-friendly 45 to 55 degrees. For runners with less endurance, the companion 8K (5.3 miles) race begins at 8:30 A.M. on the Benjamin Franklin Parkway. The marathon always happens on a Sunday; on the previous Friday and Saturday the public is invited to a Health and Fitness Expo at Eakins Oval, 23rd Street and the Parkway. Wear your sneakers and join in the Verizon Family Fun Run for kids 4 to 12 on Saturday morning. It's non-competitive, short-distance, and participation is free.

Philadelphia Museum of Art Craft Show
Pennsylvania Convention Center
1 Convention Center Place
(215) 684-7930
www.pmacraftshow.org
This premier show exhibits and sells the works of 195 of the finest craft artists in the country. Each year they are selected from a field of more than 1,500 artists working in wood, glass, pottery, and other media, and proceeds are used for purchasing works for the Museum of Art's permanent collection, and to fund art conservation, publication, and education projects. The show lasts four days with a Preview Party the previous Wednesday.

DECEMBER

Army/Navy Game
Lincoln Financial Field
www.phillylovesarmynavy.com
Take your blood pressure medicine before this game because it's one of the most charged rivalries in any sport. After 105

games prior to the 2005 match, both Army and Navy had each won 49 games, and there were seven ties. And after the 2005 fight, all we can say is—well, grrrr. Philadelphia hosts the game in 2006, 2008, and 2009. The Web site is hilarious; it displays a ticker counting down the days, hours, minutes, and seconds until the chance for revenge.

A Longwood Gardens Christmas
Route 1, Kennett Square
(610) 388-1000
www.longwoodgardens.org

The holiday begins in late November at the luxurious Longwood Gardens, and lasts through the first week of January, lighting up the winter nights with some 420,000 glittering tree lights and fountains dancing to holiday music. In the heated Conservatory, thousands of poinsettias are placed among amaryllis, narcissus, begonias, and tulips—what a pleasure to see them in this season! In the historic Chimes Tower, the 62-bell carillon plays holiday music on the half-hour.

ARTS

Since the city's early years, when Ben Franklin wowed neighbors with his writings and fresh ideas, creativity has ruled this town. So we should be accustomed to the hundreds of galleries, theaters, concert stages, and music schools that seem as numerous here as the shiny pennies tossed on Franklin's grave.

Still, the numbers and excellence of artistic efforts in Philadelphia give rise to a creative power that has a momentum, constantly expanding and attracting new venues and new faces. There are the icons—the institutions in the visual and performing arts, including the venerable Philadelphia Museum of Art and the grand dame of concert halls, the Academy of Music.

Smaller institutions, too, have earned acclaim across the country: the Barnes Foundation is still a well-kept almost-secret, while the Michener Museum, in author James Michener's Bucks County hometown, puts the spotlight on Philadelphia Impressionism. And among urban arts programs, few have gained as much national attention as the Mural Arts Program (MAP).

Since its inception in 1984 as an anti-graffiti project, MAP has transformed more than 2,400 blank, dreary walls with lively murals of historic scenes, stunning landscapes, and local legends. Today the public art program has grown to collaborate with corporations, foundations, and schools in using murals and the mural design process to engage the community, stop blight, and beautify the neighborhoods, with the help of more than 1,000 youths each year.

Another community-based arts initiative is the Old City Arts Association, formed in 1991 as the Old City neighborhood—once a commercial waterfront district—began morphing in the 1970s and '80s from warehouses to artists' lofts, galleries, design and architecture firms, and condos. Suburbanites hang around the city after work for "First Friday" open houses in the galleries, and "First Saturday" gallery tours give visitors and residents a chance to talk with artists, curators, and gallery owners in depth. (For more information, visit www.oldcityarts.org.)

For contemporary art exhibits, Philadelphia's major art schools—including the Pennsylvania Academy, Moore College of Art, Temple University's Tyler School of Art, and the University of the Arts—are great stops, in addition to the Institute of Contemporary Art and the Philadelphia Art Alliance.

Music and the performing arts are no less prolific in Philadelphia, borne out by the long collections of listings in this chapter. Not only are they enthusiastically supported by patrons and visitors, but they also work together to keep their position in the community strong, through the Greater Philadelphia Cultural Alliance.

Formed in 1972 by nine cultural organizations, the Alliance's original intent was to coordinate historical and cultural activities for Philly's Bicentennial Celebration. Today more than 300 nonprofit arts and cultural groups belong to the Alliance, working together in a

---

Philadelphians call it the "Calder family public-art triple-play": At one end of the Benjamin Franklin Parkway, in the Philadelphia Museum of Art's great stair hall, hangs the famous Alexander Calder mobile. Farther down the Parkway sits father Alexander Stirling Calder's lovely Swann Fountain. And from the top of City Hall, grandfather Alexander Milne Calder's statue of William Penn keeps vigil over his city.

"Campaign for Culture," an ongoing marketing effort to increase awareness and attendance at cultural institutions and events.

One of the more interesting aspects of the Alliance is its advocacy role. While working relationships with regional and state decision-makers might be difficult for small galleries and dance companies, the Alliance enables its members to speak collectively, as a strong community, in working for the preservation and development of cultural organizations.

PERFORMANCE VENUES

Academy of Music
1420 Locust Street
(215) 893-1999 (tickets), (215)
790-5800 (tours)
www.academyofmusic.org
Modeled after La Scala Opera House in Milan, Italy, the Academy of Music is without question the "grand dame" of performance halls. Opened in 1857 in the heart of Center City, it's the oldest continuously operating opera house in the United States, home to the Pennsylvania Ballet, the Opera Company of Philadelphia, and "Broadway at the Academy," an annual series of live touring shows. The lady has seen her share of historic moments: Philadelphia daughter Jeannette MacDonald, then age 6, made her singing debut here; and John Phillip Sousa introduced "The Stars and Stripes Forever" on the Academy's stage. If you visit during the holidays, see *The Nutcracker* here.

For culture on a budget, log on to www.phillyfunsavers.com and find the best half-price tickets for the week ahead. Special museum exhibits, sporting events, concerts, theater productions, all are fair game. Register at the site to get the half-price deals by e-mail every Thursday.

Annenberg Center for the Performing Arts
3680 Walnut Street
(215) 898-3900
www.pennpresents.org
The Annenberg's mission is to showcase international artists; in one season you might hear the Jerusalem Symphony Orchestra, The Klezmatics, Ladysmith Black Mambazo, and a Chinese version of "STOMP." Founded in 1971, the Annenberg's stage actually consists of three theaters—Harold Prince Theatre, Zellerbach Theatre, and Irvine Auditorium—at the University of Pennsylvania, just west of Center City. Tickets for most productions cost in the $30 to $40 range.

Kimmel Center for the Performing Arts
Broad and Spruce Streets
(215) 893-1999
www.kimmelcenter.org
It's new, it dazzles, and with a 150-foot vaulted glass roof, it's Center City's shiny gem. Built as the new concert hall for the Philadelphia Orchestra (which formerly was housed in the Academy of Music, down the street), the center's main stages are the 2,500-seat, mahogany-walled Verizon Hall, and the 650-seat Perelman Theater with a revolving stage. Also housed here are the Philadelphia Chamber Music Society, the Chamber Orchestra of Philadelphia, Peter Nero and The Philly Pops, and PHILADANCO. For visitors, that means music choices ranging from k.d. lang and Johnny Mathis to Bobby McFerrin, Yo-Yo Ma, and the Oslo Philharmonic.

Mann Center for the Performing Arts
52nd and Parkside Avenue
(215) 893-1999
www.manncenter.org
Seating 14,000 in the "shell" and under the stars, the Mann Center, summer home of the Philadelphia Orchestra, is one of the country's largest outdoor amphitheaters. Willie Nelson has performed in this Fairmount Park center, as have such acts as the Indigo Girls, Harry Connick Jr., Alanis Morissette, the Barenaked Ladies, Tony

Bennett, Lynyrd Skynyrd, Norah Jones, and dozens of other entertainers from late May to September. Ticket prices range from $20 to $75.

Merriam Theater
250 South Broad Street
(215) 551-7000
www.paballet.org/season/merriam.aspx
Today it's the principal home of the Pennsylvania Ballet, but the Merriam Theater at the University of the Arts, located on the "Avenue of the Arts" next door to the Academy of Music, has a proud history. World-famous entertainers who have performed on this stage include John Barrymore, Helen Hayes, Katharine Hepburn, Mickey Rooney, and Al Jolson, among many others. Built in 1918, the Merriam is no mere movie theater and performances here have their own special rules, including a strict late-admittance policy: Once the curtain goes up, late-arriving patrons must wait to be seated by ushers during an appropriate break or intermission.

Tweeter Center at the Waterfront
1 Harbour Boulevard, Camden, New Jersey
(856) 365-1300
www.tweetercenter.com
Situated next to the New Jersey State Aquarium along the Delaware River, the Tweeter Center is, well, a different bird. In summer it's a 25,000-capacity outdoor amphitheater, hosting such entertainers as Pearl Jam, Black Eyed Peas, Jimmy Buffett, and Ozzfest. The sprawling lawn features giant video screens, and the view of Philly's skyline and the Ben Franklin Bridge is one of the best. In cooler seasons, Tweeter converts to an intimate indoor theater seating just 1,600 patrons. Prepare to start the evening with pricey parking, up to $20.

ACTING COMPANIES

Bushfire Theatre of Performing Arts
224 South 52nd Street
(215) 747-9230
Bushfire Theatre produces original plays depicting the African-American experience. Sometimes the season includes classics, such as *Raisin in the Sun,* but more often the dramas, comedies, and musicals performed here are more contemporary. Bushfire is closely involved with the community through acting workshops and puppet shows. When you visit, check out the "Walk of Fame" honoring African-American artists of stage, movies, and television. Call for ticket prices.

Freedom Repertory Theatre
1346 North Broad Street
(215) 978-8497
www.freedomtheatre.org
In a historic mansion anchoring the northern end of Philly's "Avenue of the Arts" resides this renowned African-American theater. Its signature drama, inspired by Langston Hughes's gospel play *Black Nativity,* has become a Philadelphia tradition; its other presentations in a given season range from classics by authors such as James Baldwin to stage adaptations of popular films. Since its beginning in 1966, the Freedom has been recognized by the NAACP and other groups for its work with local children. Ticket prices are $20 to $30.

Painted Bride Art Center
230 Vine Street
(215) 925-9914
www.paintedbride.org
We could have listed Painted Bride in every category, since this alternative performing arts organization presents poetry, dance, theater, and jazz alike, as well as mounting art exhibits. Started as a cooperative gallery on South Street in 1969, "The Bride" moved to its Old City home in 1982—but this is no amateur venue. Performers—who usually stick around after the show to socialize in the gallery cafe—have included Carlos Santana, the late Spalding Gray, and Penn and Teller. Call for ticket prices.

Philadelphia Fringe Festival
Performances throughout Philadelphia
(215) 413-1318
www.pafringe.org

Of all the new-and-experimental theater events around the country, the Fringe—with some 700 dance, theater, visual arts, music, and storytelling presentations—might be the biggest. For 16 days each September, juried and non-juried works are performed in galleries, cabarets, restaurants, and street corners, as well as traditional theaters. Modeled after the famous Edinburgh Fringe Festival, Fringe was started in 1997 as a five-day event. Today the expanded show includes clowns, magicians, and other kiddie fare.

UNIVERSITY THEATERS

Temple Theaters
1301 West Norris Street
(215) 336-2000
www.temple.edu/theater

Villanova Theatre
Lancaster and Ithan Avenues, Villanova
(610) 519-7474
www.theatre.villanova.edu
For an affordable theater experience, don't overlook Philadelphia's university theaters. Both offer full seasons and a wide mix of productions: Temple, whose theater program is the longest-running theatrical producing organization in the city, featured *Hamlet* and *The Heidi Chronicles,* among other productions, in one recent season. Villanova on the Main Line, which offers one of the country's few master's degree programs in theater, in that same season offered *Our Town* and *Urinetown.* Tickets range from $12 to $25.

If touring the city has you on physical and sensory overload, step inside the Curtis Center, 601 Walnut Street, and feel instantly inspired: Sit for a few moments and stare at the magnificent Favrile glass mosaic, The Dream Garden. *It's based on a Maxfield Parrish painting and was assembled by Louis Comfort Tiffany in 1916. Relax and enjoy one of Philly's best "hidden" examples of public art!*

DANCE COMPANIES

At Marah Dance Theatre
(215) 338-8780
www.atmarah.org
From tension to resolution, you can always watch a good story unfold when At Marah performs. The company dances in venues that span Philly and the globe, reaching in years past to Russia, Poland, and England. Named after the biblical folk story in which Moses transformed bitter water into a sweet potion, At Marah exhibits an athletic style and a universal search for spiritual fulfillment. Call for ticket prices.

Headlong Dance Theater
1170 South Broad Street
(215) 545-9195
www.headlong.org
Don't try to label Headlong's style, because this eclectic, irreverent dance company won't be pigeonholed! Their repertoire draws from influences as varied as ballet, sports, sign language, jazz, tap, and Ghanaian dance—not to mention life experiences. "Headlong is clearly not your typical dance company . . . " wrote a *New York Times* reviewer. Indeed, one piece, *Hotel Pool,* is performed at—you guessed it—a hotel pool. For *Story of a Panic,* based on a short story by E. M. Forster, dancers studied tapes of people reacting to natural disasters. This company is an original. Ticket prices vary by location.

Koresh Dance Company
104 South 20th Street
(215) 751-0959
www.koreshdance.org
Intensity and "big themes" characterize this company's repertoire. Begun in 1991 by Israeli immigrant Ronen Koresh, the company's subjects often bring to mind biblical themes, the Holocaust, and struggles in the Middle East. While Koresh now tours the country, only performing in Philadelphia two to four times a year, visitors are welcome to drop into the studio for a

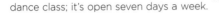

dance class; it's open seven days a week.

Pennsylvania Ballet
1101 South Front Street
(215) 551-7000
www.paballet.org
Founded in 1963, the company has never veered from its vision of a diverse classical repertoire with a "Balanchine backbone." Their strategy works, as more than 100,000 devotees attend their performances every year. Performing at both the Academy of Music and the Merriam Theater, the ballet also tours throughout the Northeast. In any season the schedule will include such classics as *Swan Lake* and *A Midsummer Night's Dream,* alongside more contemporary offerings as *Rodeo, Company B,* and the ballet's signature dance, *Carmina Burana.* Ticket prices range from $20 to $99.

PHILADANCO!
9 North Preston Street
(215) 893-1999
www.philadanco.org
One of Philly's most energetic and triumphant ambassadors, PHILADANCO! (officially The Philadelphia Dance Company) travels the globe, winning legions of new fans on each tour. PHILADANCO! is no less sought after on its home turf—especially among dancers: More than 600 audition each year for the company's rare vacancies. Since 1970, founder Joan Myers Brown has aggressively promoted her agenda of excellence in African-American dance, and the sold-out performances demonstrate her success. PHILADANCO! is the resident dance company at the Kimmel Center's Perelman Theater; during the holidays, take the family to see the joyous *Xmas Files.* Call for ticket prices.

Philadelphia Folklore Project
1307 Wharton Street
(215) 468-7871
www.folkloreproject.org
While dance is one of the Philadelphia

Give the kids a cultural treat at the Philadelphia International Children's Festival, typically held in early May each year at the Annenberg Center. Known as one of the top kids' fests in the world, the celebration brings in dancers, musicians, storytellers, and jugglers from all corners of the planet. They can sample foods from the Caribbean, Senegal, and the Middle East, and learn handicrafts from international artisans (3680 Walnut Street, 215-898-8900; www.pennpresents.org/events/childfest).

Folklore Project's (PFP) primary forms of expression, its presentations literally know no limits. Gospel singing, basket weaving, tap dancing—any form of folk culture is fair game for PFP, which has archived a remarkable 45,000 artifacts relating to Philly's Italian, Lithuanian, Cambodian, Latino, African-American, and other ethnic communities. Its aim is to preserve the city's folk life through performances, workshops, exhibitions, and other full-scale public events, almost all of which are suitable for children and families.

Voloshky Ukrainian Dance Ensemble
700 Cedar Road, Jenkintown
(215) 643-4397
www.voloshky.com
The marriage of authenticity and new ideas drives this company's choreography. Inspired by the spirit of their Ukraine heritage, dancers employ modern athletic training to become even better than their folk and classical dance ancestors. Taras Lewyckyj—who came to Voloshky as a dancer in 1974 and became its artistic director more than 20 years later—told the city's tourism office, "Since Ukraine became an independent country again, we've been liberated as artists too. We no longer need merely to preserve. We can create new traditions . . ." With this troupe, art truly imitates life!

Philly's Public Art Tells the City's Story

Public art wasn't invented in Philadelphia, but this is definitely the city where it became "official." Back in 1872, the Fairmount Park Art Association formed as the country's first private, non-profit organization to plan public art—but by the turn of the century, the association's scope took in the entire city. Important works by Frederic Remington, Alexander Milne Calder, Alexander Sterling Calder, Jacques Lipchitz, Daniel Chester French, Isamu Noguchi, Jody Pinto, Pepón Osorio, and Augustus Saint-Gaudens eventually followed.

Philly can boast more public art than any other city in America, says the Smithsonian Institution. It's no surprise—they've been installing art here for 300 years.

Long before the Fairmount Park Art Association set out to beautify the park with art, Philadelphia was erecting statues to honor heroes and the city's legacy of freedom. No other city had spent public monies on a fountain sculpture until 1809 when William Rush created his, *Water Nymph and Bittern,* for the square where City Hall now stands. (His fountain was moved to the Philadelphia Museum of Art.)

For the next two centuries, it seemed every major artist created public art for Philadelphia, some provoking public outcry. No controversy surrounded Frederic Remington's large-scale bronze in Fairmount Park, *Cowboy* (1908), though some did wink that his

model, Chester County native Charlie Trego, was the manager of Buffalo Bill's Wild West Show.

That wasn't the case in 1934, when J. Otto Schweizer's *All Wars Memorial to Colored Soldiers and Sailors* was installed in an almost-hidden corner of Fairmount Park. Only after decades of protest was the statue finally moved in 1990 to its original proposed, prominent spot on the Benjamin Franklin Parkway. Grumbles were heard, too, when the famous *Rocky* statue was moved from its roost atop the Philadelphia Museum of Art steps to the Wachovia Spectrum sports arena.

Every public art piece seems to come with a story: For the Joan of Arc statue on the east side of the Museum of Art, the model was 15-year-old Valerie Laneau—who, at 77, also was burned to death while trying to light a lamp in her home.

The big moment for public art in Philly came in 1959 when the city's Redevelopment Authority established a program requiring private developers to devote one percent of their construction costs to art—and the same year, the City Council voted to make it official. No city anywhere had actually legislated public art into development budgets before, and Claes Oldenburg's *Clothespin* was one of the first pieces installed under the new program. As a result of city leaders' foresight, Philadelphia today is a veritable outdoor museum.

MUSIC

Asociación de Músicos
Latino Americanos (AMLA)
2726 North Sixth Street
(215) 223-3060
www.amla.org

Latin music in this region doesn't get any better than at AMLA, where Philly's best Latin artists not only perform, but also teach, record, and host international artists. Located in "El Barrio"—the mostly Latino section of North Philadelphia near Fifth and Lehigh—AMLA is the clearing-house for the city's salsa, merengue, Latin jazz, classical guitar, and Cuban and Puerto Rican folk music, and its members teach at AMLA's Latin School of the Arts. Ticket prices vary.

Boyer College of Music and Dance
Temple University
1715 North Broad Street
(215) 204-8307
www.temple.edu/music

If awards were given for the best deals in the city, Boyer College might take top prize. Every year the school offers more than 200 *free* concerts to the public, in nearly every music category imaginable—opera, jazz, keyboard, strings, you name it—along with faculty recitals and a guest artist series that has included Ann-Sophie Mutter, Mstislav Rostropovich, and jazz star McCoy Tyner. Many teachers are members of the Philadelphia Orchestra

and the Mendelssohn Club. For a concert calendar, go to the Web site of classical and jazz radio station WRTI-90.1 FM, at www.wrti.org.

Concert Operetta Theater
The Academy of Vocal Arts
1920 Spruce Street
(215) 389-0648
www.concertoperetta.com

This company performs classic and neo-classic opera, with a twist: Its translations are all new, and the productions are minimalist, following the composers' intent. While their mission is to highlight rare operettas not often performed, they offer an unusual range: One recent season started with Oscar Straus's *Chocolate Soldier* and ended with a concert honoring Philadelphia favorite daughter Jeanette Macdonald and "honorary Philadelphian" Nelson Eddy. Ticket prices are $15 to $20.

Curtis Institute of Music
1726 Locust Street
(215) 893-7902
www.curtis.edu

This conservatory trained musical legend Leonard Bernstein, and its current students, some as young as 14 years old, perform for the public with the Curtis Symphony Orchestra and the Curtis Opera Theatre. The Institute is world-renowned; 17 percent of the principal

Taylor's Music Store in West Chester puts the "full" in full-service. Not only does Taylor's sell, rent, and repair instruments, it also carries sheet music and method books for every musical genre, classical to pop, and uses the talents of 40 instructors to teach more than 600 music lessons every week. Residents and visitors alike can help Taylor's help the community: Once a year, the shop will re-string your guitar free of charge in exchange for canned food, which is then donated to local food banks (116 West Gay Street, West Chester, 610–696–1812; www.taylorsmusic.com).

chairs in the country's top symphonies are held by Curtis graduates—and enrollment is tuition-free! The orchestra has performed at Carnegie Hall and was orchestra-in-residence at the Verbier Festival in Switzerland, but you can attend their Philadelphia concerts twice a year; ticket prices range from $5.00 to $30.00. From October to May, student recitals are held three nights a week with free admission.

Opera North
Various venues
(215) 848-9490
www.operanorth.com

This company has sponsored a number of renowned singers prior to their careers at the Metropolitan Opera, including Indra Thomas and Marietta Simpson. Formed in 1974 (and originally called Opera Ebony/Philadelphia), Opera North aims to make opera available to more culturally diverse audiences, and to provide talented minority singers the chance to perform in such productions as *Carmen, Aida,* and *La Boheme.* Some 3,000 inner-city children attend performances each year, and they stage two operas each season for the public. Ticket prices range from $13 to $25.

Philadelphia Chamber Music Society
Various venues
(215) 569-8080
www.philadelphiachambermusic.org

Venture into Chinatown to the Asian Arts Initiative, a community arts center where Philly's Asian community shares and display their culture through music, visual arts, theater, and dance. Visitors especially enjoy the Rap Series every third Friday of the month; the first Friday is Youth Artist Chillin' Day, a free two-hour program for Asian-American youth (1315 Cherry Street, Second Floor, 215-557-0455; www.asianartsinitiative.org).

With more than 60 concerts scheduled each season, no chamber music society brings more performances to its audiences than Philadelphia's. String quartets, jazz trios, pianists, and singers share the roster; you might hear Andras Schiff one night and the Tokyo String Quartet the next. The group prefers smaller settings of just 125 to 600 seats, but take heart: If the concert you want to hear is sold out, the staff often brings out extra folding chairs rather than turn people away. And chamber music is one of the best deals in town: Tickets range from just $15 to $21.

Philadelphia Clef Club of Jazz and Performing Arts, Inc.
736-38 South Broad Street
(215) 893-9912
www.clefclubofjazz.com

Back in 1935, when black musicians were denied membership in the racially segregated musicians' union, they banded together and formed Local #274, the Philadelphia Clef Club. Of more than 50 African-American musicians' unions in the country, Local #274 survived the longest—more than 36 years—listing jazz greats John Coltrane, Dizzy Gillespie, Shirley Scott, Grover Washington Jr., and Nina Simone among its members. Today the Clef Club's mission is to promote jazz as an art form, and to provide opportunities for jazz musicians, sponsoring jazz camps, youth ensembles, a seniors' orchestra, and other initiatives.

Philadelphia Orchestra
Kimmel Center (Verizon Hall)
Broad and Spruce Streets
(215) 893-1999
www.philorch.org

The orchestra's musical directors have been household names, musically speaking: Leopold Stokowski, who shaped the orchestra's sound; Eugene Ormandy, who took it to new heights through recordings and premieres; Riccardo Muti, a shining personality whose programs were refined in bold strokes by his successors, Wolfgang

Sawallisch and Christoph Eschenbach. In its gleaming new home, the Kimmel Center, the orchestra's music becomes a "surround-sound" experience with seating in-the-round, providing unprecedented close-up views of maestros and musicians. Ticket prices vary by performance.

Savoy Company
Performing at The Academy of Music
(215) 735-7161
www.savoy.org
Talk about finding your own niche: Founded in 1901, the Savoy Company is the world's oldest amateur company devoted exclusively to the works of Gilbert and Sullivan. Sir William Gilbert once recognized the group with a letter of commendation. Each season the company performs one operetta; for those who need a G&S refresher, selections would include *The Mikado, H.M.S. Pinafore, The Gondoliers,* and *Pirates of Penzance.* G&S aficionados will appreciate the group's Web site, with its links to many G&S resources and a fine kids' page. Call for ticket prices.

Spoken Hand Percussion Orchestra
230 Vine Street
(215) 923-5678
www.spokenhand.org
Each Spoken Hand performance shows Brazilian, West African, Afro-Cuban, and Indian drumming traditions at their best— sometimes separately, at other times blending together in a unique new style. Newcomers often express surprise at the intricacy of the rhythms and arrangements. Appearing in various venues throughout the region, Spoken Hand performs at the Painted Bride Art Center at least three times a year. Feel like jamming with the group? Join them Monday evenings at the University of the Arts, where they provide live background drumming for Afro-Brazilian dance classes. Call for ticket prices.

City Hall is one of Philly's largest art galleries. More than 250 sculptures by Alexander Milne Calder alone are part of its collection, and a special "Art in City Hall" program displays fine art year-round on the second and fourth floors. Since 1984 the works of more than 800 artists have been showcased through the program. For an up-close look at the interior spaces, art, and furnishings, join the free 90-minute tour that begins every weekday at 12:30 P.M. in Room 121.

ART MUSEUMS

Barnes Foundation
300 North Latches Lane, Merion
(610) 667-0290
www.barnesfoundation.org
Unlike most art museums that group paintings by artist, the Barnes displays its art alongside artifacts that enhance it visually—at the same time arranged symmetrically on the wall, all organized around themes. So, you might see American folk art among Japanese scrolls and a work by Dutch masters, exhibited with ancient Egyptian glass and a Chinese sideboard. It all follows the experimental educational philosophy of the founder, Albert C. Barnes. The collection includes works by Manet, Renoir, Degas, Cézanne, Prendergrast, and Picasso, but call for a reservation at least one month in advance: The Barnes admits only 400 visitors a day; cost is $10 per person.

Institute of Contemporary Art
118 South 36th Street
(215) 898-5911
www.icaphila.org
ICA has always been a magnet for provocative art, starting in 1965 when, two years after the museum's opening, Andy Warhol and his entourage shocked the city with Warhol's cutting-edge pieces—

the artist's first museum show. ICA's Robert Mapplethorpe photography exhibit in 1988 set off a national brouhaha over funding for the arts. Its oversize space on the Penn campus enables room-size installations, and admission is a bargain: $6.00 for adults, and just $3.00 for children, seniors, and artists. Watch local schedules for concerts and lectures.

James A. Michener Art Museum
138 South Pine Street, Doylestown
(215) 340-9800
www.michenerartmuseum.org

This Bucks County museum was first envisioned by the famous author himself and is located in his hometown. Housing the world's finest collection of Pennsylvania Impressionist paintings, artists of the "Bucks County school" are showcased, including Daniel Garber's rescued mural, *A Wooded Watershed,* and works by Edward Redfield, Fern Coppedge, and their contemporaries. One room is devoted to the Bucks County woodworker George Nakashima and his organic furniture forms. Along with the original site—a neo-Gothic guardhouse and warden's office of a 19th-century prison—the museum opened a satellite gallery in New Hope in 2003. Admission is $5.00 for adults, $2.00 for kids 6 to 18.

Pennsylvania Academy of the Fine Arts
Broad and Cherry Streets
(215) 972-7600
www.pafa.org

This is the nation's first art museum and school of fine arts, housed in a National Historic Landmark building, a beautiful High Victorian Gothic at the northern end of the Avenue of the Arts. Its treasures include

works by Thomas Eakins—a one-time teacher at the Academy—as well as Lichtenstein, Winslow Homer, John Singer Sargent, Edward Hopper, and the Wyeths. A local favorite is the Gilbert Stuart portrait of George Washington. Given the Academy's status in the art world, visitors are sometimes surprised at the colorful, almost exuberant interior, especially the grand stair hall decorated in gold leaf, silver stars, and ornate carvings. Admission is $10 to $15; kids under five are admitted free.

Philadelphia Museum of Art
Benjamin Franklin Parkway and
26th Street
(215) 763-8100
www.philamuseum.org

It's a heart-stopping sight as you drive the Ben Franklin Parkway into Philadelphia and the Museum of Art appears, welcoming you to the city. The striking Neoclassical building is just as impressive on the inside, with collections of fine and applied arts spanning more than 2,000 years. Among them are the "Arts of Asia" collection of ink paintings, delicate porcelains, jade carvings, and sculptures, displayed in a Chinese palace hall, a stone temple brought from India, and an authentic Japanese teahouse in a bamboo garden. The American collections include paintings by masters such as Peale and Eakins, shown alongside handicraft traditions such as redware ceramics and Shaker furniture. Medieval and Renaissance art, European art from 1500 to 1850, and modern and contemporary art round out the experience. Admission is $10.00 for adults, $7.00 for students and seniors, and kids 12 and under are admitted free.

Rodin Museum
Benjamin Franklin Parkway at 22nd Street
(215) 763-8100
www.rodinmuseum.org

Just down the Parkway from the Museum of Art you will find the largest Rodin collection outside Paris. Some 128 sculptures, including bronze casts of the artist's greatest works, are assembled here, as well as

---

Visit the Philadelphia Museum of Art on Sunday, when the admission price is "pay what you wish" and visitors can enjoy the Sunday Jazz Brunch in the Museum Cafe. Call for brunch reservations, (215) 684-7990.

Rodin's plaster studies, drawings, prints, letters, and books. Among the pieces on display are *Eternal Springtime, Apotheosis of Victor Hugo,* and, of course, a bronze cast of Rodin's most famous work, *The Thinker;* for many pieces the effect is enhanced by their placement in the formal garden or by the reflecting pool. A donation of $3.00 per person is suggested.

Woodmere Art Museum
9201 Germantown Avenue
(215) 247-0476
www.woodmereartmuseum.org
This stately stone mansion in Chestnut Hill houses a different sort of museum: art displayed in the realist tradition. In nine gallery halls, works by landscape painter William Trost Richards, Susan Macdowell Eakins, and Philadelphia's own Arthur B. Carles are exhibited alongside founder Charles Knox Smith's tapestries and original furnishings, and a year-round schedule of tours, lectures, concerts, and other special events round out the experience. At this museum, the hands-down kids' favorite is George Washington's original death mask. Admission is $5.00 for adults, $3.00 for seniors and students, and children under 12 are admitted free.

ART GALLERIES

Art Sanctuary
Church of the Advocate
1801 West Diamond Street
(215) 232-4485
www.artsanctuary.org
Founded by best-selling author and creative writing professor Lorene Cary (*The Price of a Child*), Art Sanctuary is a place for African-American expression in the inner city. Renowned poets Nikki Giovanni and Sonia Sanchez, and author Terry McMillan, are among the many who have brought their talents to the Sanctuary. Located in North Philly's Church of the Advocate, a National Historic Landmark, the Art Sanctuary hosts the annual "Celebration of Black Writing," a confab of writers from across the country, and is known for its self-publishing seminars and interactive workshops for budding poets and novelists. The site itself has known more than a few historic moments: Philly's Black Power conference happened here in 1968, and in 1974, the first women priests in the Episcopal Church were ordained here. Admission is $5.00 for adults; those under 17 are admitted free.

The Clay Studio
139 North Second Street
(215) 925-3453
www.theclaystudio.org
Judging from the smashed pottery and broken mirrors marking the entryway, you might think someone trashed The Clay Studio—but not to worry, it's just the artwork of local pottery artist Isaiah Zagar. Inside the gallery, exhibits are much quieter; they have included the exquisite gold-and-lapis teapots of Heeseung Lee, who says he is inspired by vintage Japanese kimonos. Other displays might be whimsical or somber, and they're all about clay—down to the Claymobile, the Studio's traveling ceramics classroom. All pieces displayed are for sale; one of the best times to see them is at an opening reception, held every first Friday of the month from 5:00 to 9:00 P.M.

Samuel S. Fleisher Art Memorial
709-721 Catharine Street
(215) 922-3456
www.fleisher.org

Never is Philly's art scene more vibrant than on "First Fridays," when Old City's galleries hold an "open house." More than 40 galleries welcome browsers and serious buyers alike from 5:00 to 9:00 P.M. for mingling and people-watching. It's a casual urban escape, free of charge, on the first Friday of every month; most of the galleries are located between Front and Third, and Market and Vine Streets.

At this gallery, even the space itself is eclectic: a series of connected buildings, including three historic row houses and a dramatic Romanesque-Revival Episcopal Church, complete with stained-glass windows and housing 14th- to 16th-century paintings as well as a collection of Russian icons. Other gallery halls exhibit contemporary art and house the country's oldest tuition-free art program, and it's all administered by the Philadelphia Museum of Art. Like its classes, admission is free.

Muse Gallery
60 North Second Street
(215) 627-5310

Originally formed as Philadelphia's first cooperative gallery for women artists, Muse stages monthly, one-artist shows in a variety of media—paintings, sculptures, photography, and mixed-media. Most of its members still are women.

Nexus Foundation for Today's Art
137 North Second Street
(215) 629-1103
www.nexusphiladelphia.org

More than 25 years after it opened, Nexus still manages consistently fresh and interesting shows. One of the movers of the Old City gallery scene, Nexus never fails to draw crowds to its curated and invitational shows by painters, sculptors, and photographers. This cooperative gallery's members often "graduate" to commercial gallery shows.

Every Andrew Wyeth fan will recognize the austere white house and green hills of the Kuerner Farm in Chadds Ford; beginning at the age of 15, Wyeth used the images in about 1,000 sketches and paintings during his career. You can tour the farm April 1 through mid-November; tickets cost $8.00 for adults, $5.00 for students and seniors, and kids under six are admitted free (U.S. Route 1, Chadds Ford, 610-388-2700; www.brandywine museum.org).

Rosenwald-Wolf Gallery at
The University of the Arts
333 South Broad Street
(215) 717-6145

If you enjoy thought-provoking art, don't overlook Philly's school-affiliated galleries—and since it's located on the Avenue of the Arts, the Rosenwald-Wolf Gallery is a convenient stop during a shopping or touring day. Artists of international renown exhibit here, including abstract painter Thomas Nozkowski, sculptor Alice Aycock, and avant-garde filmmaker Yvonne Rainer. The gallery even staged a tribute to Stanley Kubrick's film *2001*. Throughout the campus, you can find smaller galleries devoted to photography, illustration, and the media arts.

Arthur Ross Gallery
220 South 34th Street
(215) 898-2083
www.upenn.edu/ARG

Located on the University of Pennsylvania campus, this small gallery draws on the school's permanent collection for some of its shows, as well as from other private collections. One exhibit showed the work of architect William L. Price, whose mentor, Frank Furness, designed the 1890 building that houses the gallery. Originally the university's library, it features creative use of natural light and rich ornamentation of terra-cotta and brickwork. The gallery launches each new exhibit with an opening night reception, often featuring guest lecturers or book signings.

Taller Puertorriqueño
2721 North Fifth Street
(215) 426-3311
www.tallerpr.org

Latino-focused art is the mission at this gallery, home to Philly's biggest collection of Puerto Rican (and other Latin) paintings and sculptures. Education is important here; visitors can learn more about Mexico's Day of the Dead, how to dance the merengue, or other aspects of Latino dance, music, culture, or visual arts. Its two buildings house a theater, two galleries, classrooms, and the city's largest Spanish-language bookstore.

Village of Arts and Humanities
2544 Germantown Avenue
(215) 225-7830
www.villagearts.org

This joyful space appeared in 1984 when a local artist recruited neighborhood kids to clean up an abandoned lot. Gradually it was transformed into a small "art park" with sculpture gardens, mural parks, and reflective spaces. Angel mosaics shimmer with mirrors and tiles in "Angel Alley," while "Meditation Garden" blends West African architecture, Chinese gardens, and Islamic courtyards. Festivals and performances are held here during the year and, every Saturday, open dance and ceramics workshops.

Wood Turning Center
501 Vine Street
(215) 923-8000
www.woodturningcenter.org

Recognized as a major national resource on wood and other lathe-turned art, the Wood Turning Center promotes woodworking as an art form. It features changing exhibits and a permanent collection—the world's largest collection of turned objects, in fact—as well as a library offering more than 15,000 books, slides, and photos. Viewing the online gallery alone could keep a person busy for hours. Notice the few metal pieces, there because malleable metals such as aluminum and pewter also can be turned on the lathe.

SPECTATOR SPORTS

It's hard to imagine a city more passionate about its sports than Philadelphia. The professional teams alone keep fans in stadiums and in front of their televisions year-round: Phillies baseball, Eagles football, 76ers basketball, Flyers hockey, Wings lacrosse, Phantoms hockey, Bulldogs roller hockey, KiXX soccer, and, as of the 2004 season, the Arena Football League's Philadelphia Soul.

Philadelphia has a definite home advantage in its new, state-of-the-art playing venues, all of which are South Philly neighbors: Lincoln Financial Field, home to the 2006 Super Bowl contenders the NFL Eagles, and Citizens Bank Park where the Phillies play Major League baseball. Lincoln Financial Field also hosts the annual Army/Navy football showdown, with the United States Naval Academy and the United States Military Academy renewing their century-old rivalry. Not far away is the Wachovia Center Complex, where the Sixers and Flyers take on their opponents, along with the KiXX, Wings, and Soul.

And it isn't only professional sports that provide competition-style entertainment. There are dozens of colleges throughout Greater Philadelphia, and hundreds of high schools, each with its own sports teams and league affiliations. Among the most famous are the Penn Relays intercollegiate and amateur track event, and the many regattas that pull along the Schuylkill River in spring, summer, and fall.

Spectator sports are ingrained in the culture here. For some that means lining the streets to watch the Philadelphia Marathon in November; for others it means packing into Franklin Field in late April to watch the Penn Relays. If you're a sports fan visiting or living in Philly, you can find a competition and a team to cheer on, every week of the year.

BASEBALL

Philadelphia Phillies
Citizens Bank Park
One Citizens Bank Way
(215) 463–1000
www.phillies.com
We love the Phillies no matter where they play, but they're especially lovable in their new stadium, Citizens Bank Park—or, as Philadelphians say, The Cit. The grass is real, the 43,500 seats are close to the action (with cup holders, no less), and at sunset the outfield brings you one of the finest, sweeping views of Center City in town. Have a cheesesteak from Geno's while you watch the game. Single game tickets range from $15 for bleachers to $44 for the best field-level seats, plus $10 to park (ouch!).

BASKETBALL

Philadelphia 76ers
Wachovia Center Complex
3601 South Broad Street
(215) 336-3600, (215) 339-7676 (tickets)
www.nba.com/sixers
The mighty 76ers always seem to bounce back mid-season, and the thrilling 2005 season was no exception: From losing streaks in December and February, the team rallied and, led by superstar Allen Iverson and five-time All-Star Chris Webber, made it to the Eastern Conference

---

Most baseball teams send up fireworks to celebrate a home run, but the Phillies have their own version: a giant, neon Liberty Bell, swinging and ringing 100 feet above street level. The "Liberty Bell Home Run Spectacular" measures 50 feet high and 35 feet wide.

Playoffs with a 43-39 record. The season runs from October through early May; tickets range from $23 to $65.

FOOTBALL

Philadelphia Eagles
Lincoln Financial Field
1 Lincoln Financial Field Way
(215) 463-5500
www.philadelphiaeagles.com
Since they made it to Super Bowl 2005, single tickets to Eagles games might be the most difficult seats to score in this town. It's worth trying, though, to get into their stadium, with its high-tech video and sound systems, and gorgeous river and skyline views from the 100,000-square-foot plaza. Everybody wants in on this fun; though games don't start until 1:00 P.M., tailgaters are partying as early as 7:00 A.M. on game days. Almost all tickets go to season ticket holders, and those few being sold will be expensive, with the price depending on the game: Seats for the Eagles-Cleveland Browns game in the 2006–07 season, for instance, sold for $34 to $222, while tickets for the game against the Dallas Cowboys sold for as much as $755.

Philadelphia Soul
Wachovia Center Complex
3601 South Broad Street
(888) PHIL–AFL or Ticketmaster, (215) 336-2000
www.philadelphiasoul.com
If you prefer your football indoors, or if the season just doesn't last long enough to suit you, take in some "arena football"

with the Philadelphia Soul. Arena football's season takes up where AFL and NFL games stop, beginning in late January and continuing through May. The Soul is the newest addition to Philly's pro sports family, having played their first season in 2004—thanks to rock star Jon Bon Jovi, the team's part owner. Ticket prices here might be the best spectator-sport deal in town; seats in the corners and end zone sell for as low as $15, and season tickets start at $96.

HOCKEY

Philadelphia Flyers
Wachovia Center Complex
3601 South Broad Street
(215) 336-3600
www.philadelphiaflyers.com
Formed as an expansion ice hockey team nearly 40 years ago, the Flyers are still committed to Philly—and the feeling is mutual. The team has skated their way to winning the Stanley Cup twice, in 1974 and 1975, and as of this writing have made it to the playoffs every year since 1995. The season runs from October through April, but like Eagles tickets, single-game tickets to Flyers games are scarce. Call before the season starts and expect to pay between $25 and $85.

Philadelphia Phantoms
Wachovia Center Complex
3601 South Broad Street
(215) 336-3600
www.phantomshockey.com
The American Hockey League franchise was just granted to the Philadelphia Flyers to launch the Phantoms in 1995, and already the team has won two AHL championships. They were champions almost from the beginning, in 1997 setting the AHL record for the most first-season wins (49). Single ticket prices are $14 to $19, with special group and multiple-game plans available.

If you're pinching pennies but still crave baseball, head to Citizens Bank Park and ask the ticket seller about the "cheap tickets." On game days, you can pay just $10 for "Standing Room Only" tickets.

HORSE RACING

Philadelphia Park
3001 Street Road, Bensalem
(215) 639-9000
www.philadelphiapark.com
Philadelphia Park is the only horse race-track remaining in Greater Philly, and a great bargain: Admission, parking, and a program are free of charge. Races run Saturday through Tuesday, June 15 through mid-February, but the most exciting time to be there is Labor Day weekend, for the $500,000 Pennsylvania Derby, a 9-furlong race for three year olds. The race has expanded into a three-day festival, including a family carnival and free concerts. Post time for all races is 12:35 P.M.

Philadelphia Park Turf Club
7 Penn Center
1635 Market Street
(215) 245-1556
www.philadelphiapark.com
If you can't make it to the race track, stop into the Art Deco–designed Turf Club to watch and wager on the horses. Some 300 video monitors bring the betting to you in the middle of Center City, complete with wagering windows and, like the Park, free admission (or $2.00 admission to the Clubhouse area). You can also find Turf Club branches in Upper Darby, South Philly, Valley Forge, and Brandywine.

LACROSSE

Philadelphia Wings
Wachovia Center Complex
3601 South Broad Street
(215) 336-3600, (215) 389-WINGS
www.wingslax.com
Since lacrosse teams across the country were first organized into the Eagle Pro Box League in 1987, the Philadelphia Wings have been winners, taking six championships and playing in three finalist bouts. The season runs from January through mid-April; single tickets are $10 to $35. In the off-season, players teach area youngsters at lacrosse clinics.

TRACK & FIELD

Penn Relays
Franklin Field, South and 33rd Streets
(215) 686-0053
www.thepennrelays.com
Held in one of the nation's most historic stadiums, the Penn Relays have run every late April since 1893. More than 425 races are staged during the three-day competition, with runners ranging in age from under 8 years old to 80-plus. More than 100,000 have competed in the last decade alone; the Penn Relays are not only the oldest, but the largest amateur track meet in the country.

Philadelphia Marathon
(215) 686-0053
www.philadelphiamarathon.com
For thousands of runners, marathons are hardly spectator sports—but for the rest of us, a marathon is suspenseful and inspiring. Philadelphia's is held on a Sunday in mid-November and is coupled with an 8K run, along a scenic, fairly flat route (except an abrupt 120-foot elevation change at the 10-mile mark), out Kelly Drive, following alongside the Schuylkill River. On Saturday of race weekend is the Family Fun Run, a non-competitive race for kids ages 4 to 12; the first 250 to register receive T-shirts and medals. For the marathon and 8K, early-bird fees are $55 and $20, respectively, and there is no race-day registration.

SOCCER

Philadelphia KiXX
Wachovia Center Complex
3601 South Broad Street
(215) 336-3600
www.kixxonline.com
Another newcomer to the pro sports scene, KiXX joined the NPSL (National Pro Soccer League) as an expansion franchise during the 1996–97 season, and later joined the MISL (Major Indoor Soccer League). Like the Wings, the KiXX were winners from the start, reaching the playoffs in each of their

first eight years and winning the MISL's first two League Championships in 2002 and 2003.

TENNIS

Philadelphia Freedoms
Cabrini College, Radnor
(866) WTT–TIXS
www.philadelphiafreedoms.com
The Freedoms are one of 12 pro teams in World Team Tennis (WTT), the country's only professional co-ed team sport. The league was co-founded by tennis icon Billie Jean King and gives fans the chance to watch their favorite stars. Four players—two men and two women—play on each team; John McEnroe, Martina Hingis, and Patrick Rafter are among the pros on WTT teams. The season is in July; tickets go on sale in April, and general admission season tickets start at $99.

PARKS AND RECREATION

Nearly 325 years ago, William Penn made it known that he would be Philly's first environmentalist, reserving land for four public squares and a town square in his plan for a "greene countrie town." As the city grew, conservationists and private landowners did their best to incorporate and preserve even more green space. The concept of major parks took hold here as early as 1855 with the dedication of 100-acre Lemon Hill Park, precursor to Fairmount Park; four years later it already was expanding. Today, with more than 9,000 acres along the Schuylkill River, Fairmount Park is the world's biggest municipal park, offering Philadelphians every conceivable outdoor activity from rowing, rock climbing, and rollerblading to skating, picnicking, fishing, and bicycling.

Now Fairmount Park directly connects the city with its national park neighbor, Valley Forge National Historical Park (Route 23 and North Gulph Road, Valley Forge, 610-783-1077; www.nps.gov.vafo), via the new 22-mile Schuylkill River Trail. Once they reach Valley Forge, visitors find another 18 miles of trails, biking, hiking, and horseback riding at the Revolutionary War camp.

In this chapter we give you a sampling of the hundreds of recreational opportunities available in Philadelphia and surrounding communities. Because this topic could be a book in itself, we're not presenting every single activity in every single park; after all, you can hike just about anywhere. Instead, we're presenting the parks and recreation spots that are standouts—those that have new tennis courts, for instance, or offer exceptional camping facilities—and we've provided contact information for as many parks and recreation sites as possible.

Keep in mind that some activities, such as golf and fishing, are covered in their own chapters. Here we provide more recreation choices, beginning with Philadelphia's city squares and Fairmount Park, then the best of the state park system. Finally, we give a lengthy menu of special recreation opportunities—and you'll see that some of those also are located in local or state parks. We thought that including them under the activity headings, rather than with park listings, would help you find your favorite activity more easily.

PHILADELPHIA'S CITY SQUARES

If you just want a bit of greenery around you while you take a break from touring around town, you're always near one of William Penn's five original city squares—though you would be challenged to find much vegetation in Center Square, where City Hall now stands. The differences between all five of the squares are striking; though they all were created at the same time, each evolved with a different history and personality.

At Logan Square, the northwestern-most of the squares (18th and Race Streets), you can enjoy the Shakespeare Memorial and Swann Fountain, designed by Alexander Calder. Unfortunately, most people view the exquisite sculpture on the fly, as Logan Square actually is a traffic "roundabout" in the middle of the busy Benjamin Franklin Parkway, midway between City Hall and the Philadelphia Museum of Art.

In the northeast corner of the Convention Center District sits Franklin Square (Seventh and Race Streets),

CLOSE-UP

Playing With Pooch

With so much green space in and around Philadelphia, canines never had it so good. Dog-friendly trails, lakes, and meadows abound. From the unmarked, dirt side trails throughout Pennypack Park to the 65 acres of woodlands in Crow's Woods, your four-legged pals have lots of options for getting exercise and fresh air. Some tips before you head outdoors:

- To avoid lyme disease, try to keep your dog away from the overgrowth lining forest trails; stick to the middle of the trail. After each walk, check the dog's skin (and your own); a deer tick won't embed itself for at least four hours. Pay special attention to the neck, head, ears, and between the dog's toes. For more info, go to www.cdc.gov/healthy pets/diseases/lyme.htm.
- Thorns, broken glass, and stinging nettle all are doggie hazards—and while canines can't catch poison ivy, they can transmit it to you.
- Carry water for yourself and your dog; experts recommend eight ounces for every hour of hiking.

We've spotlighted a few of the more popular places for hiking with dogs:

- **Crow's Woods.** One of our favorite features of this Haddonfield park: a dis-

penser of dog-poop bags at the parking lot. Dogs can run off-leash until noon, and again from 5:00 P.M. until dusk.
- **Green Lane Park.** Trails at this northwestern Montgomery County park are challenging and often remote; all but the Hemlock Point Trail allow dogs (www.montcopa.org/parks/).
- **Valley Forge National Historical Park.** You and your pup can hike for miles, past important historical sites and gorgeous scenery; when Pooch gets tired he can take a dip in Valley Creek or the Schuylkill (www.nps.gov/vafo/).
- **Wharton State Forest.** More than 500 miles of unpaved sand roads, cutting through 100,000 acres of Pine Barrens, await dogs and their owners (www.state .nj.us/dep/parksandforests/).
- **White Clay Creek State Park (Delaware) and Preserve (Pennsylvania).** Off Route 896 on the state border are eight marked trails, from a $1/2$ mile to 5 miles in length. The 3-mile Penndel Trail connects to the preserve (www.dcnr.state.pa.us/stateparks/ or www.destateparks.com/wccsp/).
- **Wissahickon Valley.** In Philly's northwest corner, some 12 trails follow Wissahickon Creek, another swimming op for your dog, in Fairmount Park (www.phila.gov/fairpark/recreation/).

newly renovated and reopened in summer 2006 as a family-friendly urban park. It's Philly's newest attraction (as well as one of its oldest); the former burial ground now boasts a new, history-themed miniature

golf course, a new carousel, and new brick walking paths.

Washington Square, the southeastern square (Sixth and Walnut Streets), sits across the intersection from Independence

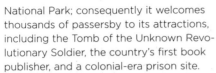

National Park; consequently it welcomes thousands of passersby to its attractions, including the Tomb of the Unknown Revolutionary Soldier, the country's first book publisher, and a colonial-era prison site.

Lastly, at the southwest corner of Penn's city sits perhaps his most famous city park, Rittenhouse Square, at 18th and Walnut Streets. It's certainly the most refined, surrounded by upscale condos, exclusive boutiques, and some of Philly's hottest restaurants.

MUNICIPAL PARK

Fairmount Park
(215) 683-0200
www.phila.gov/fairpark/

Calling Fairmount a park is a bit like calling the Mona Lisa a painting: Fairmount is *the* park—actually 62 neighborhood parks strung together—including rivers, gorges, 57 miles of trails, ballparks, golf courses, tennis courts, almost 30 colonial mansions, the Philadelphia Orchestra's summer amphitheater, famous Boathouse Row, a youth hostel, a Japanese teahouse, and the Philadelphia Zoo, the country's oldest. It's bigger than New York's Central Park.

The Schuylkill River basically divides the park into East and West Fairmount Park. The park extends north of the city starting at the Museum of Art, and is easily accessible using the Montgomery Drive, Kelly Drive, and West River Drive exits of Interstate 76, among other roads. Fairmount Park is so long, though, that your best bet is to call first for a map (or use the Web site) and orient yourself before you start exploring. A few highlights to watch for:

- *Forbidden Drive.* Beginning in Manayunk and stretching north for miles, this scenic bike and pedestrian trail takes you through beautiful Wissahickon Valley, including the only covered bridge in a major U.S. city.
- *River Drives Recreation Loop.* For 8.4 miles, this paved riverside path takes

Check out the Joan of Arc statue on the east side of the Museum of Art: 19-year-old St. Joan, you remember, was burned at the stake in 1431 after being captured by the British in the Hundred Years' War. The model for this statue, 15-year-old Valerie Laneau, also burned to death—at age 77, trying to light a lamp in her home.

walkers, cyclists, bladers, and runners past Boathouse Row, the Azalea Garden, and great river vistas.
- *Belmont Plateau.* The skyline view from the Plateau is so breathtaking that the United Nations once discussed building its offices here. It's a favorite destination for picnics, baseball games, and running.
- *Wissahickon Gorge.* Biking and horseback riding are the main activities here today, though some 25 mills once were powered by Wissahickon Creek—making this America's first "industrial park." Check Fairmount Park's Web site for biking and riding permits, or the site of Friends of the Wissahickon (www.fow.org).
- *Pennypack Environmental Center.* Birding is the big draw along Pennypack Creek; if you're a camper you can make a weekend of it. One of two nature centers in Fairmount Park, the Pennypack Center began as a bird sanctuary in 1958 and today offers a new reference library, as well as storytelling and classes in the outdoor amphitheater.

STATE PARKS

Fort Washington State Park
500 Bethlehem Pike, Fort Washington
(215) 591-5250
www.dcnr.state.pa.us/stateparks/Parks/fortwashington.aspx

The site of a temporary fort built by George Washington's troops in 1777, Fort Washington is known as a major flyway for all 16 species of raptors that migrate on the East Coast. Trout fishermen also know it for the exceptional spring fishing in Wissahickon Creek, which runs through the park. At the highest elevation in the 493-acre park is an observation deck, providing a scenic overlook and views of the park's butterfly garden.

French Creek State Park
843 Park Road, Elverson
(610) 582-9680
www.dcnr.state.pa.us/stateparks/parks/frenchcreek
Great trails and fishing distinguish this huge (7,339 acres) park. Hopewell and Scotts Run Lakes are well stocked, and there's swimming in the park's large pool. Eight miles of trails are dedicated to horseback riding, and more miles are used for hiking and bicycling. French Creek's newest distinction: Thanks to two popular courses that wind through the hilly, wooded terrain near Hopewell Lake, the park is known as the "Orienteering Capital of America."

Neshaminy State Park
3401 State Road
(215) 639-4538
www.visitpaparks.com
Here where the freshwater Neshaminy Creek meets the Delaware River in Bucks County, ocean tides are visible—it is a tidal estuary—even though the park is 100 miles upstream. A full-service marina provides easy water access for boaters, and spray fountains and a large pool help visitors cool off in the summer heat. The 330-acre park's 4 miles of woodsy trails are a bit strenuous, but walkers can stretch

If you'd like some evening entertainment after your hike (and in cold months, too), the Playmasters Theatre Workshop, located nearby in The Playhouse on State Road, stages productions year-round. Contact Playmasters for a show schedule (215-245-7850).

their legs on the paved drive that once led to a mansion.

Nockamixon State Park
1542 Mountain View Drive, Quakertown
(215) 529-7300
www.dcnr.state.pa.us/stateparks/parks/nockamixon
With 1,450 acres and four public launching areas, Lake Nockamixon in Bucks County offers plenty of sailing opportunities. Because of its size, it's a popular spot for catamarans and windsurfing, and the warm water makes it a good fishing spot. No boat? No problem; you can rent a small paddle boat. If sailing tires you out, the park offers 10 modernized cabins for overnight rental.

Ridley Creek State Park
Sycamore Mills Road, Media
(610) 892-3900
www.dcnr.state.pa.us/stateparks/parks/ridleycreek
This 2,600-acre park has something for everyone—fishing, horseback riding on a 4.7-mile equestrian trail, tobogganing, playgrounds—but our favorite part is the colonial Pennsylvania Plantation. This land has been farmed continuously for more than 300 years and was recently restored using only 18th-century tools. Staff in this "living history" site bake bread, card wool, and mend fences, portraying the lives of the Pratt family who occupied this 1710 Quaker plantation for three generations.

Tyler State Park
101 Swamp Road, Newtown
(215) 968-2021
www.dcnr.state.pa.us/stateparks/parks
What we like about Tyler State Park in Bucks County is its homey, welcoming air. You'll see families using the park year-round, either tossing balls, fishing from the banks of the Neshaminy Creek, canoeing, or just relaxing with a picnic lunch. Miles of trails are ideal for cross-country skiing in winter, and the creek usually freezes for ice skating.

RECREATION AND EXERCISE

Bicycling

Bicycle Club of Philadelphia
640 Waterworks Drive
www.phillybikeclub.org

You needn't become a member to join this club's group rides, many of which begin at the Italian Fountain behind the Philadelphia Museum of Art. Nor do you need to be a professional-level cyclist; novice riders are welcome. If you do want to be a member, though, the benefits go far beyond socializing with 1,000 fellow cyclists; the group advocates cycling as alternative transportation, and enjoys discounts on bikes and maintenance. The monthly newsletter keeps members updated on news and events.

River Drives Recreation Path
1 Boathouse Row (along Kelly Drive and Martin Luther King Drive, formerly West River Drive in Fairmount Park)
www.phila.gov/fairpark/

For 8 miles, this path follows the Schuylkill River, from the Museum of Art and past the East Falls Bridge. You will encounter smiling bladers, dog walkers, and joggers on the path; if it's a calm day you'll get to watch rowers practicing along Boathouse Row. Be aware that at noon, cars are permitted on the lower portion of the path to give them access to the zoo—but on weekends, the 4-mile stretch of MLK Drive is off limits to vehicles.

Sturdy Girl Cycling
26th Street and Benjamin Franklin Parkway
www.sturdygirlcycling.com

It started as a weekly ride among friends and quickly became an award-winning club. Their mission is to empower women to cast off their fears and enjoy cycling. Women of all skill levels are welcome; you only need a bicycle and helmet. If you

When you visit Ridley Creek State Park, don't miss the cluster of historic buildings. They once were a small, 18th-century mill village known as Sycamore Mills. Today the village, like the entire park property, is listed on the National Register of Historic Places.

want to be a better rider, the group offers clinics, workshops, and races.

White Clay Creek Preserve and State Park
405 Sharpless Road, Landenberg
(610) 274-2900
www.dcnr.state.pa.us/stateparks/parks/whiteclaycreek.aspx

Mountain biking is popular on White Clay Creek's 40 miles of trails that start in Chester County and end in Delaware. Fishing in the trout-stocked stream is another choice here, as is hiking. Halloween brings a crowd for the park's "Historic Haunting," performed at the London Tract Meeting House burial ground.

Wissahickon Valley Park, Fairmount Park
(215) 683-0200
www.fow.org

Steep, wooded trails are great challenges to mountain bikers in Wissahickon Valley. Trails can get a bit crowded, as they're open to all types of bikes as well as pedestrians, especially along Forbidden Drive. If you want to ride the upper trails, you'll need a trail permit; call the Fairmount Park Commission for details (215-683-0200); they'll provide you with a trail map and list of trail-use regulations when you get the permit.

Bowling

Center Bowling Lanes
7550 Center Avenue
(215) 878-5050

This bowling alley jumped on the hottest

trend in Philly dining—BYOB—and immediately became cool. Their New Year's Eve party is wildly popular; make your reservations early. Think of this place as a nightclub with pins.

Strikes Bowling Lounge
4040 Locust Street
(215) 387-BOWL
www.strikesbowlinglounge.com
When was the last time you heard a bowling alley described as "cutting edge"? This is another bowling lane/night spot, with billiards, full-service restaurant, and a bar. Menu items include Healthy Chick (grilled chicken), Wild Chick (with wild mushrooms), and Hot Chick Freedom (can you say, jalapeños?).

Camping

Green Lane Park
Routes 29 and 63, Green Lane
(215) 234-4528
www.montcopa.org/parks/green%20
lane.htm
There is a fee to camp at this Montgomery County park, but it's worth it because you'll probably wear yourself out hiking the 18 miles of sometimes-steep trails. The 20-mile Perkiomen Trail leads to Valley Forge National Historical Park—or you can rent a boat on the reservoir. Shower and laundry facilities are near the campsite; if you come the weekend after Labor Day you can enjoy the free Scottish-Irish festival, complete with bagpipes and sheep dog trials.

Mason Dixon Trail
719 Oakbourne Road, West Chester
(302) 239-5994
www.masondixontrail.org
Not everyone is aware that the Mason-Dixon Line, separating the North from the South in the 1800s, is marked by an actual trail. If you start at the Brandywine River in Chadds Ford, you can follow it all the way to Cumberland County. The trail is

wooded and well maintained; camping is available wherever it meets state parks; that info is on the Web site.

Pennsylvania Highlands
Highlands Coalition
520 Long Street, Bethlehem
(609) 818-9898
www.highlandscoalition.org or
www.outdoors.org/pa_highlands
This 3.5-million-acre greenway stretches from south-central Pennsylvania into Connecticut, passing through Nockamixon, Delaware Canal, and Ringing Rocks Parks. It's all been classified as "significant" by Congress because the hills help supply clean drinking water to Eastern Pennsylvania. Camping is available in the state parks overlapping the Highlands; you'll find a map on the Web site.

Tohickon Valley Park
Cafferty Road, Point Pleasant
(215) 297-0754
www.buckscounty.org/government/
departments/ParksandRec/
Twenty-two family or individual campsites are provided at this hillside park overlooking Tohickon Creek, and two additional sites for larger groups. Cabins also are available. The park is adjacent to Ralph Stover State Park, which is famous for the challenging rock climbs at High Rocks, so Tohickon Valley is a popular crash site for climbers. Twice a year, white-water fans gather here to attack the class three and four rapids. Fishing, birding, and pool-swimming are other activities.

Climbing and Hiking

Appalachian Mountain Club
Germantown Pike and Butler Pike
Plymouth Friends Meeting House
(617) 523-0636
www.outdoors.org/pa_highlands
If you'd like to join a group hike, the Delaware Valley chapter of AMC has more than 5,000 members in this region—part

of a network of 12 chapters and 94,000 members across the Northeast—who are wild about outdoor recreation and conservation. Day hiking, backpacking, white-water canoeing and kayaking, biking, snowshoeing, ice and rock climbing, and conservation clean-ups are just a few of their scheduled activities; if you become a member you can keep up through the quarterly chapter newsletter, *Footnotes.*

Batona Hiking Club of Philadelphia
215 South Spring Mill Road, Villanova
http://members.aol.com/Batona/
"Every Sunday, rain or shine" is the motto of this informal hiking club. It works for them: They haven't missed a Sunday in more than 50 years. They actually plan two hikes each week—an easy walk for beginners and families, and a more challenging trip for advanced hikers. They also organize canoe and backpacking outings, and have sponsored hiking vacations to destinations such as Scotland and Costa Rica. Hikes are planned for the entire year; a list is available for a small fee.

Delaware Canal State Park
11 Lodi Hill Road, Upper Black Eddy
(610) 982-5560
www.dcnr.state.pa.us/stateparks/parks/delawarecanal.aspx
This 60-mile strip of park follows—you guessed it—the Delaware Canal, along the Delaware River from Easton to Bristol in Bucks County. If you're looking for a scenic place to walk or bicycle, the towpath along the canal takes you through farmland and historic towns; you'll never get bored walking here.

Evansburg State Park
851 May Hall Road, Collegeville
(610) 409-1150
www.dcnr.state.pa.us/stateparks/parks/evansburg.aspx
Here on the banks of the Skippack Creek in Montgomery County, you will find an irresistibly relaxing mix of meadows, croplands, catfish and trout fishing, and

If you overnight in Tohickon Valley Park during the March and November white-water events, try to stay in Cabin Four. It gives the best view of the rapids during the white-water releases.

miles of hiking and biking trails. If you want more vigorous relaxation, Evansburg also offers four regulation baseball fields, a golf course, and 15 miles of designated horseback riding trails. Note the eight-arch stone bridge spanning the creek on Germantown Pike: Built in 1792, it's the country's oldest bridge in continual heavy use.

Gwynedd Wildlife Preserve
640 South Swedesford Road, Ambler
(215) 699-6751
www.natlands.org/preserves/preserve.asp?fldPreserveId=46
This Main Line preserve is an oasis, sandwiched among fast-growing suburbs like Blue Bell and North Wales. The 234-acre land supports warm-season grasses and wildflower meadows, two wetlands, and woods of mixed Pennsylvania hardwoods. Don't look for paved paths; this is a re-emerging ecosystem to explore on foot.

Horse Shoe Trail
600 West Germantown Pike,
Plymouth Meeting
(610) 278-3557
If you've ever considered hiking the Appalachian Trail, this is a good starting point; the 140-mile Horse Shoe Trail will lead you there from Valley Forge. You'll pass some great historic sites, including Hopewell Furnace National Historic Site and the Wharton Esherick Museum, and encounter deer and other wildlife—especially as you cross through the Middle Creek Wildlife Management Area. If you're afraid of heights, take a deep breath before you cross the cable bridge at French Creek.

Batona Hiking Club may be informal, but they're organized. Leaders of hikes form car pools for getting to that week's gathering spots, which can be as far away as the Poconos or the Jersey Shore. Be prepared to reimburse the driver a few dollars for gasoline.

Ralph Stover State Park
6011 State Park Road, Pipersville
(610) 982-5560
www.dcnr.state.pa.us/stateparks/parks/ralphstover.aspx
Rock climbers across the region know about Ralph Stover in Bucks County, and the 200-foot sheer rock face at High Rocks. White-water fans, too, migrate here after a heavy rain for the challenges of Tohickon Creek, and the catfish and bass fishing along the millrace is excellent. If you're having a picnic, you'll get a great view of Tohickon Creek's horseshoe bend from the picnic area.

Ringing Rocks Park
Lonely Cottage Road and Ringing Rocks Road, Upper Black Eddy
(215) 757-0571
It's a geological spectacle—a seven-acre, open field of boulders piled 10 feet high, set in a 120-acre forest near Bucks County's highest waterfall. The park comes by its name honestly; a third of the rocks "ring" when tapped by a hammer. Those are considered the "live" rocks; the other two-thirds—made of the same material, but for some reason don't ring—are referred to as "dead" rocks. Scientists haven't figured it out, either.

Disc Golf

Edgeley Field
Diamond Street and Reservoir Drive
(215) 683-0205
www.fairmountpark.org/Ultimate Frisbee.asp

Miniature golf was never this much fun! Disc golf is "golf" played with a Frisbee, and it's all the rage for players of any age and skill level. At Edgeley Field, though, it gets competitive; you register with the Philadelphia Area Disc Alliance at the start of the spring, summer, or fall season and are assigned to a team. You'll find serious "ultimate Frisbee" players at Edgeley Field; several teams have gone on to compete in the national and world events.

Sedgley Woods Disc Golf Course
33rd and Oxford Streets, East Park
www.fairmountpark.org/DiscGolf.asp
Disc golf is a more relaxed sport at Sedgley Woods—the second oldest disc golf course in the United States—in Fairmount Park. The terrain is more wooded and rough here, so the course is a challenge. You can play during any park hours or join the Thursday doubles league. Bring your own Frisbee.

TWO ADDITIONAL DISC GOLF COURSES

French Creek State Park (two courses)
843 Park Road, Elverson—Chester County
(610) 582-9680
www.dcnr.state.pa.us/stateparks/parks

Tyler State Park (one 27-hole course)
101 Swamp Road—Bucks County
(215) 968-2021
www.dcnr.state.pa.us/stateparks/parks

Gardens and Arboretums

Bartram's Garden
54th Street and Lindbergh Boulevard
(215) 729-5281
www.bartramsgarden.org
This National Historic Landmark is America's oldest living botanical garden. Washington, Jefferson, and Franklin all visited this Fairmount Park property when it was the 18th-century homestead

and farm of John Bartram. Along with the stone farm buildings, guests can visit the river trail, wildflower meadow, and wetlands.

Highlands Mansion and Gardens
7001 Sheaff Lane, Fort Washington
(215) 641-2687
www.highlandshistorical.org
Planned in 1796 as an "elegant farm" with panoramic views of the surrounding countryside, Highlands is a local favorite among gardeners. The two-acre formal garden, "Pleasure Ground," was originally planted in 1840 and since has been re-created and enclosed with stone walls.

Morris Arboretum
100 East Northwestern Avenue
(215) 247-5777
www.upenn.edu/arboretum
Actually a center for the study of art, science, and the humanities, Morris Arboretum in Chestnut Hill is maintained by the University of Pennsylvania. The 92-acre landscaped Victorian garden is a visual feast with winding paths, streams, a hidden grotto, and some of Pennsylvania's oldest, most rare trees. Check the Web site for jazz concerts and other performances held on the grounds.

Tyler Arboretum
515 Painter Road, Media
(610) 566-9134
www.tylerarboretum.org
Rare plants, ancient trees, and 20 miles of hiking trails—seven in all, ranging in length from 0.9 to 8.5 miles—make this 450-acre arboretum in Delaware County a local favorite. It was planted in the mid-1800s by two brothers, first as a way of preserving their own collection of trees and shrubs, and then as a systematic planting of more than a thousand varieties for public benefit. More than 20 of the brothers' original trees survive today.

Health Clubs, Pilates, Yoga

BodyWedge Total Conditioning
Gold's Gym, Plymouth Square Shopping Center
200 West Ridge Pike, Conshohocken
(610) 940-6787
www.goldsgym.com
Only the already-fit should register for this cardio and strength training workout. The "BodyWedge" is a ramp-shaped, foam exercise aid that helps you work on your core, balance, and muscles at once. Mostly women attend, but it's a good muscle-building workout for anyone.

East Eagle Yoga
18 East Eagle Road, Havertown
(610) 789-6789
Yoga instruction at East Eagle is private, individual, and by appointment only. First, however, the teacher will want to know about your stress, flexibility, and posture issues—all in your own home and for any level, including beginners.

Endurance Spinning
William G. Rohrer Center for HealthFitness
2309 Evesham Road, Voorhees
(856) 325-5300
www.fitness.virtua.org
The name is a perfect description: Endurance. For one solid hour, riders keep up their heart rates in a fast-paced spinning session. Some like to bring their own bike shoes. The instructor will show you the right moves and breathing techniques for getting the most out of the workout.

Platoon Fitness
P.O. Box 580A, Villanova, PA 19085
(888) 752-8666
www.platoonfitness.com
If you've always wondered how torturous boot camp might be, a few months' membership in Platoon Fitness will clue you in. Push-ups, bear crawls, runs, every strenuous move there is—rain or shine, snow or

heat wave, all before dawn. Some people actually think it's fun.

Striptease Aerobics
Mitch's Market Street Gym
322 West Market Street, West Chester
(610) 918-2900
www.mitchsgym.com
Bring your "stripper gear" to this fitness class—high heels, tight skirt, thigh-high hose—because after a lengthy warm-up, you'll change clothes and start strutting, thrusting, and gyrating. The workout aspect is deadly, and the striptease is a sensual way to get fit. And hey, it's never too late to learn a new skill, right?

12th Street Gym
204 South 12th Street
(215) 985-4092
www.12streetgym.com
Take the "Burn It Up" class here and dance like the stars. Each week you'll learn a different routine—perhaps slide-steps like the Temptations one week, a prom dance from *Grease* the next—and if you think you'll look ridiculous, at least you won't be alone. It sounds like fun, but count on a super-calorie-burning workout.

Yoga Babies with Gail Silver
Yoga Child
903 South Street
(215) 238-0989
www.yogachild.net
Teacher Gail Silver dedicates her practice to yoga for the family, and Yoga Babies is for moms and babies not yet at the crawling stage. Changing diapers or nursing during the class is just fine, and the infants seem to enjoy being lulled by the instructor's voice.

Horseback Riding

Biamonte Dressage
3346 Aquatong Road, Solebury
(215) 794-5229
http://biamontedressage.com
Both indoor and outdoor arenas are used at this summer day camp for kids who want to perfect the art of dressage. Campers learn not only how to ride well, but how to care for horses—and there are some non-horse activities as well, such as arts and crafts.

Chamounix Equestrian Center
98 Chamounix Drive,
West Fairmount Park
(215) 877-4419
www.fairmountpark.org/Chamounix Equestrian.asp
One of several riding facilities in Fairmount Park, Chamounix offers lessons, public boarding, and a kids' summer camp. None of the park's riding centers offer horse rental, but you do have easy access to the bridle trails and polo fields. In recent years, Chamounix has gained widespread attention for its "Work to Ride" program, providing at-risk kids a positive outlet and a chance to learn responsibility, motivation, and self-esteem in working with horses.

Harry's Riding Stables
2240 Holmesburg Avenue
(215) 335-9975
If you're a rider without a horse, this is the number to put in your Rolodex: Harry's is the only stable in Philadelphia city limits offering horse rentals to visitors. Located near Pennypack Park, Harry's is open seven days a week, and about 20 horses are available to rent every day.

Haycock Stables, Inc.
1035 Old Bethlehem Road
(215) 257-6271
www.haycockstables.com
Located adjacent to Lake Nockamixon State Park in Bucks County, Haycock Stables offers one- to two-hour rides for equestrians of any ability level along its 20 miles of trails. They specialize in groups, "seven to seventy-seven," so they're an option for family reunions or corporate outings. Let them know if you have first-time riders in your group and they'll have the best mounts and staff assistance ready.

Monastery
Wissahickon Park
1000 Kitchens Lane
You'll take a ride back in time at the Monastery, a rare example of a three-story Germantown farmhouse built in 1752. German Baptists ("Dunkards") used this site in the early 1700s, forming a "kloster" or monastery here; later it was a corn and sawmill for more than a century. Today, a non-profit organization oversees the house and stable, located within Fairmount Park.

Paddling: Canoeing, Kayaking, Rafting

Boathouse Row Boating
1 Boathouse Row, Lloyd Hall
(215) 928-1124
Get an inside glimpse of one of the country's premier rowing communities, while you learn rowing from local champions. A walking tour of Boathouse Row begins the lesson, followed by a one-hour class on a "learn-to-row" barge down the Schuylkill River, every Friday, Saturday, and Sunday, mid-June through Labor Day.

John Heinz National Wildlife Refuge
8601 Lindbergh Boulevard
(215) 365-3118
http://heinz.fws.gov
Established to protect Pennsylvania's largest freshwater tidal marsh, the Refuge offers a canoe ramp and, with 300 recorded species of birds, an excellent spot for birding. Fishing, and 10 miles of trails for walkers and joggers make the marsh—a primary stop in the Atlantic flyway—a good place to retreat for the day.

Lehigh Gorge State Park
Route 903, Jim Thorpe
(800) WHITEWATER
www.poconowhitewater.com
Rafting isn't always intense on these rapids, but they have been known to provide Class II and III thrills. Pocono Whitewater Rafting

If you're taking a boat into marsh waters, always check the tides, or you could risk getting stranded on mudflats. You also should wear long sleeves and pants, and don't skimp on the insect repellant.

organizes three- to four-hour rafting trips and, when the ride is over, includes a free barbecue on the riverbanks.

Northbrook Canoe Company
1810 Beagle Road, West Chester
(610) 793-2279
www.northbrookcanoe.com
You can take your pick of scenic trips down the Brandywine River, riding by canoe, kayak, tube, or splashboat. Novices might prefer a one-hour glide down the waterway; more serious paddlers can make a day of it with a six-and-a-half-hour run.

Peace Valley Park
170 Chapman Road, Doylestown
(215) 345-7860
www.peacevalleynaturecenter.org
You'll have plenty of wildlife for company on Lake Galena; white-tail deer, wading birds, and songbirds call these riverbanks home. You might also encounter sailboats and windsurfers; you can rent paddleboats and canoes, or bring your own—as long as the motor is three horsepower or less. The lake is well stocked with catfish, bass, walleye, and bluefish.

Swimming

Bucks County River Country
2 Walters Lane, Point Pleasant
(215) 297-5000
www.rivercountry.net
You can swim, tube, kayak, raft, or canoe along the Delaware River with Bucks County River Country; the company will shuttle you upriver so you can float down

Does the inner-you want to blast your best friend? Take out your aggressions at Skirmish, a year-round paintball complex in the Poconos. This is no backyard playground; you'll have 700 wooded acres for staging your own private war. Take it to four mock villages, a five-sided fortress ("The Pentagon"), two castles—including a three-story number complete with bridge, ramparts, and spiral stairs—or a vast forest full of creeks, swamps, and thickets (Route 903, Jim Thorpe, 800-SKIRMISH; www.skirmish.com).

with the gentle current—it's a great hot weather diversion. Life jackets are provided (and required for children under 12). Water shoes are recommended, and River Country suggests that participants check their car keys at the River Supply Store so they don't get lost in the water.

Philadelphia Recreation Centers
(215) 683-3600

Many of Philly's 100-plus municipal rec centers have pools that are open to visitors. For the address of a public pool near you, call the Recreation Department's number, above. (Note to visitors: Most hotels in Philadelphia have swimming pools; those that do not usually offer pool privileges at a health club or spa nearby. If your hotel does not have a pool, check with the concierge.)

For kids (and adults) on boards and blades, more than 20 skate parks operate in the Greater Philadelphia area. They're located in West Chester, Doylestown, Conshohocken, and Easton, as well as inside the city. For a listing with addresses and phone numbers, go to www.phila.gov/skateparks.

Quarry Swim Club
Route 654 and Crusher Road, Hopewell
(609) 466-0810

Prepare for icy-cold water at this spring-fed rock quarry. You can purchase six-day passes for adults or kids, or buy a season family membership and laze all summer long in your inner tube. Pretend you're Butch Cassidy and the Sundance Kid and plunge in.

Tennis

Aquatic & Fitness Centre
601 Righters Ferry Road, Bala Cynwyd
(610) 664-6464
www.afcfitness.com

Tennis isn't the only offering at this health club; you can also take classes in aerobics, spinning, a variety of mind/body disciplines, even Argentinian tango. Adult and junior tennis clinics are held year-round; the Centre charges a $15 guest fee but check the Web site for a one-week free guest pass.

Frosty Hollow Park and Tennis Center
4503 New Falls Road, Levittown
(215) 949-2280

Tennis is the main focus at this facility, with 10 all-weather courts, a practice court, a "lobster" machine, and ball hoppers. But picnicking and walking also are popular at this 95-acre park. Six courts are lit for night play, and clinics, individual instruction, and tournaments are on the menu.

Magarity Tennis Club
825 Bethlehem Pike, Flourtown
(215) 836-5585
www.magaritytennis.com

Six courts and a Pro Shop comprise this tennis club, with instructors on hand for individual help as well as single, double, and workout drills. Play costs $15 per hour and players must call ahead to reserve their courts.

**Northeast Racquet Club and
Fitness Center
Krewstown Road and Grant Avenue
(215) 671-9220
www.northeastracquet.com**

At 125,000 square feet, Northeast is the largest athletic complex in the area, with facilities for lacrosse, basketball, hockey, indoor soccer, exercise classes, and aquatics, as well as tennis and racquetball. Courts are built with a plexi-pave surface, and junior programs and adult camps are on the schedule.

GOLF

ot many states are as green as Pennsylvania, with lush, rolling hills in every region. The creation of golf courses—a *lot* of golf courses—is as natural a development here as skiing resorts in the Rockies.

Greater Philadelphia's golf courses accommodate every skill level, from world-class pro to beginning duffer—and so it has been since the area's first course, the members-only Philadelphia Country Club, was formed in 1890. The seventh club to join the nascent United States Golf Association, the original Philadelphia Country Club was located in Bala Cynwyd and moved to its current site in Gladwyne in 1924. But it was in 1939, when it hosted the U.S. Open, that the club gained national acclaim: Byron Nelson won his only Open title (in 11 appearances) that year, beating Craig Wood and Denny Shute—an achievement marked by a plaque at the site.

The greatest names in golf have played on Philadelphia's courses, from Sam Snead to Babe Didrikson Zaharias, Arnold Palmer, and Tiger Woods. Some of the biggest names in golf course architecture have made their imprint here, too: World-renowned architect Rees Jones sculpted the famous Tattersall Golf Club in West Chester around natural wetlands, pastoral hillsides, and wooded forests, incorporating 54 bunkers, three ponds, and mounds on every hole.

The architectural pedigree of the Aronimink Golf Club in Newtown Square is quadruply blessed, having been designed in 1928 by Donald Ross, and later by Dick Wilson, then by George Fazio, and lastly by Robert Trent Jones. Fazio, uncle of likewise famous golf course architect Tom Fazio, also designed the Downington Golf Club in Downington.

Philadelphians also are fortunate to have Golf Philly, a network of six public golf courses that have been in an upgrade mode since 1999, when Meadowbrook Golf, Inc., one of the largest golf management companies in the world, signed on to operate the courses and one driving range. Today golf course conditions, according to one report, "are in the best shape that they have been in for over 20 years . . . ," with finely groomed tee areas and fairways that are consistently maintained.

Golfers at the public courses will note, too, the addition of tall grasses and wildflowers in the open areas between holes, both beautifying the courses and enhancing their levels of difficulty. The clubhouses have been renovated as well, and their pro shops stocked with competitively priced goods for sale. Nearly $3.5 million in capital improvements have been invested in the six courses collectively, upgrading their images considerably. Meadowbrook also has made the six courses proactive in their community and initiated a major marketing campaign.

Below are brief profiles of the areas's best courses that are open to the public. There isn't one that doesn't provide a gorgeous backdrop of scalloped hills, layered in greens and blues. The golf courses of southeast Pennsylvania are some of the best places to see rural Pennsylvania at its most scenic. Even golf widows and widowers might want to come along as caddies-for-the-day, just to take in the beautiful panorama. Unless otherwise noted, greens fees quoted are in-season rates; taxes are extra.

PRIVATE COURSES

Aronimink Golf Club
3600 Saint Davids Road,
Newtown Square
(610) 356-6055
http://1stop4golf.com/343-Aronimink-Golf-Club.htm
With Donald Ross first designing this par-70

course in 1928 and Robert Trent Jones being its last designer, you know it's going to be tough. The first hole is a par 4, luring you in with an elevated tee shot to the valley below, followed by more than 100 bunkers, slopes, and doglegs throughout the 7,152-yard course. It's rated in the country's top 100 courses by *Golf Digest* and has hosted a number of pro tournaments over the years, including the 1962 PGA won by Gary Player, the USGA Junior Championship in 1997, and the Senior PGA in 2003. Located 15 miles west of Center City, Aronimink's greens fees are high—about $175—but playing there is a rare treat.

Bella Vista Golf Course
2901 Fagleysville Road, Gilbertsville
(601) 705-1855
www.bellavistagc.com
How can a golfer resist playing at a course whose name translates to "beautiful view"? The Jim Blaukovitch-designed course was once a 19th-century farmstead, transformed to a par-70 layout with a slope of 146. Old-world charm was retained in the design, with the farm's main house now serving as the clubhouse—with full service bar and restaurant added—along with locker rooms, club fitting and repair, and a great view of the 18th hole, giving it a "country club" feel. Greens fees range from $23 to walk on weekdays, to $62 with cart weekends, with special "after-5:00" rates.

Bucks County Country Club
2600 York Road, Jamison
(215) 343-0350
www.golfbucks.com
Designed by William Gordon in the early 1960s, Bucks County Country Club has a rolling terrain and layout similar to those classic course designs of the 1920s. The back nine have been revamped with a more contemporary target-oriented configuration, with elevation changes and longer fairways to make them more challenging. It's not a particularly long course (6,252 yards), but with undulating greens and bunkers, it's not easy to score well here. A

new clubhouse opened in 2005, with pro shop, locker rooms, and a restaurant and banquet room. Greens fees range from $20 weekdays to $52 weekends plus cart fees; on Ladies Day (Tuesday) and Seniors Day (Wednesday), ladies and seniors play for $35, respectively, including a cart.

Downingtown Golf Club
85 Country Club Drive, Downingtown
(610) 269-2000
www.golfdowningtown.com
Ranked one of the top five courses in America by *Golf Digest* (1998), this George Fazio–designed course has hosted numerous pro tournaments in the last two decades: the 2002 USGA Amateur Championship Qualifier, the 1998 USGA Mid-Amateur Qualifier, and the 1996 USGA Senior Open Qualifier among them. Built in 1967, Downington is a par-72 course of fair difficulty, 6,619 yards long, with elaborate bunkers and open-feeling fairways. Depending on the time of day, fees range from $39 to $69, with special junior, senior, and twilight fees. And if you're one who needs to get out there every day, look into their special membership scheme: Weekday memberships are $2,280, individual-associate memberships are $465, and seniors can join for $1,875.

The Golf Course at Glen Mills
221 Glen Mills Road, Glen Mills
(610) 558-2142
www.glenmillsgolf.com
When a course is ranked among the country's top 10 by both *Golf Digest* and *Golf* magazine, as well as rated Pennsylvania's finest course by *Golf Digest*, you can't blame golfers if their expectations are high when they come to this 6,636-yard, par-71 course. They're not disappointed—but they wouldn't be, knowing the course was designed by the great Bobby Weed. Between the seemingly constant elevation changes and the water on the back nine, this course is a great challenge and great fun, complete with driving range, putting green, and men's and women's locker rooms. Weekday fees are $75 with a cart,

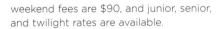

weekend fees are $90, and junior, senior, and twilight rates are available.

Hickory Valley
1921 Ludwig Road, Gilbertsville
(610) 754-7733
www.hickoryvalley.com
Voted "best budget course" in 1999 by *Philadelphia* magazine, Hickory Valley's two 18-hole courses put golfers where they most want to be: surrounded by nature, uncompromised by condo developments along the fairways. But nature in this instance is a diva, down to the cart service that roams the course, delivering snacks and drinks while you golf. The greens are fast, both courses are walkable (6,676 yards on the Presidential course, 6,442 on the Ambassador), and the courses offer woods, streams, water hazards, wildlife preserves, and a four-star *Golf Digest* rating. Fees range from $14 to $36 at the Ambassador, $22 to $33 at the Presidential.

Honeybrook Golf Club
1422 Cambridge Road, Honey Brook
(610) 273-0207
www.honeybrookgolf.com
When you golf at par-70 Honeybrook, consider a round of golf in the morning and shopping for cheeses and handicrafts after lunch, because the course sits amidst the Amish farms of Chester County. It's a pastoral, pristine area; protected wetlands and the west branch of Brandywine Creek snake through the course itself, enhancing the challenge. A chipping green and putting green are available, and the golf shop and pub were recently renovated. Fees for the 18-hole, 6,341-yard course are $25 to $34 weekdays and $32 to $65 weekends.

Island Green Country Club
1 Red Lion Road
(215) 677-3500
www.islandgreencc.com
Philadelphia's newest golf course is the Jim Blaukovitch-designed Island Green—its first addition in more than 50 years, in fact, with a shiny-new, 8,000-square-foot

If it seems as though the gods of golf are looking over your shoulder as you play Philadelphia's courses, you might be sensing energy from golf legend Arnold Palmer. The all-time champion was born in Latrobe, Pennsylvania, in the foothills of the Allegheny Mountains.

clubhouse and features such as transplanted trees that already affect play. From the 6,615-yard championship tees, five par-4 holes measure more than 400 yards each, and one of the par 5s, at 560 yards, is considered one of the toughest holes in the region. The Island Green Golf Academy was a hit since it opened, due in large part to its director, longtime PGA pro and Comcast Sportsnet personality Jay Friedman.

Linfield National Golf Club
66 Church Street, Linfield
(610) 495-8455
www.linfieldnational.com
Combining the traditional elements of water, trees, and changing elevations with features of a links-style course make the 6,164 yards play much longer than they appear at Linfield National. New owners in 2001 also purchased an additional 54 acres adjacent to the course, planning to build an adult golf course community. Improvements have gradually been made to the course, and the clubhouse was renovated in 2004 with a pub-style restaurant (Mulligan's at the 19th Hole) and pro shop. Fees are $24 (walk) to $39 with cart weekdays and $47 weekends, with special junior-senior rates; a 20-play membership including cart costs $549.

Loch Nairn Golf Club
U.S. Route 1, 5 miles south of Longwood Gardens
(610) 268-2234
www.lngolf.com
Known as a "championship shot maker's course," Loch Nairn offers tree-lined fairways, wetlands, bent grass greens,

streams, and lakes, demanding precision shots on every hole of the par-70, 6,076-yard course. The 19th Hole Tavern is just as pleasant, with a terrace that overlooks the first tee and a 50-inch-screen TV. A large practice green, showers, and fully stocked golf shop complete the offerings. Fees are in the budget range, $31 with a cart weekdays, $49 weekends, and special junior, senior, and twilight fees.

Pilgrim's Oak
1107 Pilgrim's Pathway, Peach Bottom
(717) 548-3011
www.pilgrimsoak.com
Designed by Dr. Michael Hurdzan, this par-72, 6,766-yard course carries a challenge on every hole, according to a *Philadelphia Inquirer* writer: "From tee to green, the player is confronted with water—spooky-looking water—that eventually becomes marsh and wetlands . . . " Located in southern Lancaster County, the course also features a 160-seat pavilion, driving range, putting green, and chipping green. Best of all, these thrills are affordable: Fees are $34 to $46 weekdays, $59 weekends or holidays, and junior and senior rates are available.

Tattersall Golf Club
1520 Tattersall Way, West Chester
(610) 738-4410
www.tattersallgolfclub.com
The August 2000 debut of this Rees Jones–designed course was eagerly awaited, and accolades quickly followed,

including *Golf Digest*'s award for "Best New Golf Course in the Country." Built on the highest point in Chester County, the dramatic elevation changes are highlighted by natural wetlands, bentgrass greens and fairways, 54 bunkers, three ponds, and challenges on every hole of the 6,826-yard layout. Yet the course achieves such harmony with the land and wildlife that Tattersall is a certified member of the Audubon Cooperative Sanctuary. Depending on the season, greens fees range from $68 to $80 weekdays, $77 to $95 weekends, and always include a cart.

Wyncote Golf Club
50 Wyncote Drive, Oxford
(610) 932-8900
www.wyncote.com
Designed by award-winning golf course architect Brian Ault, Wyncote echoes the features of a typical inland Scottish links course, complete with moguls, mounded bunkers, and wetlands. Stretching 7,149 yards from the back tees, Wyncote is a par-72 course, rated four-star by *Golf Digest*. PGA pro Robert Passarelli heads the pro staff, and the clubhouse amenities include a pub and full-service restaurant, locker room, and golf shop. Rates with cart are $30 to $60 weekdays, depending on the time of day, and up to $78 weekends.

PUBLIC COURSES

With nearly $3.5 million in capital improvements the images of Philadelphia's six public courses, collectively managed and marketed as Golf Philly, has been seriously upgraded; formerly known as courses to avoid, Golf Philly now are courses of choice.

Greens fees vary by course, but for avid golfers the best value is the Golf Philly Golf Permit. For one annual fee, golfers can play all six Golf Philly courses for the entire season—and the price is so low that it's a savings if you only golf twice a month. The permits are sold at three levels: a "limited" permit bestows

The Golf Course at Glen Mills has a unique distinction in its relationship to Glen Mills School, founded in 1826 and the oldest residential school for troubled youths in the country. Students receive vocational training in turf management and golf course operations, and net proceeds from the golf course are given to the students' scholarship fund. At this course, golfers can play well (or not) and do good!

golf privileges weekdays at any hour, and after 1:00 P.M. on weekends and holidays, for $1,000. A "weekday senior" permit gives privileges to golfers 62 and older, weekdays only, for $600. Junior and college student permits also are available, with privileges on weekdays and after 1:00 P.M. weekends and holidays, for $350. Day fees are included in the course profiles, below, but junior, senior, and twilight fees also are available at all six courses.

Cobb's Creek Karakung Course
7200 Lansdowne Avenue
(215) 877-8707
www.golfphilly.com/karakung.html
Length is not the challenge on this par-72, 5,762-yard course; it's the elevation changes and small greens. Built in the 1920s, Cobb's Creek Karakung features 26 bunkers, a creek, natural wetlands, moundings, and plenty of trees, so proper club selection is key. It's said that in the 1930s, golfers who were pronounced "not good enough" to play at Karakung's sister course, the Olde Course, were sent here to hone their skills until they were ready for the "big sister." Greens fees are economical: $18 on weekdays ($28 with a cart), $23 weekends (or $33 with cart).

Cobb's Creek Olde Course
7200 Lansdowne Avenue
(215) 877-8707
www.golfphilly.com/oldecourse.html
Adjacent to Cobb's Creek Karakung, Olde Course was the first public golf course in Greater Philadelphia, and is considered the premier course in the Golf Philly collection. It was designed in 1916 by famed architect Hugh Wilson (who also designed Karakung) and was deemed the "6th-Best Municipal Course in the U.S." by *Golfweek* magazine. The first challenge of Olde Course is the creek, especially a factor in the first six holes, but it's the lengthy fairways that exasperate even the strongest players—especially on the 14th hole, a grueling 638 yards. Fees are $28 to walk and $38 with a cart weekdays, and $33 and $43 weekends.

Tattersall Golf Club sits on 372 acres once owned by noted 18th-century agriculturist John Beale Bordley, who in 1793 established the first agricultural society in the United States. The stone clubhouse was the Bordley House; now fully restored, it was built in 1702 and is registered with the Pennsylvania Historical and Museum Commission.

F. D. R. Golf Club
20th and Pattison Avenues
(215) 462-8997
www.golfphilly.com/fdr.html
It's tempting to assess the par-69 Franklin D. Roosevelt Golf Club as an easy, "grip-and-rip" layout, but don't be fooled; the flat, open course makes for unpredictable winds and fast greens, creating their own challenges. Established in 1940 as a public works project, F. D. R. offers wide fairways and oversize greens that are protected by bunkers. Wetlands and a canal also run through the Florida-style layout of this 6,004-yard course. The reward for your efforts: great views of Philadelphia's skyline framing your shots. Greens fees are $23 to walk and $33 to ride weekdays, and $28 and $38 weekends.

John F. Byrne Golf Club
9500 Leon Street
(215) 632-8666
www.golfphilly.com/jbf.html
Named for a famous Philadelphia City Councilman, John F. Byrne Golf Club was the Holmesburg Country Club until the 1960s, when the City purchased it. Designed by Alex Findlay, it boasts one of the area's most interesting layouts; wedged into (and around) a valley, the rolling terrain is made even more challenging by the Torresdale Creek, which comes into play on 10 holes. Oversize bunkers, wetlands, and strategically placed trees add complexity to this par-72, 5,189-yard course. Fees are $23 to walk and $33 with cart on weekdays, and $28 and $38 weekends.

Juniata Golf Club
1391 Cayuga Street
(215) 743-4060
www.golfphilly.com/juniata.html
Juniata features the only double green in Greater Philadelphia, but that's certainly not its only distinction. Designed by famous golf architect Ed Ault in 1930, Juniata Golf Club is a short (5,275 yards) but challenging par 66, with undulating greens, an uphill 6th hole, and Frankford Creek, which comes into play on six holes. Sixteen bunkers guard the greens of this classic course. Fees are $18 to walk and $28 with a cart weekdays, and increase to $23 and $33 weekends.

Walnut Lane Golf Club
Walnut Lane and Magdalena Street
(215) 482-3370
www.golfphilly.com/walnut.html
At 4,509 yards, this is the shortest of Philadelphia's golf courses, but therein lies its challenge: the mastery of the short game. Par is just 62 at this course, located inside Wissahickon Valley Park, and because of several holes nestled in hillsides and valleys, Walnut Lane is often regarded as the city's most scenic course. It's another Alex Findlay design, complete with wavy greens, deep bunkers, and century-old hardwoods lining the fairways. Fees are $18 to walk and $28 with cart on weekdays, and $23 and $33 weekends.

HUNTING
AND FISHING

With Philadelphia positioned in the middle of the concrete corridor between New York City, Baltimore, and Washington, D.C., its first image is hardly that of a hunting or fishing destination. The southeast corner of Pennsylvania is the most densely populated region of the state and a gateway to the other big-city East Coast tourist spots.

That said, however, the Philadelphia countryside is rich in natural resources, sprinkled with a number of hunting and fishing lodges to accommodate sportspeople. One of the more popular stopping points is The Warrington, a comfortable country lodge in central Bucks County.

Big-game hunting in Pennsylvania most likely means deer, and the place to hunt is Nockamixon State Park in Bucks County, with more than 3,000 acres available to hunters during deer season. Adjacent to Nockamixon is State Game Land 157, offering another 2,000 acres.

Small-game hunting usually takes hunters to Northampton County, about 15 miles northeast of Allentown (a 90-minute drive from Philadelphia), to State Game Land 217. These grounds run along the Appalachian Trail, offering an abundance of waterfowl, rabbit, ruffed grouse, and pheasant.

Fishing opportunities are even more plentiful across the entire Lehigh Valley region, and many outfitters also will equip visitors for canoe, raft, or kayak adventures (see the Parks and Recreation chapter). For large fish, especially tiger muskellunge, Nockamixon Lake in Nockamixon State Park, Bucks County, is a popular place. East of the city, you can try catching the big one at Chambers Lake in Hybernia County Park, Chester County, amply stocked with bass, chain pickerel, and yellow perch.

For river and stream fishing, head north of the city to Saucon Creek in Northampton County—a peaceful setting, especially the portion that flows through Saucon Park in Bethlehem. Or, you can even fish right inside Philadelphia; Fairmount Park offers 34 miles of waterways with plenty of fishing opportunities along the Pennypack Creek, the Wissahickon Creek, or the Schuylkill River.

HUNTING

The first thing every hunter in Pennsylvania needs is a license, easily obtainable from the Pennsylvania Game Commission (www.pgc.state.pa.us). That's not the only essential the Commission provides, however. Each license holder is given, free of charge, *A Digest of Pennsylvania Hunting & Trapping Regulations,* and for $2.50, hunters also can receive a copy of the state's Game and Wildlife Code.

The Game Commission's Web site is a good place to start; its FAQs are especially helpful and easy to understand. They explain, for instance, information about Hunter-Trapper Education Classes, links to regional wildlife conservation offices, and rules about picking up deer

Finding lodging near designated hunting grounds is easy; hunters can either stay in hotels and inns with non-hunting visitors, or at campgrounds and hunting lodges in rural areas, including state park camping facilities. For information, call (888) PA-PARKS or visit www.dcnr .state.pa.us/stateparks/, or call for a current Pennsylvania Visitors Guide at (800) 210-8351.

Every hunter needs target practice from time to time, and one good resource is the Rock Run Sports Club (255 South Mount Airy Road, Coatesville, 610-383-1000; www.rockrunclub.com). Five indoor ranges are provided for shooting with a pistol, shotgun, or archery equipment.

that's been killed by a vehicle on the highway. It's a good resource, too, for homeowners living near hunting areas, as some questions explain options if hunters are trespassing on residential property, how to tell if an animal is rabid, and which activities are not permitted on State Game Lands.

Generally, hunters are not permitted within "safety zones," including the area within 150 yards of an occupied home, camp, commercial building, or school; the distance is reduced to 50 yards for archery hunters. On game lands, authorized activities include hiking, photography, canoeing, fishing, and berry-picking, but mountain biking and horseback riding usually are restricted to specific trails, during certain time periods. Swimming, tree-cutting, camping (except in designated Appalachian Trail sites), and most motorized boating are illegal.

As for discerning whether an animal has rabies, that diagnosis can only be made by analyzing the animal's brain tissue in a lab. There are, however, symptoms that hunters can watch for; they include nocturnal animals wandering aimlessly in the daytime, those too sick to react to human presence, animals aggressively pursuing fast-moving objects, and any animal frothing at the mouth. If in doubt, keep your distance and call the Game Commission in that area, or local or state police.

The number of deer a hunter might see on an outing is determined by so many factors that it's impossible to predict. Setting up in an area overrun with deer helps, as does stationing near a well-used food source. But deer react to conditions in different ways, and the size and

distribution of local deer populations, hunter pressure, fog, deep snow, adequate shelter, and the availability of food, all influence the animals' availability.

It is compulsory in Pennsylvania to report the taking of a deer, though authorities acknowledge that up to 50 percent of hunters do not report their harvests. To properly manage deer and their habitats, the Game Commission frequently examines about 40,000 harvested deer, more than 10 percent of those legally taken, to help managers follow trends on the herd's living conditions.

An entirely different set of laws and regulations rule the hunting of small game, including squirrel, mourning dove, ruffed grouse, rabbit, pheasant, hare, quail, woodchuck, and crow. Hunting parties are limited to six persons, and hunters of dove and woodcock must have a migratory game bird license in addition to their general hunting license.

Hunters of different animals must follow different rules regarding dress: Woodcock hunters, for instance, must wear a solid fluorescent orange cap on their heads, visible 360 degrees, and other small-game hunters must wear at least 250 square inches of fluorescent orange on their head, chest, and back combined—with the exception of dove and crow hunters, who are not required to wear any orange.

Hunting of quail, woodcock, and grouse are forbidden in certain counties. In all areas, it is illegal to hunt waterfowl—all wild ducks and wild geese—while in possession of lead shot, even if the hunter also is hunting small game, and no waterfowl hunting is permitted on Sunday. Because the regulations vary by animal and geographic area, it's important for all small-game hunters to be familiar with the regulations before they set out.

FISHING

As a fishing state, they don't come more bountiful than Pennsylvania, with more than 83,000 miles of streams and rivers,

4,000 inland lakes and ponds covering 160,000 miles, and another 470,000 acres of Lake Erie. And the regulations governing the sport are every bit as complicated as those for hunting!

To familiarize yourself with the rules, the best resource is the *Pennsylvania Summary of Fishing Regulations and Laws,* known as the Summary Book. (See http://sites.state.pa.us/PA/Exec/Fish_Boat/fishpub/summary/.) It gives a good overview, using clear charts showing the season dates, sizes, daily limits, and regulated waters of various fishing programs. The Big Bass Program, for instance, is subject to special regulations applying to largemouth, smallmouth, and spotted bass in certain waters (rivers and streams are regulated differently from lakes), and approved trout lakes in the Big Bass Program are only open on certain dates.

Brook, brown, and rainbow trout are abundant in countless creeks and smaller rivers in southeast Pennsylvania, and the *PA Region Guide*—available by writing P.O. Box 67000, Harrisburg, PA 17106, or through the Pennsylvania Fish and Boat Commission's Web site (http://sites.state.pa.us)—contains links to hot spots for trout in each of the Commission's six regions, as well as lists of streams stocked with trout in the Stocking Lists, and Special Regulation Areas. The online maps at the site are especially helpful.

Smallmouth bass and other river fish—pike, walleye, muskie, catfish, carp, and others—are likewise plentiful on the Allegheny, Delaware, Susquehanna, and Juniata Rivers; the *PA Region Guide* also lists hundreds of boat access points along the rivers. The guide provides information on specific waters and their conditions as well.

Those who want to stay closer to the city will want to check Fairmount Park's Web site, www.fairmountpark.org/Fishing.asp, which lists all of the fish species found in the Pennypack and Wissahickon Creeks, along with their scientific names and whether each species is "fishable"—i.e., whether it has been caught

Everyone over the age of 16 needs a license to fish in Pennsylvania. Applications, lists of agents, and other info about their services are found at the State Fish and Boat Commission's Web site, http://sites.state.pa.us/PA_Exec/Fish_Boat/. Most Fishing License Issuing Agents are commercial businesses that can supply fishing gear; many even sell bait.

with rod and reel. The list is surprisingly lengthy, with fishable species including brown and rainbow trout, channel catfish, largemouth and smallmouth bass, rock bass, striped bass, and white perch.

And visiting fishermen, listen up for one of southeast Pennsylvania's best angling secrets: Huge striped bass come to Philadelphia each spring to spawn in the lower Delaware River. They've made a comeback in recent decades: An estimated 36,000 were landed in 2002. And they would make quite a meal if catch-and-release weren't required; bass more than 30 inches long and weighing more than 30 pounds are common. For fish of that size, opt for medium-heavy spinning rods, with spinning reels carrying 12- to 20-pound test line.

The Commission's Region Guide for southeast Pennsylvania shows public access along the Delaware, but these sites are particularly known as hot spots:

- Neshaminy State Park Marina. This boat launch is popular and, while shore angling also is available here, some may find the boat traffic an intrusion.
- Delaware River Access (Station Avenue). Located at the southern tip of Bucks County, this is a favorite spot for shore anglers.
- Frankford Access. This is a Commission access in northeast Philadelphia. One advantage here is good wheelchair access.
- Linden Avenue Access. At this Philadelphia City access, park areas are nearby for family picnicking.

You can walk to this popular angling spot from your hotel: the Schuylkill River dam at the Philadelphia Museum of Art. In the spring this place gets downright crowded. There is, however, a fish passage facility at the dam, and angling is prohibited within 100 feet of the passageway.

• Ridley Park Access. Don't look for shore angling space here, but this ramp is a good Delaware County access point.

Philadelphians know other hot spots, though some are not beginner-friendly.

Trenton Falls, for instance, is the head of tidewater on the Delaware River. It's located far upstream in Bucks County and is extremely rocky. Newcomers will fare better between Trenton Falls and Poquessing Creek, which marks the boundary between Philadelphia and Bucks County. It's a creek confluence—known as striper "resting places"—and will be safer for boaters. Another productive confluence is where Pennypack Creek meets the Delaware, and it's a good spot for shore anglers.

At any spot along rivers and streams, be aware that fishing near some bridges may be illegal. U.S. Coast Guard regulations prohibit angling near some large commercial and naval vessel routes.

NEIGHBORHOODS AND RELOCATION

Whether you've decided to make Philadelphia your new home or just want to get to know the city better, there's a wealth of interesting information, not always apparent to the casual visitor, that is sure to enhance and amplify your view of the city.

For one thing, you can still get great housing deals here—especially considering that Philly is an East Coast city. For renters especially, prices are more like those in the Midwest than on the coasts: You can find a spacious-enough apartment in Center City for well under $1,000. Couple the city's housing affordability with its restaurant, theater, and concert prices, and you have the makings of an affordable, yet sophisticated, lifestyle.

At the same time, buying in Philadelphia can be a wise investment. In some neighborhoods, such as West Philadelphia, prices have skyrocketed 150 percent in the last 10 years. In East Falls, the neighborhood off Kelly Drive just outside of Manayunk, you can find spacious starter homes needing work for a little over $200,000—but prices are climbing fast. And while you will likely pay more than $300,000 for an apartment in Center City—a 200 percent jump over the last 10 years—try buying an apartment in New York or Boston for that price! Philly definitely is a renter's and condo buyer's market; some 10,000 new apartments and condominiums have been created in Center City since the Republican National Convention was held here in 2000, thanks in large part to the media's positive coverage of Philadelphia's assets.

In Greater Philadelphia, there is no shortage of resources to help you relocate, and one of your first calls will be to find a Realtor to help you search for a new home:

**Greater Philadelphia
Association of Realtors**
1341 North Delaware Avenue, Suite 308
(215) 423-9381
www.gpar.org

Delaware Valley Realtors Association
3475 West Chester Pike, Suite 220
Newtown Square
(215) 956-9176
www.delvalrealtors.com

**Montgomery County
Association of Realtors**
3031A Walton Road, Suite 302
Plymouth Meeting
(610) 260-9931
www.mcarealtors.org

Once you are connected to a Realtor, you'll want to find out how to make things happen in your life here—and if there were a contest to see which city makes that info most accessible to residents, Philly would win, hands down. All you need to do is go to www.phila.gov/helpme, the "help page" of the Mayor's Office of Information Services. You will find dozens of links here, clustered conveniently together, for one-click access if you need to:

• get a birth certificate
• pay a parking ticket or traffic violation
• find a job, health center, recreation center, zipcode or disability resources
• pay your taxes
• get a construction permit
• report an abandoned auto, waste collection problems, discrimination, or fraud
• get a pothole fixed
• register to vote, or dozens of other resident services

And if that site doesn't provide all the answers to a successful life in Philadelphia, you can go to www.phila.gov/residents/index.html, for even more information on paying your bills, bus and train schedules, driving directions, news and weather, animal care, schools, emergencies, human relations, and additional community resources.

EMERGENCIES

Like all cities across the country, the all-purpose phone number for health and safety emergencies is 911. For other safety matters:

- For non-emergency police, call (215) 686-3010.
- Accidental poisoning, call (215) 386-2100.
- Fire and rescue, call (215) 922-6000.
- If you need an ambulance, call Network Ambulance Service (215-482-8560) or SEPTA Paratransit (215-580-7700).
- For pet emergencies, the University of Pennsylvania Veterinary Hospital (215-898-4685) will make referrals.
- To reach a doctor quickly, call the Philadelphia County Medical Society (215-563-5343). All hospitals in Philadelphia have an emergency room.
- For a dental emergency, contact the Philadelphia County Dental Society (215-925-6050).

Outside Philadelphia, you can get public safety information from the Citizens Crime Commission of Delaware Valley (215-627-6532) or the Crime Victims Center of Chester County (610-692-7420).

TAXES

Philadelphia City Taxes

The gross earned income of Philadelphia residents is taxed at 4.4625 percent, regardless of whether the income was earned in Philadelphia or in a surrounding city, and unearned income is taxed 4.5000 percent for a school tax. Non-residents who work in the city pay a 3.8801 percent tax on gross income earned in Philadelphia.

Real estate in Philadelphia is taxed $8.264 per $100 of assessed value, plus a 4 percent real estate transfer tax (of which 1 percent goes to the State of Pennsylvania). Surrounding cities all have their own income and property tax structures; you can call their municipal offices for information, or call the State of Pennsylvania's Fact and Information Line at (888) PA-TAXES or visit www.revenue.state.pa.us.

State Income and Sales Tax

Pennsylvania taxes eight classes of income (including earnings, interest dividends, and other income) at 3.407 percent, and a 6 percent state sales tax is applied to items sold in Pennsylvania. Exceptions to the sales tax include food, clothing, drugs, and textbooks. In addition, Philadelphia charges a 1 percent sales tax. For more information, call the State's Fact and Information Line at (888) PA-TAXES or visit www.revenue.state.pa.us.

If you move to a town in Delaware, you will pay a graduated personal income tax of between 2.2 percent and 5.5 percent for incomes under $60,000, and 5.95 percent if you earn more than $60,000. Delaware does not charge a state sales tax; for more information, call the Delaware Division of Revenue/Public Service (302-577-8200) or visit www.state.de.us/revenue/index.htm.

New Jersey residents pay a graduated income tax ranging from 1.4 percent (for incomes under $20,000) to 6.37 percent if you earn $75,000 as a single. The State charges a 6 percent sales tax, exempting food, clothing, and medicines. For more information, call the New Jersey Tax Hot

Line (609-292-6400) or visit www.state.nj.us/treasury/taxation.

UTILITIES

Natural gas and electricity now are deregulated in Pennsylvania, New Jersey, and Delaware, so consumers can choose their own energy providers and packages. It's a daunting task, but there's plenty of help: First, get background from the Web site for your state:

- Pennsylvania: www.eia.doe.gov/emeu/ states/main_pa.html
- New Jersey: www.eia.doe.gov/emeu/ states/main_nj.html
- Delaware: www.eia.doe.gov/emeu/ states/main_de.html

You also will find information on deregulation, and what it means to consumers across the country, at www .electricitychoice.com. For more state organizations, contact these offices; their staff can answer your energy-related questions:

- Pennsylvania Public Utility Commission, (717) 783-1740; www.puc.paonline.com
- Pennsylvania Electric Choice, www .utilitychoice.org
- New Jersey Board of Public Utilities, (973) 648-2026; www.bpu.state.nj.us
- Delaware Public Service Commission, (302) 739-4247; www.state.de.us/delpsc

VOTER REGISTRATION

Since the Pennsylvania Voter Registration Act was passed in 1995, it's never been easier to register to vote by mail, in person, or online. Forms are available in libraries, U.S. Postal Service offices, borough or city offices, or online at www.fec.gov/votregis/vr.htm. You also can register to vote (in any state) when you renew your driver's license, as long as you will be 18 years of age by Election Day, will have been a U.S. citizen for at least

one month before the election, will live in your election district for at least 30 days before election day, and have not been imprisoned in the last five years on a felony conviction.

The League of Women Voters is a nonprofit, nonpartisan organization that provides voting information, among other services. Their contact info for the Philadelphia region:

- League of Women Voters of Pennsylvania, (717) 234-1576; www.pa.lwv.org
- League of Women Voters of Delaware, (302) 571-8948; www.de.lwv.org
- League of Women Voters of New Jersey, (609) 394-3303; www.lwvnj.org

For questions on voting in your locality, call your local Board of Elections:

- Philadelphia County Board of Elections, (215) 686-3460
- Bucks County Board of Elections, (215) 348-6154
- Chester County Board of Elections, (610) 344-6410
- Delaware County Board of Elections, (610) 891-4659
- Montgomery County Board of Elections, (215) 686-3460

DRIVER'S LICENSES

In Pennsylvania, New Jersey, and Delaware, new residents must obtain a local driver's license within 60 days of establishing their permanent residence. The phone numbers and Web sites below will put you in touch with the proper agencies; they can tell you where to find the most convenient license bureau for you.

- Pennsylvania Department of Motor Vehicles (DMV), (800) 932-4600, (717) 391-6190 out-of-state; www.dot3.state.pa.us
- New Jersey Motor Vehicle Commission, (888) 486-3339, (609) 292-6500 out-of-state; www.state.nj.us/mvc

- Delaware: New Castle Division of Motor Vehicles, (302) 326-5000
- Delaware: Greater Wilmington Division of Vehicles, (302) 434-3200; www.dmv.de.gov

RESOURCES FOR SENIORS

Although Philly isn't a Florida-style magnet for retirees, Philadelphians tend to stay here in their later years, mostly because they love the place. One of the primary resources for older residents is the Philadelphia Corporation for Aging (PCA), which operates a popular Helpline (215-765-9040) covering referral services for senior benefits and programs of all kinds. PCA's Web site also contains links to information and contacts for older adult protective services, long-term care access, and elder abuse: www.pcaphl.org.

When you need to learn about or access government services for the elderly, your best bet is to contact your area's Office on Aging. In Philadelphia, that resource is the PCA; for the state suburbs, the contact numbers follow:

- Pennsylvania Department of Aging, (717) 783-1550; www.aging.state.pa.us
- Bucks County Office of Aging, (800) 243-3767; www.buckscounty.org/seniors/area_agency_aging-index.html
- Chester County Department of Aging, (800) 692-1100, ext. 6350; www.chesco.org/aging/index.html
- Delaware County Services for the Aging, (800) 416-4504; www.delcosa.org
- Montgomery County Office of Aging and Adult Services, (610) 278-3601; www.montcopa.org/mcaas/
- New Jersey Department of Health and Senior Services, (609) 943-3345; www.state.nj.us/health/
- Delaware Department of Health and Social Services, (302) 577-4791; www.state.de.us/dhss/index.html

Other key numbers for seniors residing in the Philadelphia area:

RETIRED SENIOR VOLUNTEER PROGRAMS (RSVP)

- Bucks County, (215) 340-1210
- Chester County, (610) 436-6646
- Delaware County, (610) 565-5563
- Montgomery County, (610) 834-1040, ext. 14
- Philadelphia West, (215) 854-7077
- Philadelphia East, (215) 331-7787

SENIOR CENTERS

- Pennsylvania Senior Centers, www.paseniorcenters.org
- New Jersey Senior Centers, (877) 222-3737
- Delaware Senior Centers, (302) 577-4791

EMPLOYMENT

- Action Alliance for Seniors, 1201 Chestnut Street, 2nd floor, Philadelphia, (215) 557-0751
- Associacion Nacional pro Persona Mayores, 3150 North Mascher Street, Suite 100, Philadelphia, (215) 426-1212
- Experience Works, (610) 670-7705
- Mayor's Commission on Aging, (215) 686-8450; www.phila.gov/aging/index.html

NEIGHBORHOODS

Just try to find a definitive list of Philadelphia's neighborhoods; it doesn't exist because everyone defines "neighborhood" differently. No doubt, many who live in New Hope, a Bucks County town more than 40 miles outside of Center City, consider their borough a suburban Philadelphia neighborhood. Blue Bell, a burgeoning Main Line community, is considered part of Philly even though it's about 15 miles outside the city.

There are, in fact, more than 125 communities outside the city that are considered part of Greater Philadelphia, scattered across the countryside in Bucks, Chester, Delaware, and Montgomery Counties. Rather than select individual towns to profile here, we thought it would be less confusing to provide a general look at each of those counties, with relevant comparisons and notations about some of the more prominent towns within each county, before we present individual city neighborhoods.

You can get a good idea of the housing styles, costs, and amenities of various areas if you know what you're looking for in a home, and keep a couple of trusty resources on hand. One of those would be *Philadelphia* magazine, which publishes an annual guide to housing values in Greater Philadelphia; its 2005 guide noted that, overall, prices in city neighborhoods rose 19 percent the previous year, while prices in suburban towns increased 12 percent.

You can also refer to several Web sites for up-to-date information; one reliable site is www.phillyneighborhoods.org. It's a bit cumbersome to negotiate your way around this site, partly because neighborhood data is presented by the area of the city (North, Northwest, South, etc.) rather than by the neighborhood's name. But if you match those directional areas with the neighborhood in which you're interested, you can access information on libraries, police stations, after-school programs, health centers, even census and crime data.

You can also find informative neighborhood summaries at www.aroundphilly.com and at the site of the Greater Philadelphia Tourism Marketing Corporation, www.gophila.com.

Bucks County

A river doesn't exactly "run through it," but the drive along the eastern edge of Bucks County takes you up the scenic Delaware River, one of the prettiest and most relaxing drives anywhere.

The 600,000 residents of Bucks County are surrounded by 300 years of history; this is where Washington crossed the Delaware. Some think of Bucks towns as artsy outposts of Philadelphia, while others, thanks to former residents James A. Michener and Pearl S. Buck, have a more literary image. They're both right; Bucks County also is home to some of the best antiquing in Southeastern Pennsylvania. The Franklin Mills outlet stores are located here, as are the upscale shops of Peddler's Village and half a dozen wineries.

If you follow River Road (Route 32), it will bring you to New Hope, a rather commercial but still funky artists' colony, 42 miles from Center City and across the river from Lambertville, New Jersey, which is famous in its own right for its antiques shops. For the past five years, homes in New Hope have been appreciating at about 10 percent per year; if you found a house there for $400,000 it would be a bargain. That's about double the average price of a house in Bensalem, located about 15 miles closer to Philadelphia.

Doylestown, the county seat, is west of New Hope. It's not as touristy as New Hope, and while housing isn't quite as expensive as in New Hope (the 2004 average was just over $362,000), prices here also are increasing at about 10 percent a year.

Chester County/ Brandywine Valley

History and scenery are the drivers for visitors to the Brandywine Valley, and of course a significant factor in the housing styles and prices across this region. Wineries are beginning to draw tourists across the Brandywine region, and at the southern end of the valley are the famous Longwood Gardens and Winterthur Museum.

Some of Southeastern Pennsylvania's hottest relocation destinations are found here. Think old stone houses, horse farms, covered bridges, towering sycamores, and swinging gates. In most hamlets average home prices run $250,000 to $350,000, though one of the better deals here is the city of West Chester, where prices still average out at $250,000. Chester County has its own share of American history; the Battle of the Brandywine, a key battle in the Revolutionary War, was fought here. A more current claim to fame: QVC's corporate headquarters are located in West Chester, a thriving small city of nearly 160,000 people.

In Malvern, another upscale Chester County town, home prices average about $265,000—but, while they've increased 15 percent since 2000, they only rose 1 percent between 2004 and 2005. The hottest community in terms of housing prices probably is Franklin, with current prices averaging near $400,000 and increasing more than 30 percent between 2004 and 2005. Franklin's five-year boost in average home prices was more than 45 percent.

Delaware County

Rolling green vistas and city-style congestion are the two images of Delaware County. Few towns here have familiar names, though readers may recognize some of the Main Line communities in Delaware County: Wayne, Radnor, and especially Swarthmore.

You can find quiet streets and great schools in Delaware County. In Radnor and Wayne, homeowners pay an average of $500,000 for the privilege, while Swarthmore homes still sell for $300,000 or less, on average. There are exceptions, of course; the five-bedroom quasi-mansions along Elm Avenue in Swarthmore bring a cool mil. And don't look for any typical college-town traits in this famous college town; Swarthmore has no record stores or cafes, and it's been dry for more than 50 years so you definitely won't find college bars here. What you will find, like so many of Philly's suburban towns, is a downtown corridor lined with flower baskets and entrepreneurial shops.

Montgomery County

Colonial history and 21st-century technology juxtapose in Montgomery County, with Valley Forge, scene of Washington's winter encampment, setting the historic tone. Just as lofty are the educational institutions in these parts, with home prices reflecting the prestige: In Villanova, 2005 prices averaged nearly $700,000, while nearby along Route 30 (the "Lincoln Highway"), homes in Bryn Mawr averaged sale prices of $600,000.

Not every town in Montgomery County commands such high prices, though in fast-growing Blue Bell, they average more than $400,000 and are gaining about 10 percent in resale value every year. Conshohocken, once an industrial outpost, is becoming a mecca for new office buildings and homes in surrounding neighborhoods reflect the change: In 2005 they sold for an average of just over $219,000, but they've gone up 75 percent in the last five years.

Philadelphia Neighborhoods

CHESTNUT HILL

One of Philly's newly hot areas, Chestnut Hill has a small-town Main Street feel, with plenty of art galleries, tearooms, restaurants, and specialty shops lining the cobblestoned upper Germantown Avenue. It's a National Historic District and the highest point inside the city limits. The lifestyle fits the surroundings, with frequent small-venue concerts, parades, poetry readings, and other neighborhood events scheduled year-round. More than in many neighborhoods, people who settle in Chestnut Hill seem eager to be involved in the community. Home prices reflect the growing desirability; the average price of a home already had jumped to more than $425,000 in 2004, an 88 percent boost over the previous decade.

B3 AND THE GAYBORHOOD

Just in the last couple of years, the area east of Broad Street is being referred to as B3—"Blocks Below Broad"—including the "Gayborhood," generally encompassing the blocks between Lombard and Walnut Streets, from 11th to Broad Street. The gay reference isn't new; even in the early 1900s, gays and lesbians gathered in the bars along Locust Street. Each October the neighborhood throws an "Outfest" of flea markets, art shows, and parties.

Outside the Gayborhood boundaries, B3 is filling with upscale home furnishings stores, great restaurants, and businesses such as the gelatería Capogiro (119 South 13th Street), that draw customers from all over the city. Also here is Philly's oldest independent bookstore, Robin's (108 South 13th Street), open here since 1936 and known for its collection of African-American books. On B3's fringe are the row homes of Antique Row. Even though this is the heart of Center City, home prices averaged $301,000 in 2004—not exorbitant, though that's a 170 percent jump over the previous decade.

GERMANTOWN AND MT. AIRY

This is Philadelphia's Historic Northwest. One of Philly's oldest settlements, Germantown was first settled by German immigrants who were lured here by William Penn's vision of religious tolerance. Although the old homes have great character and architectural detail, much of the neighborhood is in need of rehab; homes here sell for under $100,000— barely a 50 percent jump in 10 years.

Mount Airy has fared better. It's one of Philly's truly diverse neighborhoods—not just racially, but also economically and in terms of ages and family structures. One of Philly's largest Jewish clusters lives in Mt. Airy, and the housing here is as diverse as the people, ranging from apartments to mansions. Homes sell for about $200,000, a modest increase of 5 percent from year to year.

MANAYUNK

Follow the Schuylkill River for 4 miles from Center City and you'll land in Manayunk, another National Historic District, now gentrified with more than 65 boutiques and about 30 restaurants along the Main Street corridor. The town overlooks the Manayunk Canal; it's an enjoyable place to spend the afternoon and a relatively affordable neighborhood to live in. Homes averaged about $200,000 in 2004—but that was a 33 percent increase over the previous year and a 250 percent jump over 10 years, so Manayunk definitely has been discovered.

NORTHERN LIBERTIES

Northern Liberties is so new as a "hot" neighborhood that it isn't even indicated on the tourist maps. But it's not a place tourists would seek out; it's just a neighborhood with a few bars, a few bistros, a few shops, and home prices under $150,000. Located along Second Street between Spring Garden and Poplar, it's not glamorous—just homey and welcoming. The most popular watering hole is Standard Tap (901 North Second Street), described by *Philadelphia* magazine as "the neighborhood bar everyone wishes were in his own neighborhood."

OLD CITY

This is the most historic square mile in the country, with the Liberty Bell, Independence National Historical Park, and Elfreth's Alley calling this neighborhood home. It's also one of the most popular areas with the under-40 crowd, especially on the first Friday night of every month when galleries open their doors for an artsy walk-around. Homes here—virtually all row houses—sell for more than $400,000, and the average price is climbing about 22 percent every year.

SOUTH STREET AND SOUTH PHILLY

The mini-neighborhoods here all have their own distinct personalities. There's the ever-bohemian South Street, loud but offering quality restaurants and shopping amid the tattoo parlors and record stores. Here and in adjacent Queen Village, a quiet buffer between South Street and the Italian quarter, home prices flirt with the $300,000 mark—and they could be either row houses, single homes, or condos.

In South Philly, homes are less expensive; you can get a single home that needs work for less than $250,000, and walk to the Italian Market for lunch.

RITTENHOUSE SQUARE

This is the tony neighborhood ringing lovely Rittenhouse Square—elegant condos, graceful mansions, designer shops, and fine dining. If you take a bench in the park, you'll be treated to some of the best people-watching in the city. An apartment here costs at least $500,000. Housing prices are more stable here than in most neighborhoods; they seem to have leveled out at about a 4 percent increase for the past few years—though they did double during the boom years a decade ago.

UNIVERSITY CITY

Once Philadelphia's first suburb, the trees, huge houses, and wide pillared porches still make University City an inviting neighborhood to settle in. You'll be joined by thousands of University of Pennsylvania and Drexel University students who have created the need for shopping clusters, bookstores, and restaurants with a great ethnic mix, from Middle Eastern to Indian, Vietnamese, and Thai cuisines. It's a fairly quiet neighborhood in spite of the huge student population. You can find homes here for under $200,000, but the average home price jumped 238 percent between 1994 and 2004, so its days of being an affordable neighborhood may be numbered.

EDUCATION

They grow 'em smart in Philadelphia. With more than 860 public elementary, middle, and high schools in more than 60 public school districts in the five-county Greater Philadelphia area—not to mention hundreds more charter, parochial, and private schools—educating kids is a top priority.

Higher education in Philly started before the country itself was formed, with Benjamin Franklin's founding of the University of Pennsylvania in 1740. Today more than 80 colleges and degree-granting institutions are located here—27 of them within Philadelphia's city limits—graduating 50,000-plus students each year. Future leaders come to Philly's six postgraduate business schools, five law schools, and five medical schools from all over the world.

But it's in the early years that education helps shape the mind. With so many hundreds of public schools, it would be impossible to profile individual schools, or even the area's 80 school districts, in a guidebook—but don't be overwhelmed, because there are easy resources for researching education in Greater Philadelphia. If your child will be joining the 196,309 students already attending Philly's city schools, your first stop should be the Web site of the school district of Philadelphia, www.phila.k12.pa.us. There you will find the policies and programs guiding the system's 273 public schools, including 175 elementary, 43 middle, 43 neighborhood and magnet high schools, 5 vocational/technical schools, and 7 special-needs centers.

PUBLIC SCHOOLS

The menu of innovative programs sponsored by Philadelphia Public Schools is impressive. By all accounts, it is the first school district in the United States to make African-American studies mandatory for all high schoolers; Philly's is a one-year course. Another interesting offering is FamilyNet, a Web page accessible through the school system's site, which allows families access to a student's school data including report card grades, attendance, test scores, and instructional resources.

Perhaps the most momentous program of the Philadelphia schools is its "Declaration for 2008: No Excuses," a series of goals in educational excellence. It is a bold initiative that includes effectiveness measures for teachers, the creation of gifted and high-achievement programs in *all* schools, new sports equipment and musical instruments and programs, and modern classrooms. The main office for the school district of Philadelphia is at 21st Street and The Parkway (215–299–7000; www.phila.k12.pa.us).

Another invaluable Web site is www.paprofiles.org, which is, frankly, a wondrous creation. This statewide site is massive, with links to data on every public, charter, and private school in Pennsylvania. Set aside time to explore here; you will find links to PDF files containing school systems' and individual schools' enrollment, programs, and contact information. It gets quite specific, including each school's technological and library resources (down to the number of computers available to students at any school, and how many of them are equipped with CD-ROM capabilities), enrollment figures, class size, staffing, the state's school assessment scores—even teacher absenteeism rates are available.

Alternatively, you can research individual counties outside Philadelphia—Montgomery, Chester, Delaware, and Bucks—that are considered part of Greater Philadelphia. The schools in every Pennsylvania county work through

Registering for Philadelphia's Public Schools

Every school district has its particular process for getting kids registered. If your child needs to register in a school that is in the Greater Philadelphia region but not in the Philadelphia city limits, contact one of these county offices for information on enrolling:

- Bucks County Intermediate Unit
  705 North Shady Retreat Road, Doylestown
  (215) 348-2940
  www.bucksiu.org
- Chester County Intermediate Unit
  455 Boot Road, Downington
  (484) 237-5000
  www.cciu.org
- Delaware County Intermediate Unit
  200 Yale Avenue, Morton
  (610) 938-9000
  www.dciu.org
- Montgomery County Intermediate Unit
  1605 West Main Street, Norristown
  (610) 539-8550
  www.mciu.org

Every child who is new to the Philadelphia region must register for school. Each city has its own policies and procedures; in the Philadelphia public schools, students who move during the summer from one city neighborhood to another must re-register, as well as those transferring from private, parochial, or charter schools. Kindergarten students must be five years old by September 1 of the upcoming school year in order to register.

Children register for Philadelphia public schools at the school itself. The neighborhood schools are open during the summer to register new students; if you do not know which school your child will attend, you can contact:
Philadelphia Public Schools
440 North Broad Street
(215) 400-4000
www.phila.k12.pa.us

Parents can also contact the school district's Regional Office in their neighborhood:

- Center City, (215) 351-3807
- Central, (215) 684-8487
- Central East, (215) 291-5680
- East, (215) 961-2066
- North, (215) 456-0998
- Northeast, (215) 281-5903
- Northwest, (215) 248-6684
- South, (215) 351-7445
- Southwest, (215) 727-5920
- West, (215) 471-2271

When you register your child in Philadelphia public schools, you should bring some proof of the child's age, such as birth certificate, baptismal certificate or other religious document, passport, or immigration documentation. You also should bring proof of a current address such as parent's driver's license, recent utility bill, or voter registration. That proof must display the parent's name and address.

If your child is entering Philadelphia public schools for the first time, you also should bring proof that the child's immunizations are current, and a recent report card to help ensure that the child is placed in the correct grade.

a clearinghouse known as an "Intermediate Unit," so called because these offices are an intermediate step between local school systems and the state. If you are planning to enroll your child in any Philadelphia-area school, see previous page for contact information.

CATHOLIC AND CHARTER SCHOOLS

If you're planning to send your child to a Catholic school in the five-county Greater Philadelphia area, you will have more than 220 elementary and secondary schools from which to choose, not to mention five special education schools and nine learning disability centers. To learn more about your options, contact the Archdiocese of Philadelphia's Office of Catholic Education (222 North 17th Street, 215-965-1740; www.catholicschools-phil.org). Or, if you will be living or sending your child to a Catholic school in New Jersey, contact the Diocese of Camden's Office of Education (631 Market Street, Camden, 856-756-7900, ext. 6288; www.njcatholicschools.org). In Delaware, the contact is the Diocese of Wilmington Schools Office (1626 North Union Street, Wilmington, 302-573-3133; www.cdow.org).

Another option available in Pennsylvania, New Jersey, and Delaware is the charter school system. These are independent schools, funded by the public school districts where they are located but with a curriculum designed by local teachers, parents, and other citizens. Nearly 80 charter schools operate in and around Philadelphia, most targeting a specific subject area. Charter schools are approved by the state education departments. To learn more, visit their Web sites:

- Pennsylvania, www.pde.state.pa.us/charter_schools
- New Jersey, www.state.nj.us/njded/chartsch
- Delaware, www.doe.state.de.us/Charter Schools/list.html

OUTSTANDING HIGH SCHOOLS: A SELECTION

**Agnes Irwin School
Ithan Avenue and Conestoga Road, Rosemont
(610) 525-8400
www.agnesirwin.org**
In the upper tiers both in terms of tuition ($19,950 plus) and academic excellence, this private, all-girls school is a Main Line star. In one program, alumnae are enlisted to counsel students on picking a college major, living/studying abroad, and other aspects of university life.

**Baldwin School
701 West Montgomery Avenue, Bryn Mawr
(610) 525-2700
www.baldwinschool.org**
Another all-girls school with tuition in the $20,000 range, Baldwin was founded in 1888 as a prep school for Bryn Mawr College. While Baldwin is known for its art curriculum, this is an academically tough school; a third of its graduates go on to major in math or science.

**Central High School
Ogontz and Olney Avenues
(215) 276-5262
www.centralhigh.net**
This isn't your parents' inner-city public school. Every student gets continual, up-close attention from counselors, beginning in the middle of junior year. Their aim is to put college in the kids' minds and not let up until the students know what they'll be doing after high school.

**Conestoga High School
200 Irish Road, Berwyn
(610) 240-1000
www.tesd.k12.pa.us/stoga**
This Chester County public school specializes in choices—meaning, enough electives that juniors and seniors feel they've sampled a number of college majors before they graduate from high school. Many can even elect to spend a month

during senior year in an internship.

Council Rock North and South
North: 62 Swamp Road, Newtown, (215) 944-1300; www.hsnorth.crsd.org

South: 2002 Rock Way, Holland, (215) 944-1100; www.hssouth.crsd.org
The Council Rock School District of Bucks County apparently has found the key to creating a high-achieving public school: Pay your teachers well. Those teaching at the Council Rock high schools, which share a curriculum, earn about $75,000 per year. The focus here is on college prep, complete with career fairs and seminars on financial aid.

Episcopal Academy
376 North Latches Lane, Merion
(610) 667-9612
www.ea1785.org
Like most parochial schools, Episcopal Academy students attend chapel three times a week, true to the school's motto: "Mind, Body, Spirit"—but at these services, there are presentations by guests such as an ethicist or a U.S. senator. Students from many religious backgrounds attend the Academy, and all are required to take rigorous athletic courses.

Friends Select School
17th Street and the Ben Franklin Parkway
(215) 561-5900
www.friends-select.org
Location, location, location—that's a major factor in Friends Select's programs. Students often visit their lofty neighbors, the Philadelphia Museum of Art and Penn's Museum of Archaeology and Anthropology, and they intern at Center City institutions such as the Pennsylvania Ballet and the Philadelphia Stock Exchange.

Germantown Friends School
31 West Coulter Street
(215) 951-2300
www.germantownfriends.org
Quaker values guide interactions at this school: There are no academic rewards, no class rankings, no competitions that would divide students from one another. Volunteerism at neighborhood institutions, such as Boys & Girls Clubs, is stressed.

Julia R. Masterman Laboratory and Demonstration High School
17th and Spring Garden Streets
(215) 299-4661
www.masterman.phila.k12.pa.us
Every student who attends Masterman expects (and is expected) to go on to college. This school is about the competitive academic environment—few extracurricular activities or "soft" classes; the emphasis in this small magnet school is on advanced studies in the basics—science, math, literature.

Lower Merion High School
245 East Montgomery Avenue, Ardmore
(610) 645-1810
www.lmsd.org/schools/lowermerion
Lower Merion is one of those schools that colleges aggressively pursue. That makes students at this private school more competitive; Lower Merion consistently ranks among the region's top schools, and in 1999 it made the *Wall Street Journal*'s list of the country's top 10 high schools.

COLLEGES AND UNIVERSITIES

Not many visitors realize that Philadelphia is one big campus! And there's a Web site to prove it: www.onebigcampus.com.

The program makes sense. Greater Philadelphia is home to more than 80 colleges and universities, with 300,000 students and 55,000 degrees awarded each year. One out of six doctors in the country was trained in Philly, but along with the conventional degrees, you will find courses of study that didn't even exist a generation ago, such as Penn State's graduate degree in "rural sociology," or Philadelphia University's advanced studies in "digital design."

"One Big Campus" is the initiative of the Knowledge Industry Partnership, a coalition formed to put Philly's "knowledge industry" to work for the region (www.kiponline.org). It recognizes that education draws talent to this region—about 20,000 students new to Philadelphia each year—and that this pool of talent and brain power is a force that can contribute to Philadelphia's growth, productivity, and prosperity for decades to come.

To that end, One Big Campus aims to create positive first-hand experiences for new and current students that will keep them here after graduation. This wide-ranging goal begins with advice on shopping for a college, to a "Visit Journal" (for tracking impressions of campus visits), and guidebook-style information on enjoying and connecting with the city.

Part of the higher education landscape are some 50 graduate schools. Some are narrowly specialized, such as the Pennsylvania College of Optometry and the Palmer Theological Seminary. Others cast a wide net; Drexel University alone offers 45 different graduate programs, from chemistry and clinical psychology to math, nutrition, and food science.

For those considering graduate school in Philadelphia, GradSchools.com can serve as your preliminary one-stop shopping resource (http://philadelphia.grad schools.com). An easy-to-search menu on the home page helps you browse the graduate programs of every grad school in the region.

For undergraduate info, www.onebig campus.com gives in-depth profiles of Philly's 80 colleges and universities. Here is a sampling of area colleges:

Arcadia University
450 South Easton Road, Glenside
(877) ARCADIA
www.arcadia.edu
Founded in 1853, this co-ed school offers students a chance to study abroad, in either London or Scotland, their first year.

Ranked one of the top 25 northern regional colleges by *U.S. News & World Report,* Arcadia offers 75 majors to its 3,400 students at its 71-acre campus.

Bryn Mawr College
101 North Merion Avenue, Bryn Mawr
(800) 262-1885
www.brynmawr.edu
Bryn Mawr's 1,350 students, all female, come from almost every state and 40 countries—and with a student–faculty ratio of 8 to 1, they're sure to get all the personal attention they need to succeed. Their graduate programs range from classical studies and art history to physics, math, and conflict resolution.

Chestnut Hill College
9601 Germantown Avenue
(800) 248-0052
www.chc.edu
This co-ed, Catholic liberal arts college has provided a holistic education since 1924. They pride themselves not only on preparing students for careers, but on "creating students for life."

Cheyney University of Pennsylvania
1837 University Circle, Cheyney
(800) CHEYNEY
www.cheyney.edu
Founded by a Quaker philanthropist in 1837, Cheyney is America's oldest historically black school. It offers 30 bachelor of arts degrees and a master's degree in education. The emphasis is on training future leaders who will work for the good of the people.

Drexel University
3141 Chestnut Street
(215) 895-2000, (800) 2-DREXEL
www.drexel.edu
Almost always making *U.S. News & World Report*'s list of top doctoral universities, Drexel is a leader in innovative curricula, integrating technology into the student experience wherever possible. Undergrads are encouraged to balance theory with practical experience, while graduate

studies include e-commerce, interior design, TV management, publications management, and "decision sciences."

Haverford College
370 Lancaster Avenue, Haverford
(610) 896-1350
www.haverford.edu

This undergrad-only co-ed college, the first founded by the Quakers in 1833, is known not only for its liberal arts education but also its manicured 216-acre campus. More than 400 species of trees and shrubs are here, plus a lovely pond and nature walk.

LaSalle University
1900 West Olney Avenue
(215) 951-1500
www.lasalle.edu

This private Catholic university focuses on both intellectual and spiritual development of its 6,200 undergraduate and graduate students. A liberal education is emphasized; majors include theology, professional communication, Central and Eastern European studies, and bilingual and bicultural studies.

Lincoln University
1570 Baltimore Pike, Lincoln University
(610) 932-8300
www.lincoln.edu

Established in 1854, Lincoln is the oldest historically black university in the United States and counts such luminaries as Langston Hughes and Thurgood Marshall among its alumni. It is a small school with only 2,000 students, and aims to prepare them for success in a high-tech global society.

Moore College of Art and Design
20th Street and The Parkway
(215) 965-4000, (800) 523-2025
www.moore.edu

More than 150 years after its founding in 1848, Moore remains the first and only accredited women's visual arts college in the United States. Students connect with a network of women artists and designers

who will help them in their careers for years to come.

Pennsylvania Academy of the Fine Arts
118 North Broad Street
(215) 972-7625
www.pafa.edu

The Academy's certificate program offers two years of classical training, then a term of practical fine arts work in a private studio. Partnerships enable students to earn a BFA degree from the University of Pennsylvania, or a two-year MFA.

Philadelphia University
School House Lane and Henry Avenue
(800) 951-7287
www.philau.edu

Digital design, taxation, fashion apparel studies, textile design, and textile engineering are among the eclectic offerings at this school whose motto is, "No Boundaries!" To that end, they follow an interdisciplinary academic approach in their 40 undergraduate and graduate programs.

Swarthmore College
500 College Avenue, Swarthmore
(610) 328-8000, (800) 667-3110
www.swarthmore.edu

At this Main Line icon, about 1,400 liberal arts students absorb an education that *U.S. News & World Report* consistently ranks among the top three such programs in the country. Its studies range from Arabic to plasma physics, from microbiology to dance.

Temple University
1801 North Broad Street
(888) 340-2222
www.temple.edu

Temple is a mega-school, with more than 34,000 students attending its 17 schools and colleges. The university offers 130 bachelor's degrees, 100 masters, and 50 doctorates, with campuses in Tokyo and Rome. The flagship campus is in North Philly. Temple also is known as a major research and health care center.

University of the Arts
320 South Broad Street
(800) 616-ARTS
www.uarts.edu
Creativity is the buzzword at this unique school, the only fully accredited university that focuses on all of the arts, including digital, filmmaking, jazz, crafts, dancing, acting, performing, design, visual, illustration, writing, and multimedia, among others.

University of Pennsylvania
3451 Walnut Street
(215) 898-7507
www.upenn.edu
This Ivy League school's beginnings were lofty enough: Founded by Benjamin Franklin, Penn is the country's first university. Not surprisingly, given its heritage, innovation and entrepreneurialism are strong here. Its Wharton School is one of the top three business colleges by anyone's standards.

University of the Sciences in Philadelphia
600 South 43rd Street
(215) 596-8800
www.usip.edu
Founded in 1821, this small school (about 2,800 students) was the country's first college of pharmacy. Today it offers 16 majors in arts and sciences, health sciences, and pharmaceutical sciences, including majors in pharmacy administration and bioinformatics.

Villanova University
800 Lancaster Avenue, Villanova
(610) 519-4000
www.villanova.edu
More than 6,300 students attend Villanova, earning degrees in wide-reaching fields such as accounting, environmental engineering, transportation engineering, philosophy, Spanish, theater, and health care. It

was founded in 1842 as an Augustinian university and is comprised of four colleges: Nursing; Engineering; Commerce and Finance; and Liberal Arts and Sciences.

FREE LIBRARY OF PHILADELPHIA

Central Branch
1901 Vine Street
(215) 686-5322
www.library.phila.gov
Growing up in any American city means frequent trips to the library, and with more than seven million items, few have more to offer than the Free Library of Philadelphia.

Chartered in 1891, the Free Library grew over the years—thanks in large part to the generosity of Andrew Carnegie—to 54 branches, including a Library for the Blind and Physically Handicapped. Books are just one reason to visit the library; its collections also include film, magazines, and rare art.

Among its holdings, one of the more interesting collections is the Auto Reference Collection, with more than 34,000 pieces of automobile-related sales literature, including books, posters, ads, and magazines.

Another notable resource is the Children's Literature Research Collection of 65,000 non-circulating children's books, published from 1837 to the present. And, drawing visitors from across the country is the Fleisher Collection of Orchestral Music, the world's largest lending library of orchestral performance materials.

But published materials are not the only offerings. Each year thousands of Philadelphians participate in the Free Library's Adult Education and G.E.D. (high school equivalency) classes, and its after-school programs providing homework assistance, computer literacy, and other enrichment skill instruction.

CHILD CARE

Whether you're traveling or just settling in a new city, child care is always a big question mark. The factors are complicated: Is the agency or center licensed? What are the hours when traveling parents can get child care assistance, and how far is the center from the hotel? Should you get references from other parents—and if you're not from that city, how can you find references?

In most cases the questions are the same as when you're searching for child care at home. You'll want to know about the caregiver/child ratio, the history and safety record of the agency, and staff experience. You should find time to visit the center beforehand, to be sure the premises are cheery and clean, and to see if the center's philosophy and activities are a good match for your child. In these matters, your intuition is always your best guide.

In Philadelphia several online resources can make the research easier for you. One is Child Care Aware (CCA), a national organization that helps parents find child care in their communities (800–424–2246; www.childcareaware.org). CCA also is an excellent resource in learning how to ascertain which child care centers will suit your needs and your child's personality. The site offers articles to help you become a better informed parent, such as information on licensing and accreditation and what they mean, how to choose the best day care, and an "average rates finder" that will tell you what to expect to pay for child care in your zip code.

For comprehensive listings of all things parenting, from birthday party performers to baby furniture, nursery schools, clinics, and au pair and nanny agencies, order a copy of the *2007 Family Phone Book* from *Parents Express,* a Philadelphia-area monthly parenting magazine. You'll also find a handy checklist for helping you select a child care facility. For your free copy, call (215) 628–8330, or access the guide online at www.parents-express.net.

IN-HOTEL CHILD CARE

Not many Philly hotels offer child care for guests, but most of those that do are likely to use the services of Your Other Hands, Philadelphia's only bonded babysitting and nanny service, according to its staff.

Even though they engage the same service, each hotel puts its own signature on the child care. Loews Philadelphia Hotel, for example, will provide its own modified care in the form of a concierge watching your child for several hours, as well as using Your Other Hands. Loews keeps a lending game library for kids of guests and offers special menus, tours, welcome gifts for kids under 10, and, for those younger than 4, child-proof kits.

The Four Seasons Philadelphia also uses Your Other Hands with a three-hour minimum. Younger kids can take their pick from a red wagon full of toys at check-in, and will get complimentary milk and cookies at bedtime—and when the nanny is there, the itinerary is up to you. The kids can play in the pool, stay in the room, or walk to the Franklin Institute with their new friend, for about $17.50 an hour for watching two kids, plus a transportation fee for the nanny to get to the hotel. There's a three-hour minimum, with fees increasing for extra kids, plus tip.

Your Other Hands also works with the Marriott Center City, Society Hill Sheraton, and the Rittenhouse Hotel—but parents can call on the service, too, if the family is staying elsewhere. Depending on the ages and number of kids, fees start at $15 per hour when the nanny is hired by individuals, plus transportation and tip (215–790–0990; www.yourother hands.net).

NATIONAL CHILD CARE CHAINS

Bright Horizons
950 Walnut Street, Suite 102
(215) 955-6556
www.brighthorizons.com
With more than 600 locations nationwide and in Canada, Ireland, and the United Kingdom, Bright Horizons specializes in worksite child care—but they do take drop-ins for parents on vacation or on a business trip. The Center City facility is open weekdays, 6:30 A.M. to 6:30 P.M., and they work with kids six weeks to 12 years old. The fee depends on the number of children, ages, and time they spend with Bright Horizons. Their Early Childhood Program offers a highly regarded curriculum, "The World at their Fingertips," which encourages all kids to be active in their communities. Bright Horizons also has centers in Bensalem and King of Prussia.

The Learning Experience
915 Old Fern Hill Road, Building C,
West Chester
(610) 692-5004, (800) 865-7775
www.thelearningexperience.com
Taking the approach that children develop to their highest potential if they're allowed to learn at their own pace, The Learning Experience operates dozens of day care centers in the Mid-Atlantic states. Features include "Make Believe Boulevard," where kids can "work" at the firehouse, post office, market, or in shops, and a "Fun 'n Fit" program, teaching children that fitness is fun. Kids over five can participate in organized after-school sports, computer games, and arts and crafts.

ONLINE RESOURCES

A citywide babysitting subscription service, www.Babysitters.com, serves parents whether they typically need a sitter at the last minute, or plan their nights out weeks in advance. They can search the detailed babysitter profiles for someone who suits them, or post a job. Parents also will be interested in the "How To" series for both sitters and parents, with step-by-step advice on doing background checks, how much to pay a sitter, how to interview, and tips for working with a new family. Babysitters.com covers sitting for infants to children aged 12 years; a subscription costs $39.95 for the first three months and $8.95 per month from then on.

For longer term help, www.4Nanny.com is a nanny clearinghouse where parents can advertise for a nanny ($25 and up for a 30-day classified), research and compare fees of nanny agencies, and learn from sample work agreements and an "Ask the Experts" forum. FAQs here start with the basics, such as the differences between a nanny and an au pair. Prospective nannies, too, will find the site useful; they can post a resume, and both parties can learn the pros and cons of live-in verses live-out nannies.

Another service, www.4sitters.com, covers the globe, helping parents locate babysitters, nannies, home day care providers, house sitters, and even pet sitters worldwide. Parents will find the sitter "rating system" helpful, along with sitters' posted resumes—which viewers can review free of charge. Once you see that there are suitable nannies in your area, more information on them is available with a membership, $49.99 for the first three months, $9.99 per quarter thereafter.

HEALTH CARE Ⓗ

Because of the medical technology and research centers affiliated with Philadelphia's major universities, this city is fortunate to have more than its share of mega-hospital systems, large and small independent hospitals, and a wealth of walk-in and alternative care facilities.

From state-of-the-art neonatal care to expert diagnostics, Philly has health care covered. With 20 hospital systems—and multiple hospitals within each system—it would be impossible in this guide to provide detailed information on each center in Greater Philadelphia. However, we have given contact information for walk-in centers and hospital systems, with notes on their locations, hospitals, and, in some cases, special notes about the care offered.

WALK-IN HEALTH CARE CENTERS

Broadview Family Medical Center
2152 North Broad Street
(215) 232-8700

John F. Kennedy Walk-In Clinic
112 North Broad Street
(215) 568-0860
The JFK Clinic is one of many outpatient clinics in Philadelphia devoted to substance abuse services.

Philadelphia Health Care Centers
(215) 685-6790, for general information or to locate a center near you, 8:30 A.M. to 5:00 P.M. weekdays.
These centers are designed to serve Philly residents only. Their services and hours vary by location; some centers offer wide-ranging care, from family planning to dental, pediatric, and HIV testing. Call before you go, to be sure the center nearest you can treat your problem, and bring along personal identification as well as proof of address, family size, income, and any documents regarding your Medicare, Medicaid, or health insurance status, if applicable. For more information on individual centers and to locate them on a city map, visit www.phila.gov/health/units/ahs/HealthCenter_map1.htm.

- Health Care Center #1, 1400 Lombard Street (Broad and Lombard), (215) 685-6570. STD care, HIV testing, and family planning only. English spoken.
- Health Care Center #2, 1720 South Broad Street, (215) 685-1803. English, Vietnamese, and Cambodian spoken.
- Health Care Center #3, 555 South 43rd Street, (215) 685-7500. English, Spanish, Vietnamese, Cambodian, and French spoken.
- Health Care Center #4, 4400 Haverford Avenue, (215) 685-7600. English spoken.
- Health Care Center #5, 1920 North 20th Street, (215) 685-2933. English spoken.
- Health Care Center #6, 321 West Girard Avenue, (215) 685-3803. English and Spanish spoken.

Spectrum Health Services, Inc.
1415 North Broad Street, #224;
(215) 235-7137
5619-25 Vine Street, Progress Haddington Plaza; (215) 471-2761
www.spechealth.org
The two centers operated by Spectrum Health offer primary care. If more in-depth treatment is appropriate, Spectrum maintains referral agreements with nearby

---

For an overall look at health care providers across Philadelphia, visit http://philadelphia.zani.com/Health. Hundreds of centers and services are listed at the site, from biofeedback labs to blood banks, and dietitians to sports psychologists.

hospitals. Their services include general medical, prenatal, family planning/GYN, pediatric, and geriatric care.

HOSPITAL SYSTEMS

Albert Einstein Healthcare Network
(part of Jefferson Health System)
5501 Old York Road
(215) 456-7090
www.einstein.edu
Four hospitals in Philadelphia and Montgomery Counties belong to this network, including Albert Einstein Medical Center (tertiary care and teaching hospital), Belmont Behavioral Health Center (psychiatric care), MossRehab/Einstein at Elkins Park (rehabilitation and acute care), and Willowcrest (subacute care). Einstein also operates a number of satellites and outpatient centers and Germantown Community Health Services, a primary health care center in northwest Philly.

Crozer Keystone Health System
Healthplex Pavilion #2
100 Sproul Road, Springfield
(610) 338-8200
www.crozer.org
All of Crozer Keystone's five hospitals are in Delaware County: Community Hospital in Chester (behavioral health sciences), Delaware County Memorial in Drexel Hill (acute care), Crozer-Chester Medical Center, which has the only regional trauma center in Delaware County (tertiary care), Springfield and Taylor Hospitals (both acute care).

Jefferson Health System
259 Radnor-Chester Road, Radnor
(610) 225-6200
www.jeffersonhealth.org
Hospitals and hospital groups are banded within the Jefferson Health System umbrella, including the Albert Einstein Healthcare Network, Frankford Health Care System, Thomas Jefferson University Hospital, Magee Rehabilitation Hospital, and Main Line Health in Montgomery

County, almost the only facilities in the system not in Philadelphia County. Main Line Health's partners include community hospitals in Paoli, Malvern, Wynnewood, and Bryn Mawr, while the Frankford System includes a satellite in Bucks County.

Lourdes Health System
1600 Haddon Avenue, Camden, New Jersey
(856) 757-3500
www.lourdesnet.org
Headquartered across the Delaware River in Camden, the Lourdes hospitals all are located in New Jersey: Our Lady of Lourdes Medical Center (tertiary care), Lourdes Medical Center of Burlington County, and St. Francis Medical Center (both acute care).

Mercy Health System
One West Elm Street, Conshohocken
(610) 567-6000
www.mercyhealth.org
With hospitals in Delaware, Philadelphia, and Montgomery Counties, the Mercy system is one of the larger addressing acute care: Mercy Fitzgerald Hospital, Mercy Hospital of Philadelphia, Mercy Suburban Hospital, St. Agnes Medical Center, and Nazareth Hospital. Like all of Philadelphia's hospital systems, Mercy operates its own physician referral service; call (877) GO-MERCY.

Temple University Health System
3509 North Broad Street, 9th Floor
(215) 707-0900
www.health.temple.edu
All of Temple's university-associated hospitals are in Philadelphia: Temple University Hospital/Episcopal Campus (acute care), Northeastern Hospital (acute care), and Temple University Hospital (tertiary care), plus Jeanes Hospital, a progressive facility employing "hospitalists"—physicians who manage the care of hospital patients on behalf of other physicians. Temple Children's includes Pediatric Intensive Care, Newborn Nursery and Infant Intensive Care, and cardiology, allergy, and gastroenterology units.

Public Health Info

Wondering how to check for leaded paint in an old house you want to buy? How about school nurse programs in your neighborhood? For any questions related to public health, call one of Greater Philly's three Public Health Information Centers:

• C. Everett Koop Community Health Information Center

College of Physicians of Philadelphia (215) 563-3737
• Patient and Family Education Center University of Pennsylvania Medical Center (215) 662-4898
• Consumer Health Library Delaware Academy of Medicine (302) 571-1101

Tenet HealthSystem Philadelphia, Inc.
Centre Square, West Tower
1500 Market Street, 34th Floor
www.tenet.com
Four of Tenet's five facilities are located in Philadelphia: Graduate Hospital (acute care), Hahnemann University Hospital (tertiary care), Roxborough Memorial Hospital (acute care), and St. Christopher's Hospital for Children (pediatric tertiary care). A fifth, Warminster Hospital, is in Bucks County. Tenet's services are comprehensive, ranging from neuroscience and spine treatment, to a pain center, digestive health institute, and wound care center.

University of Pennsylvania Health System
21 Penn Tower, 3400 Spruce Street
(215) 662-2203
www.uphs.upenn.edu
Penn Health's first distinction is that it *was* the first hospital in the country, founded in 1751 by Ben Franklin and Dr. Thomas Bond to care for the "sick-poor and insane of Philadelphia." Today it's a major health care system, with five hospitals—one in Chester County (Phoenixville Hospital, acute care), the others in Philadelphia: Pennsylvania Hospital, the original (acute care), Hospital of the University of Pennsylvania (tertiary care), and University of Pennsylvania Medical Center (acute care,

outpatient heart hospital, and Scheie Eye Institute).

Additional Health Care Systems

Capital Health System
(2 hospitals in New Jersey)
446 Bellevue Avenue, Trenton,
New Jersey
(609) 394-4000
www.capitalhealth.org

Chestnut Hill HealthCare (2 hospitals,
Philadelphia and Montgomery County)
8835 Germantown Avenue
(215) 248-8200
www.chh.org

Christiana Care Health System
(3 hospitals in Delaware)
501 West 14th Street, Wilmington,
Delaware
(302) 733-1000
www.christianacare.org

CoreCare Systems, Inc. (Westmeade
Center, mental/behavioral health)
111 North 49th Street
(215) 471-2600

Holy Redeemer Health System
(Holy Redeemer Hospital,
Montgomery County)
667 Welsh Road, Huntingdon Valley
(215) 938-4650
www.holyredeemer.com

Kennedy Health System
(3 hospitals in New Jersey)
1099 White Horse Road, Voorhees
www.kennedyhealth.org

North Philadelphia Health Systems
(2 hospitals in Philadelphia,
acute and psychiatric care)
1524 West Girard Avenue
(215) 787-9000
www.nphs.com

Psychiatric Hospitals of Philadelphia
(2 hospitals, Chester and
Montgomery Counties)
660 Thomas Road, Lafayette Hill
(215) 836-7700
www.eugeniahospital.com

Universal Health Services
(6 hospitals, Montgomery, Philadelphia,
Delaware Counties, plus New Jersey)
367 South Gulph Road, King of Prussia
(610) 768-3300
www.uhsinc.com

Virtua Health (6 hospitals,
all in New Jersey)
94 Brick Road, Marlton
(888) VIRTUA-3
www.virtua.org

It's hard to imagine terminally ill children receiving better care than from the
Pediatric Advanced Care Team at Children's Hospital of Philadelphia (CHOP).
The team is a small band of doctors,
nurses, psychologists, and counselors
who only treat terminally ill kids, spending time with them in art therapy, sur-
vivor support, and even annual vigils to
honor former patients.

Special Select Hospitals

Children's Hospital of Philadelphia
(CHOP)
34th Street and Civic Center Boulevard
(215) 590-1000, (800) 879-2467,
Physicians Referral Service
www.chop.edu
Begun in 1855 as the country's first
children's hospital, CHOP is the site of
dramatic breakthroughs in pediatric medicine, such as vaccines for mumps, whoop-
ing cough, and influenza; and early
research on "shaken baby syndrome."
Specialized programs include cardiology,
oncology, plastic surgery, and neuro-
surgery, and current research focuses on
fetal surgery, pediatric HIV and AIDS, and
genetics. Both *Child* magazine and *U.S.
News & World Report* have three times
ranked CHOP as the finest pediatric hospital in the country in recent years.

Fox Chase Cancer Center
333 Cottman Avenue
(215) 728-6900
www.fccc.edu
Though it is a relatively small hospital with
100 beds, Fox Chase is one of the largest
in the country devoted exclusively to cancer care. More than 300 oncology nurses
provide care, and the multidisciplinary
staff attend to patients' total needs, with
special programs in diagnostic pathology,
pain management, and a clinical-studies
wing for developmental chemotherapy.

Philadelphia Shriners Hospital
3551 North Broad Street
(215) 430-4000
www.shrinershq.org/shc/philadelphia/
index.html
One of 22 Shriners Hospitals in North
America, Philadelphia Shriners provides
complete, orthopedic medical and rehab
services to children at no charge; their
motto is, "Empowering children in mind,
body, and spirit—all in a hospital that
never sends a bill." Specialties include

treatment for spinal cord injuries, cerebral palsy, scoliosis, limb deficiencies, spina bifida, and leg-length discrepancies. More commonly, metabolic bone disease, club-foot, brittle bone disease, and juvenile rheumatoid arthritis, among other disorders, are treated here.

Independent Hospitals—A Quick Reference

PHILADELPHIA COUNTY

Friends Hospital (psychiatric)
(215) 831-4600

Kensington Hospital (acute care)
(215) 426-8100

Kindred Hospital (long-term acute care)
(215) 722-8555

Philadelphia Veterans Affairs Medical Center (tertiary care)
(215) 823-5800

Renfrew Center, Inc. (psychiatric, intensive outpatient, day treatment programs)
(215) 482-5353

Wills Eye Hospital (specialty)
(215) 928-3000

BUCKS COUNTY

Doylestown Hospital (acute care)
(215) 345-2200

Grand View Hospital (acute care)
(215) 453-4000

Lower Bucks Hospital (general)
(215) 785-9200

St. Luke's Quakertown Hospital (acute care)
(215) 538-4500

All 50 states, and nearly 50 countries, have referred pregnant mothers to the Children's Hospital of Philadelphia (CHOP) for special procedures in its Center for Fetal Diagnosis and Treatment, where children still in the womb undergo delicate surgery for severe problems. It's one of just two such centers in the United States where, after in utero *diagnosis and treatment, babies are born "normal" against all odds.*

St. Mary Medical Center (acute care)
(215) 710-2000

CHESTER COUNTY

Brandywine Hospital (acute care)
(610) 383-8000

Chester County Hospital (acute care)
(610) 431-5000

Jennersville Regional Hospital (acute care)
(610) 869-1000

DELAWARE COUNTY

Riddle Memorial Hospital (acute care)
(610) 566-9400

MONTGOMERY COUNTY

Abington Memorial Hospital (acute care)
(215) 481-2000

Brook Glen Behavioral Hospital (mental health services)
(215) 641-5300

Montgomery Hospital Medical Center (acute care)
(610) 270-2000

Valley Forge Medical Center and Hospital (acute care, addiction center)
(610) 539-8500

Emergency and Support Numbers

ActionAIDS, Philadelphia's largest
AIDS service organization
(215) 981-0088

Al-Anon, for families and loved ones of
alcoholics
(215) 222-5244, Bucks, Chester,
Delaware, Montgomery, and Philadelphia Counties
(856) 547-0855, South Jersey
(302) 366-8484, North Delaware

Alcoholics Anonymous
(215) 222-5244, Bucks, Chester,
Delaware, Montgomery, and Philadelphia Counties
(856) 486-4446, South Jersey
(302) 655-5113, North Delaware

Animal Bites
(215) 685-6748, Department of Public
Health, Division of Disease Control, 24-
hour hotline
(215) 685-9040, (215) 685-9000 for
rodents; www.phila.gov (yuck alert:
photo of rat on site)

Breast Cancer Hotline
(888) 273-3348

CHOICE, info and counseling for preg-
nancy options, birth control, sexually
transmitted infections, and AIDS
(215) 985-3300

Commonwealth of Pennsylvania
(800) 932-0784, in-state
(717) 787-2121, out of state

Delaware Commission for Women
(302) 761-8005

Delaware County Women Against Rape
(610) 566-4342

Fathers & Childrens Equality, counseling, information, referrals
(610) 688-4748

Men's Resource Center, counseling,
information, referrals
(215) 564-0488

Mental Health Association of Southeast Pennsylvania
(215) 235-1366

Narcotics Anonymous
(215) 440-8400

New Jersey Division on Women, rape
care, sexual abuse, domestic violence
(609) 292-8840

Pennsylvania Commission for Women,
information and referrals
(888) 615-7477, (717) 787-8128

Pennsylvania Office of Attorney General, Public Protection Division, including Civil Rights Enforcement Section,
Office of Consumer Advocate, and
Bureau of Consumer Protection
(800) 441-2555 (hotline), (215)
560-2414

Philadelphia Mental Health Center
(215) 735-9379

Planned Parenthood
(215) 351-5560, (215) 351-5550, (215)
351-5580

Poison Control Emergency
(800) 222-1222

Sixth Street Mental Health Clinic
(215) 235-4581

Suicide and Crisis Intervention, 24-
hour emergency hotline, referrals
(215) 686-4420

Women in Transition, counseling
service, drug and alcohol addiction,
domestic abuse
(215) 751-1111

Women Organized Against Rape, individual and group counseling
(215) 985-3315

Womens Way, fundraising organization
for children and women's needs
(215) 985-3322

ALTERNATIVE HEALTH CARE

Probably the best source for information on alternative health care in Greater Philadelphia is the Citizens' Alliance for Progressive Health Awareness (CAPHA), a non-profit organization formed "to increase public awareness about natural/holistic health care options and sustainable living."

CAPHA's membership is open to anyone interested in integrative health care. The group publishes a directory of its practitioner network, including services in acupressure, acupuncture, Alexander technique, kinesiology, Ayurvedic medicine, biofeedback, chelation, chiropractic, colon hydrotherapy, counseling, cranio sacral therapy, holistic dentistry, feng shui, hypnotherapy, and dozens more specialties. CAPHA also sponsors health fairs and seminars on such topics as the benefits of raw foods, developing intuition, and flower essences, and publishes *Progressive Health*, a semi-annual magazine (CAPHA, P.O. Box 775, Paoli, PA 19301, 610-640-2788; www.capha.org).

MEDIA ⬛

Perhaps it's Philadelphia's prominent role in forging a new nation that initially planted the take-no-prisoners mentality in its publications. Whatever the origins, that same boldness and uncompromising journalistic integrity still drives Philly's publishing community today. Simply put, journalism here has attitude.

Take Howard Stern. Syndication of his controversial radio show began in Philadelphia in 1985, and Philly was one of the first cities to rank his show number-one in the all-important morning drive-time competition.

But in Philly, along with attitude comes excellence. On the print side, Philadelphia is where Pulitzer winners are created—18, in fact, attained by the *Philadelphia Inquirer* alone. The city's 55 radio and TV stations, too, have won their share of accolades.

And, as in every city, media outlets here are changing and evolving constantly. Philly's two sports-talk radio stations are a good example: Radio AM-610 WIP, long the area's only widely established sports-talk outlet, always has been great at inciting listeners' emotions about their beloved pro teams by emphasizing caller participation. WIP is a companion of sorts for sports fans; the station relies on engaging and involving the audience, much more than interviewing sports celebrities.

In 2005, however, WIP found new competition when Radio AM-950 WPEN, one of Philly's most popular oldies stations, switched its format to sports talk with a different approach: WPEN features more interviews than WIP, and rather than producing all of its own shows, the station also brings in nationally syndicated programs.

The verdict is pending on who will win the sports-talk wars. What we do know is that all the media in Philadelphia—as in every major city—faces new challenges in recent years from the Internet. Readers, viewers, and listeners get more information online every day, and no doubt the audiences for print, TV, and radio will pressure even more outlets to reinvent themselves.

NEWSPAPERS

Daily

Philadelphia Daily News
400 North Broad Street
(215) 854-5900
www.philly.com
The *Daily News*'s tag as "the people paper" leaves no doubt as to its priorities. Since 1925 this tabloid has carried out its aggressive, take-no-prisoners brand of journalism, and it works: With more than 500,000 readers, it's one of the top 100 dailies in the United States. Yet it's a relatively small paper for a major market, with just 64 reporters and 26 editors. Departments that make it so popular include "Philly Confidential," the "inside look at the crime beat," and famous columnist Stu Bykofsky.

Philadelphia Inquirer
400 North Broad Street
(215) 854-2000
www.philly.com
More than a million readers devour the *Inquirer* every day. It's a big paper, with 205 reporters and almost as many editors (187)—figures that hint at why this "Inky" has won 18 Pulitzer Prizes. That's a lot of editorial scrutiny, but with both the *Inquirer* and the *Daily News* sharing the same owners (notice they're located at the same street and Web addresses), we're guessing they have to work overtime to ensure the standards are above

reproach. Familiar columnists at the *Inquirer* include Gail Shister, Jane Eisner, Acel Moore, and foodie Craig La Ban.

Weekly

Catholic Standard & Times
222 North 17th Street
(215) 587-3667
www.cst-phl.com
The official newspaper for the Archdiocese of Philadelphia, the *Catholic Standard* presents profiles, news, position pieces, history, stories of church preservation, parenting advice, and other lifestyle topics such as careers and recreation. It's published 49 times a year; the paper also produces other materials such as the Archdiocese's annual *Philadelphia Directory*.

Jewish Exponent
2100 Arch Street
(215) 832-0700
www.jewishexponent.com
The *Exponent* publishes news and columns of interest to Philadelphia's Jewish community, from hard-hitting opinions to features and reviews. It also brings news from Israel to its Philadelphia readers, as well as of efforts to rescue Jews from repressive regimes around the world. Published since 1887, the paper has about 50,000 subscribers, and thousands more read it online.

Philadelphia Business Journal
400 Market Street, Suite 1200
(215) 238-1450
http://philadelphia.bizjournals.com
The *Business Journal* is part of a chain of 42 newspapers across the country, publishing local and national news. It also runs industry-specific news for 46 industries, as well as advice columns. In addition to publishing the paper online, the Web site also offers online business directories and other resources.

Philadelphia City Paper
123 Chestnut Street
(215) 735-8444
www.citypaper.net
One of Philly's two rival alternative weeklies, *City Paper* is the town's largest weekly, distributed free to 245,000 readers in more than 2,000 locations including offices, high-traffic retail outlets, restaurants, street boxes, and other public places. The target audience is "educated, affluent, and active," reading regular columns and features on politics, news, opinion, culture, the arts, food, sex, relationships, and movies.

Philadelphia Gay News
505 South Fourth Street
(215) 625-8501
www.epgn.com
For 30 years, the *Gay News* has been serving Philly's gay and lesbian community with news, entertainment, editorials, cartoons, classifieds, and other matters of special interest to the gay community. An events calendar keeps readers updated on celebrations, festivals, gallery openings, premieres, and other activities.

Philadelphia New Observer
1520 Locust Street, Suite 501
(215) 545-7500
www.pnonews.com
One of Philly's African-American and ethnic newspapers, the *New Observer* is dedicated to the "human rights of all people," bringing its readers news, op-eds, sports, reviews, profiles of community leaders, and lifestyle pieces.

Philadelphia Sunday Sun
6661-63 Germantown Avenue
(215) 848-SUN-4
www.philasun.com
The *Sun*'s target audience also is the African-American community, whom they reach with commentary, health, news, and sports coverage. The paper's aim is to "build a quality newspaper that allows African Americans to easily and efficiently find business, community, educa-

tion, government, and religious organization information, and all the weekly news."

Philadelphia Weekly
1500 Sansom Street, 3rd Floor
(215) 563-7400
www.philadelphiaweekly.com
With a circulation of about 107,000, the *Weekly* is the *City Paper*'s biggest competition for the alternative-paper audience. Like its rival, the *Weekly* covers food, art, news, opinions, music, movies, and politics. It's a free paper, distributed in yellow street boxes. The same company also publishes two small neighborhood papers, *The South Philly Review* and *The Southwest Philadelphia Review.*

PERIODICALS

Philadelphia
1818 Market Street, 36th Floor
(215) 564-7700
www.phillymag.com
If you can only read one publication in this city, read *Philadelphia* magazine. It is far and away the finest city magazine in this country, and it is essential reading for anyone who wants to understand Philadelphia. Whether they're doing an investigative report or reviewing restaurants, these writers and editors don't mind controversy. *Philadelphia*, a monthly, pioneered the art of restaurant reviewing in city mags; some go as far as to say they created the business of food buzz.

Philadelphia Row Home
P.O. Box 54786, Philadelphia, PA 19148
(215) 462-9777
www.gohomephilly.com
Covering four zip codes in South Philly, *Philadelphia Row Home* focuses on interiors and lifestyles of special interest to residents of those neighborhoods. Circulation of this free quarterly is more than 20,000; the magazine publishes decorating tips, before/after home makeovers, stories of local history, and profiles of neighborhood business people.

Philadelphia Style
141 League Street
(215) 468-6670
www.phillystylemag.com
Published quarterly, *Philadelphia Style* offers stories on beauty, fashion, home decor, and style, art, and travel. Profiles of artists and restaurateurs add into the mix; this mag is *Philadelphia* magazine without the edge.

TELEVISION

Comcast Cable is the cable provider for the city of Philadelphia (1639 Fairmount Avenue, 215-684-2723; www.comcast .com). Other locally based television stations:

- WKYW-TV 3 (CBS)
- WPVI-TV 6 (ABC)
- WCAU-TV 10 (NBC)
- WHYY-TV 12 (PBS)
- WPHL-TV 17 (WB)
- WTXF-TV 29 (FOX)
- WYBE-TV 35 (IND)
- WPSG-TV 57 (UPN)

RADIO

The following is just a partial list of the dozens of radio stations broadcasting from Philadelphia. We've included their specialties as of this writing, but they can change direction anytime. Our advice is to surf your radio dial and find your favorites.

Country

WXTU 92.5 FM

News/Talk

WWDB 860 AM (Business)
WURD 900 AM
KYW 1060 AM
WPHT 1210 AM

WHAT 1340 AM
WILM 1450 AM
WKXW 101.5 FM

WNAP 1110 AM
WIMG 1300 AM
WDAS 1480 AM
WISP 1570 AM
WSJI 89.5 FM
WKDN 106.9 FM

Oldies/Nostalgia

WSNJ 1240 AM
WBUD 1260 AM
WRDV 89.3 FM (Big Band/Oldies)
WVLT 92.1 FM
WOGL 98.1 FM
WSNI 104.5 FM

Spanish

WPHE 690 AM
WEMG 1310 AM

Top-40

WSTW 93.7 FM
WPST 97.5 FM
WIOQ 102.1 FM
WPHI 103.9 FM

Public Radio

WNJT 88.1 FM (National Public Radio)
WRTI 90.1 FM
WHYY 90.9 FM

Alternative

WVFC 1180 AM
WXPN 88.5 FM
WPLY 100.3 FM

Rock

WMMR 93.3 FM
WYSP 94.1 FM
WTHK 94.5 FM (Classic Rock)
WMGK 102.9 (Classic Rock)

Religious/Gospel Music

WFIL 560 AM
WVCH 740 AM
WZZD 990 AM (Christian Contemporary)

Hip-Hop

WRDW 96.5 FM
WUSL 98.9 FM

WORSHIP

I n a city whose most famous icons are symbols of freedom, some of the most meaningful sites are monuments to religious freedom. That's no accident: The freedom to practice religion is what brought William Penn to Philadelphia, and the concept defined the city's most important developments for decades.

Philadelphia was founded as Penn's "Holy Experiment," an "example to the nations." Centuries before cultural diversity was valued, Philadelphia was the only major city in the world that embraced people of all religions and ethnic backgrounds. Penn, a Quaker, had circulated pamphlets exalting the advantages of his new colony, and openly inviting the world to migrate to the area often referred to as "Penn's woods." By the early 1700s, every separatist sect was represented here, alongside mainstream Protestant denominations, Catholics, and Jews. Most of the early settlers even shared buildings for church services.

The city was a refuge for religious dissidents and a haven for religious expression. Tolerance toward all faiths was the cornerstone on which Philadelphia was built, and was tested for 100 years before America's founding fathers met here to write the U.S. Constitution. They saw that the experiment in religious freedom had worked beautifully, and in fact adopted William Penn's own language from his Charter of Privileges in drafting the First Amendment to the Constitution: "Congress shall make no law respecting an establishment of religion or prohibiting the free exercise thereof . . ."

The spirit of interfaith respect was honored in 1976, during the United States Bicentennial, with the organizing of the Old Philadelphia Congregations, a consortium of historic churches and temples. Member churches trace their histories to William Penn's 1701 Charter of Privileges and still work to promote religious freedom and tolerance. All are still active parishes that hold regular worship services and welcome visitors. Members of the consortium include:

CHRIST CHURCH

Founded in 1695. Bordered by a small park and a cobblestone alley, the church is a beautiful example of Georgian Colonial architecture. Among its features is the 600-year-old baptismal font brought from England in 1697, where it had been used to baptize William Penn (20 North American Street, 215-922-1695).

OLD PINE STREET CHURCH

Built in 1768, Old Pine Street Church is the only surviving colonial Presbyterian church in Philadelphia. The church was gutted by the British and remodeled in the 1830s. Step into the churchyard; many of its 3,000 graves date from the early 1700s (412 Pine Street, 215-925-8051).

MOTHER BETHEL AFRICAN METHODIST EPISCOPAL CHURCH

Mother Bethel African Methodist Episcopal Church stands on the country's oldest parcel of land continuously owned by African Americans. Founded in 1787 by former slave Richard Allen, the church served as an Underground Railroad station; Allen's tomb and fascinating artifacts are in the base-

---

Among worshippers at Christ Church were George Washington, Benjamin Franklin, and Betsy Ross, and visitors can still find their pews today. The church's eight bells are the originals that rang in 1776 to proclaim our independence from England—and they still "ring out freedom" once a week.

The churchyard outside St. Peter's Epis-copal Church contains the graves of eight Native American tribal chiefs; they died from smallpox when they traveled to Philadelphia to meet with President George Washington in 1793.

ment crypt, now a museum (419 Richard Allen Avenue [Sixth Street], 215–925–0616).

ST. PETER'S EPISCOPAL CHURCH

St. Peter's Episcopal Church was founded in 1761 to handle the overflow of affluent Christ Church parishioners who lived in Society Hill. Its style is elegant but unusual: The altar stands at one end while the elevated pulpit is at the opposite end; hence the church has no front or back. The odd "box pews" face both ways so the faithful can follow the service (Third and Pine Streets, 215–925–5968).

MIKVEH ISRAEL CONGREGATION AND CEMETERY

Mikveh Israel Congregation and Cemetery is Pennsylvania's oldest Jewish congrega-tion, dating from 1740 when Thomas Penn granted land to Nathan Levy so that Levy (whose ship, the *Myrtilla*, brought the Lib-erty Bell to the United States) could bury his infant son. The land became the Jewish community's cemetery. Mikveh Israel's first synagogue was built in 1782 with financial help from Benjamin Franklin, among oth-ers. The cemetery, several blocks away at Eighth and Spruce Streets, is part of Inde-pendence National Historical Park (44 North Fourth Street, 215–922–5446).

The cemetery of Old St. Mary's Catholic Church is higher than street level because graves are layered—i.e., people are buried on top of each other. The top layer was added in 1793 after an epi-demic of yellow fever.

OLD ST. MARY'S CATHOLIC CHURCH

The interior of Old St. Mary's Catholic Church is striking, partly due to two-story rows of stained glass windows. Furnish-ings include brass chandeliers from Inde-pendence Hall. St. Mary's started the first Catholic school in the United States in 1782 (252 South Fourth Street, 215–923–7930).

OLD ST. JOSEPH'S CATHOLIC CHURCH

Old St. Joseph's Catholic Church, in its original building, was the site of the first public Catholic mass in Philadelphia in 1733. The present church was built in 1839 and features an 1850 stained glass win-dow above the altar. A painting in the sac-risty was donated by Napoleon Bonaparte's brother, Joseph, a parishioner at St. Joseph's in the early 1800s (321 Will-ings Alley, 215–923–1733).

ST. GEORGE'S METHODIST CHURCH

St. George's Methodist Church, the oldest continuously operating Methodist church building in America, stands in sharp visual contrast to the more grandiose historic churches. Standing a mere 14 feet from the Benjamin Franklin Bridge, this small, unadorned brick church appears just the same as when it was opened in 1792. (It had been purchased in 1769 by followers of John Wesley, founder of the Methodist movement, as a partially constructed meeting house.) In 1789 it was the site of the first Methodist Book Room, predeces-sor of the current Cokesbury Book Stores. One of St. George's more notable parish-ioners was Anna Jarvis, creator of Mother's Day, who attended church here in the early 1900s (235 North Fourth Street, 215–925–7788).

Philadelphians and visitors still find William Penn's "city of brotherly love" to be a multicultural mecca. More than 800 congregations cohabit the city today, rep-resenting virtually all the faiths of the

Christ Church Burial Ground

It seems an unlikely spot for a cemetery—only a few steps from the new Independence Visitors Center in Philadelphia's busiest tourist section—but in 1719, documents placed this two-acre tract of land "on the outskirts of town."

Today Christ Church Burial Ground sits in the heart of Old City. It was created because the churchyard at Christ Church, several blocks away on Second Street, was full. The brick wall around the burial ground was added in 1772, but while the wall and iron gate protected the cemetery from vandals, the gravestones couldn't be protected from the elements—until, that is, a forward-looking parishioner came up with a plan.

Concerned about gravestone deterioration, and worried that future generations would not be able to identify the graves of Philadelphia luminaries buried there, citizen Edward Clark created a "plot plan" in 1864. His registry recorded every headstone inscription in the cemetery.

More than 5,000 men, women, and children are buried in Christ Church Burial Ground, about 80 percent dating from before 1840. Some 1,400 headstones mark the graves. Among those buried here are four signers of the Declaration of Independence, as well as John Dunlap, the man who printed the Declaration and the U.S. Constitution; composer and poet Francis Hopkinson; Dr. Philip Syng Physick, medical pioneer; and Dr. Benjamin Rush, known as the "father of American psychiatry." Commodore William Bainbridge, naval hero of the War of 1812 and captain of "Old Ironsides," also rests here.

The most famous "resident" is Benjamin Franklin, buried with his wife, Deborah. Franklin's grave is a destination in itself; visitors come to toss pennies on his plot as a small tribute to the man who preached, "a penny saved is a penny earned," and as a good-luck gesture for their own financial futures. When Franklin died in 1790, 20,000 Americans attended his funeral. Many more than that visit him every year. Nearby is the grave of John Taylor, the man who dug Franklin's grave.

Christ Church Burial Ground was closed for about 25 years but is again open daily to visitors. (When it was closed, countless would reach through the iron gate to try to toss their pennies onto Franklin's grave!) It's still a working cemetery, though the last burial was in 1994. The cemetery is mapped and divided into quadrants for easy identification, and a book of 50 biographies can be purchased at Christ Church. The burial ground is located at Fifth and Arch Streets (215-922-1695).

world, from Eastern Orthodox churches to Taoists, Mormons, and Rosicrucians. Only eight Quaker houses remain alongside 131 Catholic parishes. Of Philadelphians who consider themselves part of a religious community, 61 percent are Protestants of one denomination or another, while 25 percent are Roman Catholics, 2 percent are Jewish, and 12 percent belong to a Buddhist, Muslim, or "other" congregation.

INDEX

ABOUT THE AUTHOR

MARY MIHALY has spent more than 20 years exploring Philadelphia's neighborhoods, restaurants, boutiques, museums, and rich history. Now based in Cleveland, Mihaly has written about Philly and other cities for *Playboy, Miami Herald, New York Post, Country Living, Northern Ohio Live,* and other prestigious publications, and she shares the best of those insights in this Insiders' Guide.